# The Devout Woman

Evaluating Between Traditional and Christian Beliefs.

## Emmanuel Igwaro Odongo-Aginya

The Devout Woman by Emmanuel Igwaro Odongo-Aginya

ISBN 978-1-970072-18-1 (Paperback)
ISBN 978-1-970072-22-8 (Hardback)

This book is written to provide information and motivation to readers. Its purpose is not to render any type of psychological, legal, or professional advice of any kind. The content is the sole opinion and expression of the author, and not necessarily that of the publisher.

Copyright © 2021 by Emmanuel Igwaro Odongo-Aginya

All rights reserved. No part of this book may be reproduced, transmitted, or distributed in any form by any means, including, but not limited to, recording, photocopying, or taking screenshots of parts of the book, without prior written permission from the author or the publisher. Brief quotations for noncommercial purposes, such as book reviews, permitted by Fair Use of the U.S. Copyright Law, are allowed without written permissions, as long as such quotations do not cause damage to the book's commercial value. For permissions, write to the publisher, whose address is stated below.

Printed in the United States of America.

New Leaf Media, LLC
175 S. 3rd Street, Suite 200
Columbus, OH 43215
www.thenewleafmedia.com

# Foreword

A lot has been said about women's freedom. If there is one area of male-female propaganda, it's the claim that women were denied their freedom. The Devout Woman, by Professor Odongo-Aginya speaks contrary to that misconception. Women, especially, the Acholi of Uganda, had always been free since the symbiotic relationships between Christianity and African Traditional worship. It also dispels the notion that African women were saddled with the task of having dozens of children instead of either one or two children. Prior to the beginning of the 20$^{th}$ century, Acholi women already had independence and freedom, and were defying traditions in an age when women in the Western and Christian society were still under their male societal domination. Fictional as the setting is, but entranced in Acholi tribe of Northern Uganda cultural and traditional religion believes; this is a must read book for all persons who are open-minded and progressive.

Whether you are religious or not, and if you only have to read one book this year, pick up The Devout Woman; it's a testimony to the freedom our women world over who are devouted to their spouses or their religious believes; have always had through the centuries despite men's effort at twisting the truth and attempting to suppress women's rights in many cultures!

*Santonino Ku'Caya Banya, Ph.D.*

# Chapter One

Ogwok, the father of Acellam, was a tall thickly built man with the physic of a weight lifter. Before he died, Ogwok worked as a bricklayer apprentice with the Verona Missionaries in a new Mission about two miles from his home in Coomit village. At that time, his wife was expecting his posthumous son, Acellam. Born posthumously, Acellam, the name which his father had wanted him given, should he be a boy, was reared by his mother alone, aided by the Missionaries in the Mission, because she had refused to be inherited by Otwol, a clan brother of Ogwok according to the customs in Acholi. "I'm capable of looking after myself, the child and these animals my husband left. If only God could keep this child alive and healthy, there will be nothing I will lack. I do not want to be inherited by any man and leave this home." Anyadwe the widow of Ogwok told the elders who had given her and her son to Otwol.

During his infantile age, his mother carried him with her wherever she went. When she went to dig, she dug with him tied up on her back. Occasionally, whenever he was asleep, she put him in the shade of trees near her where she had dug, on a sack layered with some cloth to provide a semi-cushion, and checked on him as she dug. Whenever he woke up, Anyadwe always fed him on her breast milk before she either tied him on her back, or put him back to sleep on the sack. Acellam grew up healthy through Anyadwe's devoted love and care.

"This is my only treasure in this world." She one day thought, as she bathed him in the evening. She pressed him on her chest and whispered in his ear. "Nothing in the whole world pleases me more than seeing you alive. You remind me everyday and night of your father, thank God for His gift."

Acellam was baptised David, the Christian name which was chosen for him by Father Santonino the parish priest of Coomit Mission when he was only one month old. David Acellam was two years old when his mother almost got the shock of her life because Acellam had a severe attack of measles. His skin was full of rashes. His mother recited her rosary day and night pleading to the Blessed Virgin Mary to help her only child. She never fed properly during the period when her child was critically ill. She was as ill as her child was. However, her prayers were answered. David barely and slowly pulled through. Although he recovered, he was nothing but a small sack of organized bones. He could not stand on his feet as if he had not walked many months back. His legs were bony and feeble. The disease wasted the child who was once admired by many people because of his good health. The eyes were deep set in their sockets, and they stared blankly like those of a human carcass. However, his mother was happy he had recovered. She knew it was her responsibility to put back the child's good look.

David Acellam gradually gained strength and energy during the first two weeks of his convalescing period. He was able to stagger once again on his tenuous legs, and prattled to his mother from time to time breaking the monotonous silence in the hut. His mother was full of hopes that within the next few weeks, he was going to regain half of his strength.

Anyadwe used to carry her child on her back and covered him with a big elliptical calabash *Awal-Wic* (calabash specially made for the purpose). This protected the child as an insulator against the heat of the sun, and as an umbrella against the rain. The calabash was held in position over the child by means of a string looped at one of the narrow ends of the calabash.

When it was in position at the back over the child, the string was wound on the cloth used for carrying the child and the calabash was held firmly.

One dimly lit day, a thin cloud covered the whole sky evenly making the day cool and dull. There was no sign of immediate rain but a shower was expected that afternoon. Acellam was waddling on the wet compound, slipping and falling on his buttocks from time to time. His mother sat at the doorway resting her back against one of the pillars watching him. She did not attempt to stop him because she thought it was a good exercise for him to regain the power of his legs. As she sat, a thought crossed her mind. "Why don't I go and see my gardens?" I have not been to the gardens for over a month now. The weeds must have over-grown all the crops. "Acellam, come here."

She called the boy who had sat on the dampen compound playing alone. Meekly, he took a stick he was playing with and toddled towards her. "We're going to see our gardens. Okay she said. Acellam merely shook both his fists in the air, walked hurriedly as he neared her, and fell on his stomach on her thighs. She flicked off the mud adhering on his buttocks, got up, tied him on her back, went in and took her water pot, and left for the garden. She did not take the covering calabash with her because, it was cold and the rain was not expected soon even if small white clouds were gathering in the East. Slight wind quivered the leaves of trees as it blew past bringing the easterly clouds nearer. They went. She visited all the gardens, and as she expected, the weeds had overgrown most of her crops. The last garden she reached was the millet garden. The weeds were about a foot taller than the millet. She was disappointed at the sight of the weeds over-running her millet. "I must start weeding tomorrow", she thought, as she moved through the garden. David had fallen asleep on her back.

She stood and looked at the garden from all corners and bent down to uproot a few weeds. They were easy to pull because the ground was soft. Without realizing what she was doing, she found herself weeding. She did no notice that the clouds she had seen building up in the East about an hour ago had pulled near and it was ready to rain any moment. Strong waves of wind and the thunder, which roared across the clouds like a series of time bombs, warned her that they were going to be sodden in the rain. She left the weeding, took the water-pot she had brought with her and rushed to the well to draw some water. She filled the pot and stood it on the bank of the well. She had just finished washing her legs when it began to rain. It poured as if it was jetting through holes made underneath a water tank suspended in the sky. The wind was strong enough to worry the most gigantic trees in the forest.

The first few drops of the rain awakened David and he began to cry, gasping for air. His mother untied him from her back and carried him on her breast pressing his head on her left collarbone. She ran homewards, without the water pot. From time to time, she stopped and hid behind trees to shelter from the strong wind. Nevertheless, she soon abandoned the shelters because of the threats by collapsing branches of trees. She continued trudging on, occasionally being swept of course by the violent wind. With difficulties, she reached her hut before they suffocated to death in the storm. There was not a pore on their skin without water. They were worse soaked than drowned rats.

When she entered the hut, she uncovered the wet cloth she had used for covering David's head in the storm. She expected her son to stir as they had then entered the hut, but to her shock and dismay, he was as soft as rubber. His eyes were closed as if he continued to sleep in the rain. His head drooped hopelessly backwards on her arm.

His arms swung down limply and helplessly. "He's dead"! She shouted hysterically and moved wildly around the room checking for dry covering. She stripped herself off her soaked dress and was naked from head to toes. She grabbed the blanket, bundled the child in it, and laid him on the floor in the hut. She hurriedly built some fire with tears streaming down her cheeks.

"What've I done to deserve these punishments? Blessed Virgin Mary my mother, help me, to restore the life of my child." She cried as she moved around the hut.

After she had built the fire, she slipped on her frock and took the child in her hands, sat with him near the fire, uttering prayers to God for mercy. With trembling hands and thumping heart, she uncovered the child slowly. What she saw alleviated her heart; she thought she saw feeble movements of his stomach muscles and the ribs indicating respiration. She could not believe it. She wiped off tears filling her eyes to make sure the view was clear. She saw distinctly the breathing movements. She smirked and said "Thank you God, please revive him I need him alive. I need him. " She did not notice that it was a long time she had sat near the fire. The rain had closed to drizzles only, with rainwater racing across the compound carrying with it all sorts of rubbish to be dumped under the sisal fence. It was at that time that David sneezed three times consecutively, yawned and opened his eyes and closed them again. His mother smiled. Again, David sneezed and yawned. She licked his eyes with her tongue then David woke up.

David Acellam grew up without any other serious illness. It was when he was turning eight years old that his mother used to tell him plenty of stories particularly the short Christian life she lived with her husband Ogwok. She wanted him to have a clear picture of the early Christianity in the village pioneered by his father Ogwok.

"We had very happy lives in this small village especially when the first missionary arrived here." She told him one day. "We were among the early converts to Catholicism in this part of the world. The First Missionary to arrive here was Padre Santonino, an Italian Padre of the Verona Society. He was a very nice and friendly man, particularly to sick people who were suffering from contagious diseases like leprosy, tuberculosis, and yaws, which we feared most, because of their fatalities. Those who had the diseases were cast out of the human community and small huts were built for them near the forest, where their families took them food and other things. When Padre Santanino came, he did not care, he mixed with them very freely and in the end, he became tuberculous. As a result, he was withdrawn from here and taken back to Italy. It was he, with the help of your father who chose the site of this present Mission of Coomit. Our chapel was very small. We had built it ourselves during our catechetical time when Padre Santonino was still with us. The walls and the floor were mud, smeared with mixture of sand and cow-dung. The roof was grass thatched. The altar was made of two pairs of forked wood dug into the ground towards the far end of the Chapel near the Father's entrance. The finished framework which looked like a table, had papyrus mat laid on it over which were laid the alter cloths for the Mass celebrations. The chapel was dedicated to St. Joseph, the name the Mission is maintaining up until now," she narrated. Padre Santonino taught us catechism and the daily prayers for six months. It was nice, but hard to memorize the songs because most of us were old people who could hardly remember the phrases Padre Santonino kept repeating with us together slowly every day. Whenever he was leading us, we followed him, but immediately he stopped and asked us to go it alone by ourselves, one would hear your father's voice on top, and a few of us dragging behind him, leaving the rest as mute and dumb like the walls. That was one of the reasons why Padre Santonino liked him. He was a brilliant man. After about a year of catechism coaching, Padre Santonino baptized us. We were thirty in number.

"You must make efforts to remember these simple daily prayers because; these are the prayers you will be expected to recite on Sunday, at home, and all the time you want to pray. If you don't know them, you aren't going to pray." Padre Santonino told us when he was leaving.

Padre Egidio whom you see here with us now replaced Padre Santonino. He was the one who arranged for our confirmation. Bishop John confirmed us, three months after we were baptised. After our confirmation, Padre Egidio one Sunday proclaimed in the church that we should all marry in the church. We did not understand at first what he meant. "We are already married, we have paid our dowries, what is this Padre talking about?" most men complained. Nevertheless, he explained to them that they were not going to pay a single cent for the marriage or wedding as he called it. He said we were going to accept one another in the church before God's Minister, the Priest, as husband and wife, and he asked any ready couple to give in their names to him. The following Monday, your father took in our names and on the following Sunday, our banns were put up in the church. Two weeks after, we wedded. We did not have the best man or the woman of honor, nor did we have the bride maids, because that was probably one of the first ever wedding held in the district, but in this village it was certainly the first.

A special platform was made for us in the sanctuary. The Christians adorned the chapel for the occasion. Trees with flowers on them were planted at the doors of the chapel, while inside, the wasp nests, which used to dangle from the roof were all beaten down.

Before the usual mass that Sunday, Padre Egidio took us to the sanctuary and on to our special platform. I was wearing my usual Sunday dress with a small white netted veil, which Padre Egidio had tied, round my head, the long end flowing freely down my back just falling below my waistline. I thought I looked lovely in my attire, because everyone stared fixedly at me both in the chapel and outside. Your father wore his white khaki cassock and pair of buffalo skins sandals.

Following the wedding at our home, Padre Egidio, was full of nice words about us during his talk. He paid tribute to our wedding occasion, which was the first ever in this place. He urged us to love and be faithful to each other, and be good examples to others, particularly our offspring. He emphasized on family prayers at home, and Sunday, to be observed as a Holy day. In conclusion, he appealed to those who had not given in their names to do so and asked them to offer us any gifts as sign of appreciation. Later we escorted him and returned home to attend to our guests who were drowning themselves in *lacoi beer* (local traditional brew). We drunk and danced. The beer was good. It left everyone very drunk. During the merrymaking some of the guests whose homes were nearby ran to their homes and came back with whatever gifts they could lay hands on to comply with the appeal of Padre Egidio. The gifts consisted of a wide range of commodities such as chicken, goat, sheep, inanimate items like clay pots, bowls, baskets, winnowers, spears, and knives were given. One man, Kweronga, under the influence of drunkenness, brought for us a bull and a goat. He came staggering, lugging the animals and when he arrived with them, he pulled them in front of the guests and heralded patting his chest, "who among you has given as much as myself?" He asked, while staggering. Everyone laughed and applauded him for the gifts. Those whose homes were distant kept on sending in their gifts during the week until Sunday. Following our example, all the newly baptised and confirmed Christians wedded.

Several months passed and the number of Christians increased enormously in the villages. The entire pagans who were not baptised turned up to be enrolled as catechumens in big numbers so that our small chapel became too small for us. Because of this, Padre Egidio had to say two masses on Sunday instead of only one he used to offer when we were still few. The first mass for those who were near the Mission started at seven o'clock while the second mass always started at ten for those whose homes were far away. Christians were walking as far as ten miles to come to St. Joseph's chapel for worship. Notwithstanding the increase in the numbers of celebrated masses, the chapel was still over filled with worshipers up to the verandah during both masses. This gave Padre Egidio a second thought of opening up an auxiliary chapel at Latinnyer, a place that was and is still flooded with numerous zealous believers. Padre Egidio appealed to all of us to give hands to the Christians in Latinnyer to erect another similar chapel for them to ease their problems of walking long distance every Sunday, and to avoid over-crowding in the small chapel of Coomit. A meeting was held one Sunday, chaired by Padre Egidio to decide how the Coomit Christians would assist those in Latinnyer.

It was unanimously decided that the Latinnyer Christians should gather the raw materials necessary for building, once those were ready, and then, the Coomit group would go to help put up the chapel. During the same meeting, Andriano Opige was elected the headman who would coordinate and supervise the Christians of Latinnyer. After one and a half weeks, they had collected excess grass, and wood required for the building. They were very enthusiastic to get a chapel for themselves, so they worked willingly. Andriano Opige notified Padre Egidio that the raw materials were ready and that the building business could then start. His announcement automatically called for another meeting to decide the date when work should start. Padre Egidio alerted the Christians about the meeting. We were very friendly and co-operative. No one turned his back to any request concerning doing work for the spread of Christianity. This made the work of Padre Egidio very easy although he was alone here. We also elected your father as our leader. In his brief speech of acceptance, he said that he would do his best, with the co-operation of those who elected him, to see that the work was done to the satisfaction of the Christians in Latinnyer. He appealed to all of us to be industrious. In the end, we resolved that we should leave our homes on Monday the following week for Latinnyer and work should start on Tuesday. We also decided to move together because we feared that separate movement was not safe as we were passing through a belt of forested land haunted by wild animals like lions, hyenas, elephants and buffalos. Whenever they came to pray on Sunday in Coomit, the Christians from Latinnyer got up early and walked in a big crowd carrying their weapons with them.

At six o'clock the following week on Monday, all the participants left. We went and stayed away for another two weeks. We worked like ants. Everyone was happy. We seemed to get stronger as the days wore out into evenings. In a matter of one week, the building was up with the grass-thatched roof, and the walls were wattle and daubed. The second week was spent fixing an alter in the chapel, compressing the floor and plastering the walls, both inside and outside, with the mixture of sand and cow dung. When it was completed, it was the duplicate of the chapel in Coomit with the exception that it was slightly smaller. Padre Egidio was visiting us every alternative day to see the progress we were making. Whenever he visited us, he boosted our morale by working with us until late in the evening before he rode back to Coomit. We returned home after two weeks and Padre Egidio was thrilled to receive us. He congratulated us all on our co-operation and brotherly spirit, which prevailed among us.

On Sunday which followed the week we completed building the chapel, Padre Egidio herald that the inauguration of the chapel we had just built, would be the following Sunday, when one hundred catechumens, out of whom, forty were from Coomit, would be baptised in the same inauguration ceremony. He also informed us that he was inviting a priest from Gulu to come and give him a hand in the ceremony. He urged us to give our visitor a rousing welcome.

Padre Romano was the guest we were waiting for. He arrived on Saturday morning when the sun was just turning into afternoon on a triwheeled motorcycle at the back of which he was pulling a cart packed with about three large boxes.

We welcomed him and later offered him gifts. I do not know how many goats, sheep and chicken he was given but they were enough to start a sizeable farm of goats and sheep. While the chicken were more than enough to set up a poultry farm. The eggs filled about five big baskets as if they were fruits plucked from chicken trees. Padre Romano was stupendous at the sight of the gifts. He confessed he had never in his life seen so many gifts like those we gave him. He did not know what to do with the animals bleating and the birds chuckling all over the compound.

"Why did you give him so many things like that?" David asked.

"We were mad about Christianity. We thought, it was our obligation to support any Missionary and we just wanted them to feel at home and not among people who hated them. Indeed, we made their lives quite easy and enjoyable. Because they were not discriminative, they mixed with us, lived with us as they taught in the church. So, every one of us actually took them as their own guests. As a result if any one did not give any gift, he thought he was being hostile to the visitors."

"Were they appreciative when you gave them the gifts?" David asked.

"Oh, yes, very much indeed." Replied his mother.

"Did they also give you something in return for what you gave them?" Asked David.

"Yes, whenever it was applicable they gave what they could but of course we were far too many for them so they only helped those who were in dire need." Replied his mother and she went on. "They gave out old dresses, blankets, etcetera but they were also helpful in treating our minor illnesses. That was more important than the mere eggs and consumable goods we were giving them.

After we had collected all the gifts, Padre Egidio thanked us very much for what we did to welcome Padre Romano on his behalf. "He said it was a good demonstration of excellent fraternity and love we had, not for them, but for Jesus Christ, whom they were representing. He said they were not there to teach nor preach their own words, but the words of Jesus Christ. Therefore, anyone who welcomes their words was welcoming the word of Christ." Anyadwe said quoting Pader Egidio and continued. Finally, he invited us all to turn up at Latinnyer to witness the inauguration of the chapel but more so, to welcome to the church, the catechumens who were going to be baptised in the name of Christ, and to rejoice together with them.

We had already earlier sent to Latinnyer some animals and chicken to be slaughtered for the occasion. We had also sent the ingredients for *Lacoi beer* to be brewed for us by the women of Latinnyer. We left our homes at dawn, so that by early sunrise we would be in Latinnyer.

"Weren't you afraid of the wild animals?" asked David.

"That was why we went in a huge group, with the men armed with spears. No one dared walk alone through the thick forest at that hour. A few hours walk brought us to Latinnyer chapel with sun just hauling above the horizon. We arrived to the welcome of the huge bonfire built by the catechumens to be baptised. They were all awake by then. They had slaughtered the goats, sheep and chicken, and had chopped the meat in small pieces to be shared among us.

They welcomed us, took our luggage and put them in a pile while we rushed, and surrounded the fire to warm ourselves with our hands stretched over it. We needed the fire badly. We remained there chatting, and talking until it was bright enough, then we were distributed into different camps built for us by comrades at Latinnyer. They had also supplied us with all the necessary items like firewood, cooking pots, millet flour, and salt etcetera. For the meat, we were given preference of our choices. We quickly built the fire, washed the meat and before eight O'clock, the meat was on fire cooking for lunch.

Then we started preparing for the Mass. Cipirian Drallo, a Lutugu from Sudan born in Gulu, was the catechist in Latinnyer who was helping Padre Egidio teaching the catechumens at that time. His parents came from the Sudan. The early Missionaries who started the Mission in Gulu brought them in as porters. When they reached Gulu, they settled near the Mission and refused to go back to the Sudan. They remained giving all the necessary help to the Missionaries. It was at that time that Cipirian Drallo was born. As he grew up, he was taught how to read and write by the Priests, and later they trained him as a catechist to teach the catechumens in Gulu. He was very helpful, so that the Priests almost left all the teaching to him." Anyadwe explained.

"When Padre Egidio went to Gulu to ask for assistance, there was neither a priest nor a Brother who could come and give him a hand, instead they asked Cipiriano to come and help him with the teaching of the catechism, while Padre Egidio did other duties. Drallo came, and he was posted to Latinnyer. The first batch of his catechumens to be baptised were the sixty people who were baptised during the inauguration day of the church.

Drallo rang the gong which was a worn out hoe suspended from a mango tree by a rope, calling everyone to assemble along the main road to wait for the two Priests, Anyadwe continued. "We lined up along both sides of the road and soon we heard the blearing noise of the motorcycles of the two priests breaking the tranquility of the early morning air. In a matter of a few minutes, they emerged on the straight road heading towards us on their motorcycles. We applauded them to a huge welcome. On their part, they waved back to us smiling jovially as they rode past us and parked their motorcycles in the shade of the mango tree with the bell. With Cipiriano Drallo leading the prayers, we walked back towards the chapel with the catechumens to be baptised in front. They were all dressed in white. The hair on their heads and beards, if any, were shaved to expose the bare skin on the scalps and the chins respectively. Some, especially women, smeared the clear skin of their skulls with simsim oil. That made their heads glittered in the sun reflecting light like mirrors. Their Godparents walked next while the rest of the Christians walked last in the procession singing baptismal hymns. The first ceremony to be accomplished was the inauguration of the church, which was nothing but cutting a string tied across the main entrance of the chapel by Padre Romano. After this, the chapel was declared opened. Because of our great number, it was not possible for all of us to go into the small chapel because of that the mass and baptismal ceremonies were celebrated outside it. The ceremony was a lengthy one." Anyadwe said.

"The number of the catechumens to be baptised were too many." David remarked.

"Yes, it was." His mother agreed and continued, "during his preaching, Padre Romano commended Padre Egidio for his hard work in broadcasting Christianity in this part of the world, which, he admittedly proclaimed, was due to our Christian co-operation and unity. Without unity you wouldn't have got this place for worship ready sooner than you have got it." She said quoting Padre Romano. "He appealed to us to perpetuate the fraternity existing among us, and, not to allow it to collapse. Similarly, he urged the newly baptised Christians to copy our examples and join hands with us in the building up of a concrete Christian nation.

The mass went on after his touchy preaching which left all of us examining our consciences as to how well we were behaving as Christians. In the end, after the mass, every new Christian was donated a rosary and a medal of the Blessed Virgin Mary. With pieces of thread, they hung the medals round their necks making them look as holy as the saints at the doorsteps to heaven. After the mass, which ended at three o'clock, we went to prepare our late lunches and later we began to suck the *Lacoi beer* the women at Latinnyer had brewed for us.

We sucked the beers, sang and danced throughout the night until the following day when we left for home. We were seen off by the comrades from Latinnyer up to the forest, before they wished us good luck and went back. We continued with our journey and arrived in Coomit between 1 p.m. and 2 p.m. We were tired, worn out bodies. When we got home, we wanted nothing more than siesta. We threw papyrus mats, and skins in shades of trees and huts, before we fell on them, and slept.

# Chapter Two

Like most African homes, in the ancient days, the home of Gwaromoi, the father of Ogwok, which later became the home of Ogwok and his wife, and lastly it became Ajulina Anyadwe and her only child David Acellam, was heavily fenced with three rows of sisal, three yards apart running around it, leaving small gates which were always closed with heavy logs of wood so that single handed, opening and closing the gates, was like hauling a dead cow from a pit. There were a number of grave trees, one for every grave of Ogwok's kin who had died scattered in the compound making a forest by itself. The pen for the goats and sheep, was within the fence next to Ogwok's hut, while the kraal for the cattle was detached from home about one hundred yards away, and it had heavier fencing than that for the home. Their chicken had a hut built for them and hoisted on four forked poles two meters high with a small opening about a square foot at the side of the hut for their door. This structure was lifted off the ground to protect the chicken against wild cats and snakes. The door was closed using a thin sheet of tin, held in position by inclining a stone against it after the chicken had gone in by climbing on a ladder always leant against the door but removed whenever all the chiken have entered. Ogwok's hut was rectangular with one door, two small round windows with permanently fixed in perforated tin sheet shutters. One of the windows was on the bedroom side, and the other one was on the sitting room side. The sitting room had four mushroom stools for visitors. His wooden bed, had thin strips of buffalo skin, professionally intertwined across the frame formed a network which served as springs. On the bed, two old sacks, were joined mouth to mouth by sisal strings, and was packed with cotton lint to serve as a mattress. These, were the luxuries Ogwok enjoyed during his leisure time.

On top of the mattress on the bed, there was a sordid polychromatic bed sheet which was probably once white, and an old blanket torn at the edges, so that the thread used for hemming it, dangled loosely like strings from an old fish net. Stacked in one corner in his bedroom towards the foot of the bed, were his weapons, which consisted of seven spears of different sizes, the longest was two yards and two feet long. It had a skin sheath for its blade. Together with the spears, was a straight strong machete about three feet and eight inches long, eight inches being the length of the hilt. It also had a sheath for the blade, which was as sharp as a surgeon's blade. A horn, which he used to blow when necessary, and a pot of crashed tobacco near the pillar, was additional assets he had in his hut. When her husband died, Anyadwe never attempted to alter the position of anything in her husband's hut although she swept and dusted them often. She kept them as the museum specimens, which reminded her of the last day they spent together in that hut with her dead husband.

Her kitchen was only ten yards from her husband's hut. The kitchen was roundly built, with mud wall grass-thatched roof like her husband's hut. It had a single round shutter less window about a foot in diameter right on top of the cooking hearth. Inside, there was a half wall built from the main wall extending towards the centre of the kitchen, separating what served as a sitting room from where she had three vertical rows of pots piled on top of each other starting with the largest and diminishing in size up to the smallest sitting on top. The pots served as internal food stores. Each pot contained varieties of ready cleaned foodstuff, like threshed millet grains, seeds ready for planting, salt, etcetera.

This was particularly very useful during the rainy season when at times one hardly saw the sun for the whole day, so that it was difficult to dry millet before it was cleaned and ground. Two water pots were near the door. Next to them, separated by a narrow aisle of about two feet wide, were mounted two grinding stones. The one for millet and sorghum was larger and always looked whitish while that for grinding simsim or groundnut was smaller and shining with the oil from simsim and groundnut. She always left the daughter stones for grinding on the respective mother stones. Behind the grinding stones, was a rack built by Ogwok for hooking their hoes after work.

It was in this kitchen that David Acellam slept with his mother during his early life. His mother slept on the outside of the dividing wall on a papyrus mat made for her by her husband just before he died. She valued the mat dearly. Her son, David, slept in the inner part of the kitchen on an antelope skin, which was killed by his father when he was still alive.

Because they went to sleep very late the previous night when his mother told him the story of their early Christian lives in Coomit, David woke up late.

"David! David! Wake up! The sun is already high up in the sky. You are still snoring?" Anyadwe said arousing him from his sleep. He felt her grip on his shoulder, stretched, and woke up.

"Wake up", his mother repeated bending over him watching him wriggle on his sleeping skin. He got up, sat supporting himself with one hand resting on the skin, and rubbed his eyes with the other hand while yawning.

Meekly David got up, collected his sheet from the skin and walking like a child who had just learned to walk, staggered towards the string tied across the inner side of the kitchen where they always hang their dresses, and threw his sheet over it. He came back, hooked his piece of cloth in front of him on a string of cloth tied around his waist, which was his daily wear, and walked out of the kitchen after he had folded and put away his sleeping skin.

To his surprise, he found that it was almost eleven o'clock in the morning. His mother had already finished winnowing the groundnut seeds they had shelled and she had put them in one big basket. "I don't think we can do much today, the sun is already high up in the sky and it is becoming hotter. What we'll do, is, go and collect the grass from the place we dug on Saturday and burn it so that tomorrow we begin to plant the groundnuts". His mother said.

"I hope the grass is dry after yesterday's shower." David remarked lazily.

"It's two days since we dug it. I should think the grass is dry enough to be collected." She said and continued to sort out immature groundnut seeds from the good seeds to be planted. David glanced at his mother lazily and walked to the sisal fence to the spot where he had been urinating for years, so that the grass there looked like those at the fringe of a desert, with bees buzzing there like in the beehive. He discharged his urine, came back, washed his face, went and tethered the ten goats and eight sheep they had in their grazing pasture.

His mother had already finished sorting the groundnuts and was busy in the kitchen preparing food for them to eat before they went to the garden. After their food, which was a boiled leftover from supper, they went to the garden. As they worked, David kept thinking about the story his mother told him about their early Christian lives in Coomit and was perturbed as to where all the people his mother mentioned in the story had gone.

"Have they all died, migrated very far away, or have they decided to abandon the spirit of co-operation they had in the past? My uncles, not even one comes to see us. We are all by ourselves. Our neighbours, are strangers, they are not related to us, in spite of the fact that out of their sympathies for our solitude, come once in a while to sit with us for a few minutes before they go away leaving us alone." Among those who paid courtesy call on Anyadwe and her son, was a native deputy chief game warden commonly known as "chief Kinyera". He did not only come to see them, but he also assisted them in some of their needs. He had a gun, and very often, he went out in the non-reserved areas, shooting, and shared with them whatever he had shot. His kind gesture of humanity gave David Acellam a thought. He began to wonder whether he was not a relative. With all these thoughts roaming in his mind, David continued to collect the grass with his mother.

The following day, they woke up early enough because they both had good sleep. David quickly took the goats and the sheep to their grazing pasture, while his mother prepared breakfast for them to eat before they left for the garden.

It was on one of those few days during the wet season when the rain gave way for the sun, to give the plants the necessary heat energy they required, that David and his mother left for their garden to plant their groundnuts. His mother carried the seeds in a calabash on her head with her hoe hooked on her shoulder, while David, holding another empty smaller calabash in his hand, walked behind her, when they got to the garden, Anyadwe began to dig the holes about four inches deep, and three inches apart and David, put the seeds singly from his small calabash into the holes. He kicked the soil to cover the seeds with his feet. Whenever the seeds from the calabash in his hands were finished, he refilled it with the seeds from the big calabash his mother had carried. They went on, the sun rose up, towards mid-day and it became hot. His mother noticed that Acellam was tired.

"David."

"Yes mama."

"Finish these holes and we go home. This is enough for toady." She said, and straightened herself up, holding her waist, and rose up slowly with difficulty, as if some of her vertebrate bones were out of the way. She crossed herself, closed her eyes and whispered her prayers after work.

"Why do you always do that before and after work Mama?"

"I do it to ask the Lord for his protection during whatever we are to do, and after, I thank him for having helped us to complete the task successfully. We are through with today's work. Let's go home, I have got to go to the market to buy paraffin."

"Shall I come with you?"

"No, you're going to stay at home. I am going to put some millet out to dry. You will look after it and keep chicken away from it. I won't be long there." His mother assured him. Since Ogwok died, Anyadwe never ate the chicken, because she, like most ancient Acholi women, never ate chicken for they regarded them as dirty birds because being freeranged birds they eat human feaces, snakes and frogs. David was only eight years old; too young to eat a full chicken alone at a meal. Therefore, the only way they had to reduce the number of chickens at their home was to sell them, or offer them to the priests at the Mission.

Before she left for the market, after they had caught two cocks and a hen to go and sell, Anyadwe swept the compound put out un threshed millet to dry, and threw a few handful of the millet in the shadow of the trees where the hens and the cocks, were lying resting avoiding the heat of the sun, and the kites.

"David."

"Yes Mama!"

"I'm going." She said, and picked up the empty tin of paraffin which she intended to refill at the trading centre near the market, and the basket containing the two cocks and the hen with their legs tied, and began to walk to the market.

"Okay Mama." David said and sat on the wooden mortar in the shade of granary.

"If the hens and the cocks are going to be quiet like that, remember to transfer the goats and the sheep into fresh pasture. Will you?" His mother said.

"Yes Mama."

"Bye."

"Bye Mama."

Acellam sat on the wooden mortar with a long stick in his hand ready to drive away any hens or cock which dared come round to eat the millet, but none came out, they all looked comfortable and satisfied in the shade, so he thought he had better attend to the goats and the sheep. As he went, he thought about the cattle still in the kraal. Although Anyadwe and Ogwok had abandoned closing the gates leading in and out of the home with heavy logs when his father was still alive a few years back, the ones at the cattle gate were still maintained partly to avoid them wondering out at night, and partly to protect them against wild animals that might want to prey on them. "Should I go and open them up?" Acellam thought as he approached the kraal. He had never unpacked the logs at the entrance to the kraal alone because they were piled many feet higher than he was; furthermore, they were too heavy for him to lift alone. When he got to the gate and saw how high the gate was, more than twice his height, he was frightened. "How am I going to handle the job? I could climb on something and remove the logs by tilting them on one side. So long as the cattle will be out it will be alright." David thought and went straight to the kraal to open it. He came and stood next to the gate, glanced up to look at the log lying solidly on top of each other heavy enough to make minced meat out of him should any of them hit him. The sight frightened him, and gave him a twist in the stomach. When he tuned round in surrender, he saw a good tough long rod of wood lying behind him. He had brought that rod there himself about a week ago, and had forgotten it there. It encouraged him to try opening the gate with it. He lost no time, picked it up and turned to the gate. The last log on top was fairly small, he poked it from below at one end, lifted it from where it was lying slid on the other end, and crashed on sisal fence 'thud' it went down knocking away some of the sisal leaves.

"Ha! This is a bad job. I am destroying the fence. I'm not doing any useful work at all, Mama might just scold me instead when she finds that I have been battering the fence up with these logs." He whispered to himself. He almost abandoned the idea when another tempting thought of gaining praise from his mother started its way again in his head.

"That doesn't look to be inclining towards the fence, its bent outward. Therefore, if I lift it, it will definitely fall outwards away from the fence because of its shape." He approached the gate once more, poked the second log underneath and exerted upward thrust on it. It was heavy; it did not rise as easy as the first one. With some effort, he lifted it but it left the top of the rod and fell back to its original place.

He was not sure then if he would go even half way through the task because the logs were getting bigger and heavier as they descended down. He stood with the rod in his hand leaning lightly on it looking at the pile of logs hatefully.

"Let me try again", he told himself.

He inserted his rod and pushed upwards. The log lifted, slid slightly on the opposite side but as he continued pushing upwards almost smiling and counting two off the pile, the log left the top of the rod and instead of falling back to its original position, because of its shape as he had predicted, it fell short of the pile and came somersaulting crushing towards him missing him by a split of a second. He jumped and watched it tumbling down rolling on its curved side before it came to a rest right in front of the gate, away from the fence. While he stood panting, his mother, who had seen what was happening from a distance, came and stood behind him and said, "They are still heavy for you to manage alone; you'd better not try it again. See how you've damaged this sisal." She said pointing at the log lying buried under the broken sisal leaves.

"Have you attended to the goats and the sheep already?" his mother asked.

"No, I haven't gone there. I was on my way there when I thought I should release the cattle first." Replied David.

"Will you go and see them while I finish your job?"

"Yes Mama." David said and left without looking behind.

There was a he-goat among the goats, which was nearly as old as David himself was. In spite of the age, it was quite strong. It was spotted black and white, with a long tuft of hair in front of the head. It had a thick mane like that of a lion. The twisted "V" shaped horns and its colour differentiated it from a lion cub. It had a very strong odor which always remained behind even if it was far away. As a result, their grazing pasture always stank of the he-goat.

Because of its age and strength, all the other goats, and sheep, seemed to respect it, so that it always led the way for them. No other he-goat or ram dared to do so for peaceful purpose. When he left his mother opening the gate for cattle, he went straight to where he had tethered the he - goat. Nevertheless, on reaching the spot, it was not there. The grass on which he had tied the he-goat was badly ruffled as if it broke off violently and had escaped.

"But where has it gone?" David asked himself. "It is not possible for it to break loose and go away; it would be here enjoying the company of the nanny goats and terrorising the young male goats. Has someone stolen the goat or was it a lion which has caught it and it's eating it somewhere in the forest?" That thought frightened him, but all the same, he went and climbed an anthill, which stood nearby, and he saw what he could not believe at first. He thought it was a snake he was seeing but when he recalled some of the stories his mother used to tell him about pythons, that they could swallow larger animals and get anchored in one spot for months until the animal is completely digested, and bone excreted, he concluded that what he was seeing was a python lying stretched under a tree with the head, the feet of the goat, and the tether still sticking out off its mouth. David hysterically ran down from the ant-hill and untied the other goats and the sheep. Some of them were badly entangled in an attempt to break loose when the he-goat was battling with the python. Because of that, he released them from the entangled tethers and hastily he drove them out of the pasture and ran home as fast as they could. Anyadwe was already at home pounding the millet in the mortar in the shade of the granary, when she saw both the animals and David running home frightened.

"Eh what's the matter David?" she asked standing up quickly from where she was kneeling pounding the millet. She ran to David and held him by the hand and looked round but could not see the he-goat. "Where is the he-goat?" she asked, before David had time to gain his breath to answer her. "The python ..."

"What?"

"The python has killed it. It has swallowed it, only the head and the fore legs including the tether are still out. It's lying under the fig tree near the ant-hill." He told his mother with his heart pumping at the rate of a ticking wristwatch.

He thought his mother was going to be frightened, and start running to every neighborhood to call for help from the men, but her courage shocked him."Pythons aren't lions. We will go and kill it. It is very easy to finish them when they are gagged up with a lump in their stomach like that. In that stage, they are immoblised." She said and went into her late husband's hut and took two spears, gave the smaller one to David while she carried the machete and the bigger spear.

"Come on, let's go." She said and they started to run towards the anthill, mounted it, and stood side by side with their weapons in their hands. David looked down where he had seen the python and there it was, lying bulging on the chest like a maturing coconut tree with only the rope showing. His mother made the sign of the cross as if she was a crusader going to fight a Holy war, and undauntedly descended down the anthill with the machete, out of its sheath, in her right hand, the spear and the machete's sheath, in her left hand, she walked straight to the python while whispering her prayers. She walked with the courage which is very rare, if not absent in females.

The python saw her come but only stared at her apologetically. David left the anthill to follow his mother walking very carefully. He saw her approach the python, stood just opposite the bulb, and put the machete across it. With little effort, the python was in two. David did not know the machete was very sharp. It cut like acetylene gas flame playing with a thin sheet of tin. She put the tip of the machete at the side of the gagged mouth slid it laterally, immediately black and white sports showed revealing the he-goat. Encouraged by what happened, David quickened up his steps and came to take care of the harmless tail portions, spearing it at random until it stopped dancing.

By that time, his mother had completed her job, and had dragged away the he-goat covered up with wet, shining, slippery, mucoid material, which made her sick.

"What are we going to do with this mama?"

"We'll let it rot or bury it somewhere; all I wanted was the python dead which we've achieved. It could have come back for more if it went alive."

"Why? Don't you think someone in the village might like it?

I do not think the meat is bad after peeling off the skin." David suggested and frowned in disgust before he spat on the grass. She thought for a while and said, "We'll tell Opuk about it and see if he'll take it."

"Are we going to leave it here alone?"

"No, we'll drag it near home."

Opuk was one of the oldest men in the village. There was no single black hair on his head, so that at a distance, he appeared a Muslim wearing a white turban. He never grew a beard or moustache. In spite of his old age, he had not lost much of his masculine vigor. He wore around his waist a beaten up skin, which was as soft as cloth. On his wrists and ankles, he wore four metal rings, and those on the ankles used to clack when he walked. He always walked on a bamboo stick, which was as tall as he was. Occasionally, he carried it across his shoulders. His sitting stool was always suspended under his armpit by a string, which ran round his shoulder. He was a witch doctor, a strong believer in devilism, and a traditionalist, which left him the only one unbaptised in the village. It was highly believed he was possessed by devil, because one day when on their village tour, Padre Santonino and Ogwok passed through his home in an attempt to convince him to be baptised. As soon as he saw Padre Santonino, he began to shout to Ogwok. "Why have you brought that white man here, we don't want to see him. He is deceiving us all to abandon our ways of worshiping the gods of our fathers, and he wants us to adopt his. We'll never do that, take him away from us, we don't want him here." He got up, walked away into the hut, and closed the door behind him.

Opuk always associated any abnormal happening with witchcraft. As a result he always swept his compound clean before sun set, and, before dark, he patrolled round his home to note foreign objects and marks in the compound and in the morning, he got up very early before any of his family did, to check if there was anything else other than what he saw the previous evening in the compound. If he did, even if it was brought in accidentally, he always sat under the trees, which he believed his gods stay, so that they told him the name of the person who brought the object. He always came out with something anyway. Besides his witchcraft for which Anyadwe disliked him, Opuk had very effective Acholi herbs, which helped very many people in the village for which; all those who would never have visited his home did so. He lived beyond the well they fetched for their drinking water. Therefore, when they were going to Opuk's home they took with them their water vessels in order that, on their way back they could bring home some water in them. When they reached the well, they hid their vessels near a tree not far from the well before they continued to Opuk's home.

Opuk had got up from the papyrus mat he was sleeping on, under the trees in his compound, where he believed the gods of his ancestors lived. He sat on his mushroom stool. His elbows pivoted on his knees drown near his face, his hands clasped on his stooped head; he stared angrily meditatively on the ground between his legs. What am I going to do with this white men's God?

## The Devout Woman

I was respected and known for a seer in the entire village. Everyone came to me for treatment and sooth saying. I cured them and told them the truth. I warn them about our tradition and cultures. I told them that this power of seering and sooth-saying, I inherited from my uncle because the gods were pleased with me. I am to pass it on to some one else in our clan who will please the gods. Nevertheless, here are the people who have now turned against their gods, tradition and culture. Particularly Mama Acellam, the wife of Ogwok, my own nephew, the son of a woman I call my sister, perpetuated the bitter war pioneered by her husband against the gods of our ancestors by criticizing me openly in the village. She is persuading the entire village to rise against the gods.

She has convinced half of the village not to listen to me, she calls the white men's words, the words of God, Holy words, and they are the people of God. Well my uncle Gwaromoi her father in-law never did that. He was a man who was highly refuted because of his stand on the preservation of traditions and culture. Mama Acellam tells me that the white men's God is better than our gods are. The white men's medicine is better than my herbs. She stupidly believes anything pertaining to a white man is better than that of a black man. Look, she insists people must remarry in the church the house of the white men's God. I will show her that this is not true. I Opuk with the help of the gods will show these *Italiano* that their God is not better than the gods of our ancestors are. Ogwok welcomed these white men in the Village. It was he who led them in the village and helped the *Italiano* to contaminate the minds of the black people. Now these people do not know their gods, culture and traditions. The gods are angry they have just confessed it to me in the dream I have just had.

Anyway, where is Ogwok now? I am sure he would have come out clean from the fight he had with the lion if the gods were not angry with him. I warned him, but he impudently went ahead, and defied the gods warning. I regret his death but he had been foolish not to heed the warning. What is going to happen to our people? The gods are already annoyed with them. Our children will not know any traditional dance because they prefer the white men's dance; they will not know any herbs because they want the white men's medicine. They will not play *Lawala* (Acholi popular traditional game to train young men in accuratecy in spearing animal when hunting) because they will prefer the white men's game. All our culture will just be tales to tell and nothing tangible any more.

Have the gods not confessed this to me in my sleep just now? I hate the idea. Christianity what is Christianity? The white men's land is packed tight and now they are trying to get homes. They come here to tell us that all we have and do are rubbish but they want our land and everything in it. They pretend they have come to teach me about God. Who had not known about God before? Our great, great, grandfathers did before these white men were born. I am going to see the elders of the village and talk to them about this new development. It must stop. In addition, this Mama Acellam if she was not the wife of my nephew, I would have asked the gods to burn her alive with her son. All her song is about Christianity, Christianity. I am sure if no one followed these *Italiano* all of them would have packed and vanished. I hear in the house they call church, the house of their God they have statues of white men, and women, everywhere impersonating their God, and statues of black men horrible made with long tails, fingernails, and toenails, impersonating the devil. In addition, here they call me a devil because I am black, and because I have refused to yield to the white men slyly confusing God. I am proud of everything and my achievement.

Why can't these Africans see simple logic? Is Mama Acellam white? If she isn't, why does she not see that the white men are insulting us? A black man is a devil, a white man is God! The God he has come to confuse us with. In other words, we should begin to adore the white men because they are gods! I will never do that. I will be the last to join the group. In addition, I will join it in my grave. The gods have already complained to me about their shelters in my dream just now. What is going to happen to our *Abila*, our places for offering sacrifice to our gods? These *Italiano* have convinced some of these people to destroy their *Abila* and they did. What happened to Ogwok their leader? He's dead, Opiro, snake vomited all the poison in him, and he died a miserable death. His skin cracked like dry pods of beans and he exploded like thunder. The daughter of Owiny became mad; she walked naked like a nanny goat. The son of Anyamonyuk became impotent. Was it not in front of those *Abila*, they have destroyed that they buried the umbilical cords of those children when they were born? Those *Abila* with their stone doors were the shelters and the resting place for the gods; the gods who take care of these children.

How would you expect the gods to take these insults lying down? When we want rain, it is in front of our *Abila* that we offer our sacrifices to the gods for the rain. Before sowing our seeds, we put them before the *Abila* for the blessing from the gods. In addition, when we harvest our crops we give the gods food made out of our harvest in front of the *Abila*. So I hear, the white men do the same in their church to their God.

Then why do these *Italiano* tell the black idiots that their God is better, and real, and the God who made the black man's gods! When we want sunshine, it is the same place we go to for sacrifice, when one becomes mad like Owiny's daughter, it is before the *Abila* that we solve the problems, and so is the case of secondary impotence like the one of the son of Anyamonyuk. Is our *Abila* not therefore the same place, with what the white men called an altar in their church? Is it not there that the white men offer their sacrifice to the God? If anyone asks him to destroy his altar, will he accept to do so? He won't why? Because, he calls it the place where his God stays and therefore, a sacred place, a Holy place. Nevertheless, a black man goes on and destroys his *Abila* because a white man has told him to…

"May I come in?" Anyadwe sought for permission to join Opuk interrupting his thought. "Oh, Mama Acellam, that is you! You are welcome. I was coming to you now if you did not come. It's the gods who actually sent for you." Said Opuk.

"I see. You want to see me?"

"Yes very much."

"Well here I am. How is the matter with you?"

"I am very much disturbed in the head at the moment."

"About?"

"About you people here who are following these *Italiano* blindly without knowing the seriousness of the consequence. You know they are actually creating a rift between you and the gods of our ancestors. They want you to forget our gods, cultures, and tradition. Above all, they want their cultures and traditions to over whelm ours so that they find it easy to live and stay with us here.

With their cultures predominating ours, they could easily tell us that we are not worth existing because a man without, customs, traditions, and gods, is no man at all. Better dead than alive. That is why the gods keep on emphasizing that we must boot these people out. All we have to do is boycott them, and they vanish. They have nothing in their land, nothing at all, that is why they are here. I am sure if you people refuse to follow them, they will force you in everything, and this will be the time we should take up arms and fight. A man like me can't take away my land under pretext of bringing me news of Christian God." Anyadwe sneered and interrupted him.

"Is that why you were desperately in need of me?" she asked.

"Yes, so that we discuss what we can do to these white people in Coomit Mission. You see, you people will wake up too late. Look, the gods are telling me that a disaster awaits the village and unless we stop these people from spreading their wings too far, we shall all perish in it. You and I are influential enough. If we stand firm on our decision, these young people in the village will automatically follow us." Opuk said.

"What do you think you and I can do? We cannot make a decision for them, if we do, they will tell us that we are old and ancient in our thinking. Therefore, our advice is antagonistic to modern ways of living. Fighting is just out of question. These people have come to live with us in a peaceful way like brothers. They are not interested in our land. They are here to teach the words of God to you, me and anyone else who will listen to them. God is the creator and the Almighty. Now they have hundreds of thousand of jealous believers who will definitely fight along their side should you declare war on them and you can see what the result will be, a complete disaster and chaos. Honestly Opuk this should not be your worry."

"Why should it not? Don't you see what is happening? You have already denounced your own gods, the gods of your fore-fathers, the gods who cared for you from childhood until you are an old woman today."

"It's that God that they want you to know about well."

"Nonsense, how can a man who doesn't know about my customs come to teach me about my gods? Don't you see what has started happening? The destruction of *Abila*! Who has ever misbehaved with *Abila*, our sacred place of worship and offertory? Is this what you call knowledge about the new God, the Christian God? You Mama Acellam tell me, have you ever heard of anyone who destroyed his or her *Abila* at home? I know of none and when these *Italiano* ordered the destruction of the *Abila* you jumped on them and pulled them to pieces. What happened to those who have done so? I give you the names of the few. Ogwok your husband is dead. The daughter of Owiny became mad, when she defied her father's warning, and destroyed the *Abila*, and used the *Okango wood* (specific tree used for the constructing *Abila*) for cooking. She destroyed the eating pots of the gods put in the *Abila* and her father cursed her. You always hide away when you meet her patrolling the village naked. In addition, that handsome son of Anyamonyuk is now a flower in the garden, no use to any woman. There are numerous examples throughout the village and I am sure you know all about these. Therefore, Mama Acellam are we going to sit, fold our arms, and let these white men destroy our children. Should we allow them to do that? The gods are already angry with you in particular. I have always been pleading to the gods for you, they accept my explanation, but they keep telling me that if you do not change your ways of living you will die very soon or you and Acellam will lead a miserable life throughout.

The gods had trust in Acellam, and they wanted me to hand over the leadership of this village to him so that he becomes the next seer, soothsayer, and medicine man.

Nevertheless, you have spoilt everything you are a lion against the gods with your Christianity. I see a dark future for this village of Coomit. There is going to be a lot of suffering in most homes and even deaths. The gods are going to punish people."

"I have heard what you have narrated. True none in the past meddle with the *Abila*. The place they called the resting place of the gods of our ancestors. However, I do not agree with you that, the misfortune that befell these people should be taken for granted that it came about because they destroyed the *Abila*." Anyadwe said doubtfully.

"Mama Acellam, when will you grow up?" Opuk interjected.

"Well Opuk, can you tell me what you have to say about the madness of Okek. They didn't destroy their *Abila* it is intact, but he is also patrolling the village naked." Retorted Anyadwe.

"Has he not joined the white men? He is one of these who are now using the white men's name. He now calls himself Kerobino Okek.

These are names of dead white people and the white men are forcing us to use them and you people follow them and you call them Christian names, the ghosts of the dead white men will make you all mad. I tell you Mama Acellam you people of this village must rise and do something to maintain our integrity, tradition, and dignity. The white men are mistreating us."

"How?" Anyadwe asked.

"I think you have misunderstood everything about these white men and their followers.

I have been in the company of the priests, what I see is not what you believe. You see, you can criticise anything genuinely when you see it, and know the good and the bad side of it. Otherwise, you will be prejudiced, that is what I think you are now."

"You're talking like a mad woman. With the white man's God and you sink. There is no double dealing Mama Acellam. They are going to keep on visiting you people. In addition, in the mission they will tell you to destroy anything traditional, because they call them things of the devil and primitive. Theirs are the modern and belong to God. Tell me the explanation of this if you know. Why is it that these days, River Lukwor is drowning very many people? That river was very peaceful. I have lived all my life here, there has not been any incidence of anyone drown in river Lukwor, but these days, every week you hear someone has drowned in the river, why?"

"I think you will agree with me that those incidences we have been hearing were children. They were the young schoolchildren who went to learn to swim, and they always drowned at the centre of the river near the bridge where the water current is strongest. Otherwise I know of no explanation."

"Were we not children when we learned to swim in that river?" I was about ten only, and my brother was about six years old. We used to swim right to the centre of the river but none of us was drowned. Let me tell you. The gods are very angry with the people here. They are angry because of the bridge they built across the river. Secondly, the white men have taken the river away from us. You know on Saturday and Sunday you people here are not allowed to reach the river. Why? Because white men believe, you are dirty and you spoil the water. You see what I mean I suppose.

Your own river, in your own country and village, a man comes so many thousand of miles away, and takes it away from you! He orders you not to use your own river! Something you live on! It is incredible; I just cannot bring myself to think of that to be true. In addition, here you are giving me childish reasons that the people drowning in that river these days are children and because they swim right in the centre. What of Odine who drowned last week, and Akuta yesterday, were they children? These are married men with children.

Think before you talk. The whole of this village will go in tears very soon. I am telling you now. I have seen it and the gods are telling me to warn you people to boycott these white men but you force your way to them like fools. I will not be blamed if the gods take up arms against you. I will have told you all but you impertinently went your white men's ways. Besides you know, Mama Acellam, I have just been dreaming that your late husband wants some food from you, he is hungry he wants you to sacrifice for him something to eat. He would have actually asked for this from his brothers but you know just as much as I do that all his brothers are dead. Of course, none knows about Kilama a man who walked away from home some years back. No one knows whether he is alive or dead, and it is no use to think about him." Opuk concluded.

Since Ogwok died eight years ago, no one gave his ghost the food and the beer. Therefore, to Opuk the bigot polytheist witch doctor, whatever misfortune was happening in Anyadwe's home was due to nothing else other than the ghost of Ogwok in demand of food and drink.

"As you know traditionally, when an old person dies in Acholi, sometime after his or her death, close relatives give food to the spirit, which always consist of the meat of a cow, goat, or sheep. Beer is compulsory. If this is not done, the ghost of the deceased complains through signs. The signs are always ill health, or even death invades such homes unless the spirit of the deceased is fed and boozed." Opuk explained and gazed at Anyadwe who sat in front of him. "Therefore, the spirit of your husband has wisely suggested it through me that you give him food." Anyadwe was left confused, and stupefied. She laughed and said, "Anyway Opuk, we had come to see you on a different issue."

"Oh, I see" He said clearing his voice. "What is this, I must know."

In fact, Anyadwe was feeling very uneasy so much that she wanted to rush through the story and leave his home.

"It's quite a simple matter." Anyadwe stressed.

"Hmm, Opuk groaned and started to speak to the spirit of his dead nephew; Ogwok. "You were a very nice man when you were with us. You never fought nor insulted anyone. Why are you beginning to fight us now that you are away? I know, as you have just told me that you need something to eat; we shall give you all you want, but please take away sickness and bad luck. It is only when we are healthy that we can give you whatever you want. Without……"

"The thing is", Anyadwe interrupted Opuk impatiently while sitting upright from the stooping position she was sitting, and twisted her nose as if a rotten egg was smashed under her nose.

"We had a misfortune this morning, a python killed and swallowed one of the biggest he-goat we had but we killed it and took the goat out of its stomach, she said and went through the story rapidly. "Being the village elders we thought it was wise to let you know about it first before we did anything with the dead goat", she put in politely.

"Hmm Opuk said as if the "Hmm" was the introductory sound he made to begin every sentence.

"You're quite right, and you've done the right thing. You'd have made the greatest mistake if you didn't come to tell me this as you've done, or if you had meddled with the carcass before I saw it myself." Opuk said confirming his superiority in the village.

"I'm coming with you straight away now to scrutinize the inside of the goat to determine what has sent the python to kill it. Even now I see something strange about the incidence, why the he-goat, more over the biggest of them all? And why you as a woman killed the python so easily and here is the spirit of Ogwok your husband yelling for food." Opuk said. Anyadwe sighed and said.

"We must be going now Opuk, but we're passing through the vegetable garden first before we go home. I suggest you go your way. We will meet at home."

"Hmm, I think that will be alright with me because I've got a second thought. I will talk to Tongpur first. If I get him at home, we will come together."

Anyadwe didn't want to begin any more talk, so they got up and walked away almost in silence, because all the rest of the family of Opuk were away in the garden.

Anyadwe and David did not go to the vegetable garden nor did they intend to do so.

She merely gave the excuse to brush Opuk off their backs and to avoid unnecessary boring irritating talks about the gods. Instead, they went to the well. When they got to where they had hidden their water vessels, they were surprised to find that the vessels were not there.

"Have we missed the spot?" Anyadwe asked annoyed.

"No, this is the tree near which we had left them." David pointed out.

"Don't you see the grass still trampled where the vessels were lying? Who could have taken them and why anyway?" David asked.

"May be some of these hunters came across them and took them." His mother replied.

"Why?" David asked again.

"Funny people behave in funny way son." Anyadwe answered.

"What are we going to do about this Mama?"

"Nothing, what can we do? We do not know who took them nor do we suspect anyone. We'll just have to forget them."

"I do not have any other gourd for carrying water what will I use?" David asked.

## The Devout Woman

"We will buy a new one for you from Topiny. He has plenty of good gourds at his home. He brought some to the market today. They were very nice.

They arrived back home a few minutes past three o'clock.

At five o'clock every Saturday, David accompanied his mother to the Mission for confession and Benediction. They never had a clock nor watch to tell them the exact time. Therefore, they always told their time by looking at the position of the sun.

"If Opuk and Tongpur do not show up before four o'clock we'll not wait for them." Anyadwe said.

"Then what will happen to the goat?"

"What do you think they are going to do with the goat? Nothing, except to come and pronounce their lies about the spirit of your father which he had already started saying. He always had some lies to say about the spirits. A stupid old liar; I'm almost thinking of burying the goat before they arrive to hurt me," she said with hurt feelings.

# Chapter Three

A few minutes passed, the two men arrived. Opuk was in front followed by Tongpur with his black dog at his heels. Tongpur was about the same age with Opuk, but he was a little shorter and younger unlike Opuk he was neither what one would term a good Christian nor a strong believer in witchcraft. He practiced both moderately. He also did not wear the heavy bangles around his wrists and legs like Opuk. He was more modern than his friend was. The two old men were very friendly but they very often disagreed on two points. Firstly, when the extremist Opuk wanted some of the traditional functions to be done according to his personal belief, and secondly they often picked up quarrels over Tongpur's forgetfulness for which he was best known throughout the village.

Anyadwe welcomed the two old men in her kitchen, and after some petty conversation she reminded them, "Gentlemen you'd better do what you want to do quickly because we're going away to the Mission and it's getting late."

"Hmm, so you're going away?" Opuk asked.

"Yes", Anyadwe agreed.

"We shouldn't have come if you told me that you're going away. Okay bring us the goat, let us see it. I'm doing this cheerily because it's my nephew's home if it wasn't I wouldn't have sat here for the next few minutes." Opuk said viciously.

"Opuk", Tongpur broke in, "you don't have to lose your temper. She hasn't said anything wrong, she has merely told us that they are going to the Mission, and that shouldn't have annoyed you."

"Looking for what there?" Opuk asked.

"Well, Anyadwe", Tongpur said turning to her; she was sitting next to Opuk with her back resting on the wall.

"Let's have the goat." Without a word, Anyadwe got up and walked outside and the two men followed her.

David was last to walk out.

According to the way they always told their time by the sun, they were getting late for the church services that Saturday. Anyadwe led the two men to where they had left the dead he-goat. The two men began to skin the goat, and Opuk kept on commenting on all sorts of blood clots, and bruises inflicted on the goat by the python before it died, claiming they were caused by the gods, and the spirit of Ogwok. David did not say a word but walked away and brought the sheep and the goats back to the pen and tethered them. He had just pushed in the last calf when he saw his mother walking briskly towards him.

"Do you know David, they are about to finish skinning the goat. Opuk is saying all sorts of stupid things which I do not want to hear and I think Tongpur is not happy with him either. Anyway, when we finish here, you go and wash your legs and get dressed ready to go to church. There should be enough water for both of us still left in the pots."

"Are we going to leave them here at home?" David asked.

"It's their funeral, I'm not bothered. If they want to complete their work they have started, let them do whatever they please."

"Why was Opuk annoyed with you Mama?"

"Because I mentioned that we are going to church, he believes I am not interested in whatever lies he is going to say." Anyadwe said as they put the last log on the pile of logs closing the entrance to the kraal. On their way home, they stopped where the two old men were skinning the goat. They had already finished and they were seated down waiting for her, so that they could slit the stomach of the goat open in her presence to read for her the messages from the spirit of her dead husband.

"Come here Mama Acellam," Opuk called her as soon as he saw her.

"I want to open this goat when you are here, because I want to show you all the abnormalities we are going to find, and explain to you what each of them means." He said with certainty of a prophet.

"You could have as well done that without my presence." She said. David walked passed them home to do what his mother had told him. His mother reluctantly stopped. Opuk first spat on the ground and recited a few prayers to the gods to help him read the signs he was to get inside the goat accurately. He particularly mentioned the name of Ogwok to be frank and show all his needs in that goat he sent the python to kill. "Ogwok", he went on, "I'm asking you to stop fighting us now." Be a nice man as you had always been. Tell us now, and we'll know what you want, so that we give you with clean hearts, and you also take it with clean hands." He concluded and spat on the ground rapidly three times before he took Tongpur's knife and slit the stomach of the skinned goat which was lying on its back, with the legs pointing upwards.

He made the slit from the lower abdomen right up to the diaphragm exposing the liver, lungs and heart of the goat. Anyadwe wanted to walk away but Tongpur, who had sat in silence, said almost in a whisper to her, "let's hear what he is going to say."

Opuk, was very busy with the goat murmuring alone, did not hear what Tongpur said.

David went, dressed, and came back where they were interpreting signs in the goat. At the base of the liver, there was a pool of dark blood, which apparently was due to internal bleeding which resulted from the way the python killed the goat by breaking the ribs. The liver had started to show signs of autolysis, but, to Opuk, those were bad signs.

"Hmm" Opuk started. "Mama Acellam, and Tongpur, comes near." He ordered. Tongpur moved, but Anyadwe did not move. "Move nearer Mama Acellam." Opuk pleaded.

"What are you afraid of?" He asked. Anyadwe kept quiet and remained where she was.

"Mama Acellam, I'm asking you to move nearer, do you hear me?" Opuk asked impatiently

"But I'm hearing and seeing all what you are doing there; do you want me to come and sit on your back or enter inside that goat?" She said annoyingly. Opuk sighed and nearly threw the knife he was holding at her.

"You people, we are not here to fight." Let's do whatever we are doing and begin other things." Tongpur warned them.

"Hmm anyway", Opuk went on after a spell of silence in a low tone clearing his throat in between "Do you know what this black blood and the spots on the liver mean?" Anyadwe and Tongpur kept quiet and merely glanced at each other and their eyes met.

David who was already at the side of his mother looked up at his mother and knew she was very annoyed.

"Mama let's go!" He whispered pulling her lightly on the arm while looking up in her face. She looked down, smiled at him, and nodded.

"Gentlemen……"

"Hmm" Opuk interrupted her. "The black blood and the spots on the liver means that Ogwok, the owner of this goat who is already dead, is angry because he hadn't been given any food since he died. His anger is shown by the dark blood." He said and lifted the lung and saw another spot, which he pointed at with the tip of the knife. This means that he was the one who ordered the goat to be killed by the agent, which he chose to be the python. The victim was to be a human being but the gods didn't allow his plan to work as he had decided".Opuk said, probably to throw a scare in Anyadwe to make her gain interest in his words, but instead it worsened the situation especially when he said that a human being was to be the victim of the python.

"Gentlemen, we must go to church now, we are getting late, help yourselves to anything you want in the home. We do not have much water, but you can use the little we have in the pots for any washing your might need."

"When will you come back?" Tongpur put in politely.

"As soon as the prayer will be over." Opuk was as quiet as a switched off radio; he sat with the back of his head towards them.

Anyadwe hurried home washed, dressed and they were off to church running.

"What an awful day!" Anyadwe commented as they walked.

"Why?"

"I'm wondering why the day has been so terrible for me all through up to now. I do not know how it will end. You know, I lost one of the cocks on the way to market. I could not explain the loss.

"Really", David exclaimed.

"Yes" his mother replied and went on. When I told some of my friends, they believed that it fell off the basket but I was not alone, I was walking with Aculu. She would have definitely seen the cock fall. In any case, it would have cackled and fluttered while falling off the basket. Anyway, it was lost. The goat was killed, our water vessels mysteriously disappeared like the cock and this good for nothing-old liar keeps pulling my legs with the death of my husband, I have disliked him for it. Well, there we are, these are what God has planed for us today. I don't know how we are going to end it, may be yet another one is waiting for us." She concluded with tears filling the sockets of her eyes. She tried to fight them back but it was too late, she stopped, wiped the tears streaming down her cheeks with the hem of her frock, before they continued to walk to the Mission. They had reached the last turn to the Mission when his mother suddenly stopped and sat down holding her head in her hands.

"What is the matter Mama?" David asked and crossed to where she had sat.

"I'm a bit dizzy; I feel I must rest a little."

David put his hand on his mother's shoulder. "Mama, you're shivering, are you sick?"

"I think I have got too much on my head today, that's all but I will ask the sister for some medicine when we get to the Mission." After about five minutes rest, Anyadwe struggled up on her feet holding the ground firmly with her left hand while the right hand gripped on her knees, she got up, stood and closed her eyes without moving an inch. She was too giddy to move, she wanted to gain stability first before taking a step forward. David stood with his hand folded behind him, and watched his mother struggle with her sickness. He did not know what to do to help her. They continued to walk to church. The church was built in such a way that the main door was at the dead end of the church avenue, so that when one was on the nap of the avenue from the main road, one saw whatever was happening on the alter especially if the candles were alight and the door open. "Look the prayers are over!" Anyadwe yelled and quickened her steps almost breaking into a run as if she was not sick a while ago. They hurried on, when they were a few yards away from the church; they heard the jingling sounds of the altar bell, which confirmed to them that they have missed every prayer.

After a brief silence when the bell was rung, they heard the congregation singing the Benediction song. A few seconds later Padre Egidio walked out of the church reading a breviary. He was putting on his long white cassock, a coat over it, and stole round his neck indicating that he had been hearing confession. He had just finished reading a page in the book and was turning the page over with the aid of a strip of cloth fixed at one end of the book, when he saw Anyadwe and her son David Acellam coming.

"You're late today?" Padre Egidio said smiling to them and extended his hand to shake with them.

"Yes father." Anyadwe replied and added, "We had a very busy day today, and moreover I wasn't feeling fine." At that time, Padre Egidio had put his hand on top of David's head ruffling his kinky hair with his palm as he always did. He had closed the breviary and held it against his ribs, like a Professor of theology from a lecture.

"You really look sick. What is the problem?"

"I have been having headache and dizziness."

"Do you feel cold?"

"No."

"Did you vomit today or have diarrhoea?"

"No."

"May be you'll like to see Sr.Veronica for some tablets. They are about to get out of the Church. "

"Yes, I'll do that, but we must go in first." Padre Egidio nodded approvingly stooped down, patted David on his buttocks, and pushed him gently forward indicating he should follow his mother.

The time was running to past seven o'clock, when Anyadwe and David came out of the church, and went to Sr.Veronica for treatment.

Sr. Veronica, Padre Enriko and Bro. Albertini were the second group of the Verona Missionaries who joined Padre Egidio in Commit Mission to help him with the work, which had become too much for him to handle even with the help of industrious catechists like Cipiriano Drallo.

"Ajulina, we missed you during the Benediction this evening." Sister Veronica said and shook hands with her. Ajulina the Christian name of Anyadwe was preferred by Sr. Veronica, so that she always called her by it.

"I've been having a bit of headache."

"How is it now?"

"It has improved, slightly."

"Do you feel cold?"

"No."

"When did it start?"

"Just before we left for the Mission. Probably, I'm only tired."

"It could be but'll give some quinine for malaria in case it's the one. It should drive that headache away so that you are fresh for tomorrow's service."

"Thank you very much sister."

The sister entered the clinic and soon came out with the tablets and a cup of water. After her treatment for suspected malaria, they left for home.

"Do you think that those men are still at home?" David asked his mother as they walked home.

"I wouldn't know, nor would I like to think about them." His mother replied. There was no moon light, but only myriad of stars lit the night, which was bright enough for anyone with good sights to see where he was setting the foot. David and his mother were only a few yards from the path to their home, when David stepped on a sharp stick, which nearly trimmed his big toe off his left foot. Blood poured out profusely from the cut.

He screamed and fell down on his buttocks.

"What's the matter, David?" Anyadwe cried and came dashing to his aid.

"My foot, my toe," David cried. She bent down to see what had happened. With the dimly lit night, she could see the blood gushing from his toe like red water. She quickly uprooted some grass and tied the wound to stop the bleeding. She put him on her back and walked home. Was that what she was saying, "I don't know how we are going to end the day, may be yet another disaster is waiting for us!" She thought as she walked home with David on her back. When they got home, they found Tongpur was still at their home. Opuk had left with the message that he would be back on Sunday but did not indicate the time. Tongpur was roasting several pieces of meat on a long stick in the fire he had built in the compound. He had also hung chunks of the goat's meat all around the fire. His dog, which was fully satisfied with meat, lay near him with no appetite at all in the meat, which encircled the fire. It was even unable to bark so that when Anyadwe and David came in, it only lifted its head, looked at them, growled and put its head down and continued wagging its tail on the ground.

"What happened?" Tongpur enquired when Anyadwe lowered David down near him with his toe full of blood.

"He cut his toe on a sharp stick. It's a bad cut." She said

"I am sorry to hear that." Tongpur consoled them and in silence, he watched pathetically how Anyadwe was trying to nurse her son. After staying briefly, Tongpur packed the goats meat in a big basket, took it inside the hut, wished them good night before he walked away, to his home promising to see them the following day.

The night was a long one for David. He painfully dragged through it. His foot got swollen up to his ankle in the night, and standing on that foot was impossible so that he crawled on his knees and hands. That Sunday, his mother went for the first mass to inform the priest about his accident and to give her time to remain with him most of the hours during the day. She walked out leaving the door open.

When Anyadwe left, Tongpur came in almost immediately from behind the kitchen with his dog running in front of him. He walked to the kitchen where David was lying on his sleeping skin and greeted him "Good morning David, how did you spend the night?"

"Sleepless, I was in a bad pain throughout the night and my foot is now swollen up."

"Sorry about that David." Tongpur said.

"Thankyou." David acknowledged his condolence.

"Where is your mother?"

"She has gone to church." David answered. Tongpur entered the kitchen and squatted down to examine his foot like an orthopedic Professor examining a fractured foot.

"She hasn't washed the wound!"

"No. She wanted to wash it last night but she was afraid to start the bleeding again."

"Tongpur stood up and began to walk outside when Opuk arrived carrying his walking stick across his shoulders. The two men exchanged greetings and when Opuk saw David lying in the kitchen he immediately asked Tongpur as he walked in, "What happened to David?" He barked.

"He cut his foot yesterday on a sharp stick when they were returning from the church."

"Didn't I warn them? They are always wasting time walking at night. Where is the mother now?"

"She has gone to church."

"Back again! This woman is mad." The bigoted, polytheistic Opuk remarked. Opuk moved to David approaching him like someone coming to defuse a time bomb. David coiled and pretended to be in a deep sleep after he had heard their conversation. Opuk came, put down his mushroom stool, and sat on it. He collected the skin tied around his waist in front of him to cover his nakedness and shook David gently by the shoulder. David stretched groaned, turned around and opened his eyes slowly as someone waking from a sleep.

"Acellam."

"Um" David answered him with his mouth closed, the sound coming deep from within his chest.

"What happened to your foot?" he asked as he looked down at his swollen foot.

"It was cut by a stick last night."

Opuk shook his head regretfully and paused.

"I don't know why your mother can't understand, and see simple clear facts. She thinks these *Italiano* are going to solve the problems in this home? I have already told her about this but she is being stubborn for nothing. See all these gravetrees in the compound, they stand on the graves of people who should be giving your father blood to drink, and food to eat, but they are all dead. Since your father died, he has not been given food and your mother ignores him as if he never lived. All these cows, goats, and sheep belong to him, and your mother does not want to give him even a kid. I bet you, a human life is going to disappear in this home."

Tongpur had sat outside on a stone. He had been as quiet as the stone on which he sat when Opuk was lecturing to them, but when Opuk mentioned that a human life was going to disappear in the home, he was forced to talk.

"I think you are trying to know too much Opuk, you'd better begin to watch your words before you utter them because they will lead you into a big problem in future," Tongpur warned.

The two men had just finished challenging each other when they heard the spectacular sound of the motorcycle of the Priest coming. Opuk's heart sunk at the sound of the motorcycle as it approached Anyadwe's home. He immediately got up and walked away behind the sisal fence. A few minutes later Padre Enriko carrying Anyadwe on the back of the motorcycle emerged through the gate. They were riding at a slow speed and came to a stop near the door of the kitchen where David was. His mother came down from the motorcycle carrying a small first aid box in her hand.

Opuk who has vanished behind the bush near the sisal fence when he heard the motorcycle of Padre Enriko coming home cowered away in the bush to avoid him. "Is there anyone there?" Anyadwe asked Tongpur when she heard him disturbing the trees.

"Opuk has just walked that way as you came in."

"Oh well, I am not surprised if he's the one. In fact I would have been surprised if he stayed here." She said, and entered the kitchen.

Tongpur moved to Padre Enriko and greeted him before they both sat outside on mushroom stools charting. After she had transferred David outside in the compound and set him on a mat, Anyadwe went in, boiled some water, and came out with it. She put the warm water near David and began to clean his wound.

"Mama is he going to inject me?" David asked his mother.

"No, I don't think so. He's going to dress the wound only."

"But Sr.Veronica always injects children with bad sores in the Mission."

"Come on, don't worry David." She assured David as Padre Enriko moved in to dress his wound. Padre Enriko dressed his wound and left immediately.

Opuk re-appeared five minutes after Padre Enriko had left for the Mission. He was sweating like a devil in hell, with pieces of grass stuck randomly on his body and legs.

"Ho Yooooo" He moaned as he lowered himself on his stool, I have been looking for this medicine to be applied on the wound, it's a good medicine for wounds", he said and put a bundle of roots he was holding in his hand down on the mat near David.

"Mama Acellam!"

"Yes."

"Come here." Opuk called Anyadwe who was in the kitchen; she came and knelt on the mat, waiting for more commands from him.

"You crash these roots with a mortar or stone and put it in the sun to dry. Once it is dried, grind it up into fine powder. When you wash the wound, sprinkle the fine powder in the wound. It is not painful it gives dull biting pain only.

It is a good medicine; you'll use it for a few days only before the wound is cured." He said and uncovered the sheet, which was used to cover David's legs. When he saw the white bandage on David's toe, which reached as high as his ankle, he frown his eyebrows in disgust forming many creases on his forehead.

"So you've started with the *Italiano* medicine already, well go ahead, with it, I might as well take mine away." He said bending as if to grab back the roots, which were still lying at the side of Anyadwe. She did not make any move to prevent him.

"The medicine is yours, you brought it through your own sympathy, and I didn't ask you to bring it, if you want to take it, take it." She said and sneered at him. Opuk looked up at her and looked at Tongpur who was sitting in silence next to him and said nothing. Tongpur quietly got up, walked in the kitchen and brought out the basket of meat he had kept in the hut the previous night.

"What're we going to do with the meat?" Tongpur asked to change the topic.

"Share it among you and Opuk", Anyadwe replied, got up and walked back in the kitchen to prepare the lunch she was making.

The two old men shared the meat among them and wrap it in grass. After they had lunch of dried vegetables mixed with groundnut paste with *Kwon bell*, (soft bread made out of millet flour) Opuk repeated his claim that all what happened to them on Saturday, were indicating that Ogwok's spirit wanted some food from his wife, who was the only person then, who could do that.

Nevertheless, Tongpur disputed his statement and said that, all those were accidents as far as he was concerned, but to avoid future regrets, Anyadwe could do whatever Opuk wanted, so that Opuk, the staunch witch doctor, could perform the ritual ceremony.

On her part, Anyadwe told them that she would let them know of her decision later.

When the two old men left, she sat near her son in the shadow where he was lying. "These men must be crazy". She said. "How are they going to convince me about their nonsense? Some old bustards in the villages use this tricks for consuming peoples' animals. I doubt very much if they will succeed with me."

"You mean you are not going to sacrifice food to the spirit of my father?"

"No. There is nothing like that David I cannot participate in such diabolical ceremony."

"What about giving them the animal they want but don't participate in the actual ceremony."

"No, that is what I don't want and you know once I give in, I'll be required to participate fully in the actual ceremony from the beginning until the end as the wife of the deceased and above all as the host of the function."

"Just do it as a play without believing in anything you'll do." David suggested.

"No, I won't do anything like that; I don't see any sense or truth in what they are talking about. Just imagine David how can a spirit of a dead man eat? Spirits are not like us, who have senses of taste, smell, touch, pain etcetera. I know your father even if he is dead, is very dear to me, very dear indeed, that is one of the reasons why we are living the two of us only here. However, even if it were I who died before him, he was not going to accept this nonsense. A dead man is a dead man. His soul goes to hell or to heaven depending on what type of life he led on earth here," she said.

The day grew older with all the work left to Anyadwe alone. David felt sicker to see his mother labour alone with all the domestic work. He wondered when he would be well again to alleviate her from the tasks. After three days of complete rest, David's feet started subsiding. Padre Enriko came to dress his wound after every two days. After four weeks, David's foot was much improved. He was able to walk limply on it, attend to the goats and sheep and do most of the domestic work while his mother toiled alone in the garden.

Two months had passed since the dramatic Saturday when everything they touched melted away into a ruin. It was during the busy rain season when people worked from morning until dusk, when David and his mother were returning from weeding their groundnuts. They were tired. They were not expecting anyone at home. All they were thinking about was a cool bath, after returning the animals in their resting places, cook super, eat, and sleep, but to their disappointment, as soon as they entered the compound, they saw him seated near one of the granaries, his head stooped down, his walking stick clasped in both hands, stood on its end on the ground between his knees. He looked a committee member putting his points in order before an important executive meeting.

Anyadwe on seeing him did not react because she was not sure why he was there. "It could be, he came for a visit or something, but if he has come to reopen that chapter I preferred not to talk about, then I will just ask him to be expectant", she quickly thought.

"Eh Mama Acellam, you're just coming back from the garden." Opuk asked.

"Yes we are", she answered. Have you been here long?" She added.

"Ha yes, since about two p.m."

"Two p.m!" She exclaimed. The answer warned her of the motive of his visit, which she lightly suspected to be in harmony with the suspended sacrifice.

"Sorry for having kept you waiting for such a long time, but we had to stay and weed the groundnuts. We really have a lot to do. Unless we give ourselves extra hours we might not be able to harvest the millet, and weed the cotton, sow the simsim etcetera."

"Hmm, yes this is quite a busy period but I've come to remind you about what I told you about the starving spirit of my nephew. He keeps coming in my dream every day and night. I'm worried about the consequences if nothing is done within the shortest time available so that we finish up with the problem."

Anyadwe received the gist of the suggestion like someone exposed to a live wire. She fidgeted and looked at Opuk scornfully not accepting she heard what he had said.

"If you're tied up with work; I could ask my wife and my daughter to give you hands in some of your work," Opuk continued.

"Thank you very much for your kind offer and suggestion, but I must prepare myself with many things as you know it yourself. I'll be welcoming many people and if I won't have enough for them to eat and drink, the blame with rest squarely on me, so I still maintain my decision that, when I am ready, I will let you know."

"Hmm that is true Mama Acellam, but this has taken quite a long time now since we last talked to you about this. You told us you would inform us soonest, but since then we have not heard anything from you. I've just had been talking to Tongpur about it." Opuk insisted.

"I never had the time to prepare anything and nothing is ready besides the goat or sheep or, what-what would you like to give him by the way if I may know?"

"A bull, most of the time a bull is given, but in his case, as he was a very big man in the home, we'll give him a bull and a he-goat." Opuk explained.

"I see, they are there, you'll make your choice when the time comes but I'm sorry, I'm not yet ready and I don't want to accept your suggestion as yet."

"Okay Mama Acellam, I leave everything in your hand, I've done my part, don't blame me for any chastisement that the spirit of my nephew will inflict on you in this home after impatiently waiting for his food." Opuk said irritated, got up and lifted his sitting stool and, hooked it on his shoulder, and walked away to his home.

The following day was a Sunday, David and his mother were going to church when his mother said, "I think today after prayer we should pass through Topiny's home to buy for you the gourd. Topiny was also a regular churchgoer so that more often they walked together from his home to church. His trade in calabashes occupied most of his time so that his wife laboured alone in the garden while he busied himself with his calabashes at home in the shadow of trees.

That Sunday, they met him emerging from his path. He was dressed in his usual outing outfit of a black shirt, a khaki pair of shorts completed with buffalo skin sandals.

"Eh, Topiny, good morning", Anyadwe greeted him.

"Good morning Anyadwe and David how are you?"

## The Devout Woman

"We are fine. What about you?"

"I'm improving and feeling better today?"

"What have been eating you up, you look as if you haven't eaten in last seven days?"

"Ha, yes, I've been having bad diarrhoea since Friday."

"Sorry to hear that."

"I have improved quite a lot otherwise I would not have come out."

"I know, no one walks out with a running stomach."

"It embarrasses people", Topiny said and they laughed.

"We'd like to buy a gourd from you today, do you still have some?" She asked changing the topic. He croaked laughter and said, "If I run out of them then who will be your supplier? That's a factory for them you know that don't you?" Topiny asked.

After prayer, they walked back home together with Topiny. When they reached the narrow path to Topiny's home, he led them, David walked behind Topiny and in front of his mother. They were about to reach home, when Topiny's small emaciated puppy began to bark at them. As David suddenly fainted, he shouted, "Mama!" and fell down. His mother quickly lifted him up and set him on her thighs.

After one or two minutes, he opened his eyes and found himself on the laps of his mother, and Topiny kneeling beside them.

"What happened?' his mother asked.

"I don't know. I just saw trees moving and everything else red and that was all." David replied.

"Has he been falling like this before?"

"No. this is the first time. What do you think could be the cause?" Anyadwe asked worried.

"I don't know, but it could be the beginning of epilepsy even if he didn't convulse as you've seen, but to eliminate it, I would suggest you see Opuk about this, he has quite an excellent medicine for it. You see that big son of Adum, Nyeko, he was having fits twice in a day when they were still in Panyimur, but when they migrated here, I told them to try Opuk, they did, and in a matter of a week only, the boy was permanently cured. He is quite a man now. Opuk has good medicines." Topiny said emphatically. Anyadwe remained seated on the grass with David on her laps with dried pieces of grass hooked on his hair and vest while Topiny remained kneeling near them discussing what to be done to David.

"How are you feeling now?" his mother asked knocking off the dried grass gently from his hair and vest.

"I'm fine Mama."

"Can you walk?"

"Yes Mama."

Anyadwe disbelieving what he said, took him by the hand, and walked with him side by side along the narrow path.

Akello, the wife of Topiny, always went for early confession and mass on Sunday. She was at home to welcome them. Although Topiny and his wife were married a long time ago, they were unfortunate in their marriage in that the only daughter they had, died very young of measles and since then, they never had another child.

"Eh, Mama Acellam, it's a long time since I last met you, how are you and David?" she said and walked out from the grinding stone in the kitchen where she was grinding the millet, dusted her hands on her thighs on the sheet she was tying, and shook the hand of Anyadwe warmly.

"We are alright except that David has acted funny just a few minutes ago although he claims he's fine now."

"What happened?"

"He felt giddy and fell."

"He'll be all right", Akello said with a note of concern in her voice.

"I hope so." Anyadwe replied doubtfully.

"You're all welcome, my husband always tells me that he meets you on Saturday and Sundays but you never come to see me at home, I guess you must have come for something else and not to see me." She said and laughed.

"You're partly right we came to buy a gourd but more so to see you."

"Thank you very much for thinking about me." She acknowledged the visit and went on with the preparation of the lunch while Topiny led Anyadwe and David away to a hut, which he had built specifically for storing his processed calabashes and gourds of various sizes and shapes for sale. They chose for themselves what they wanted and paid before they went back to the kitchen to wait for the lunch Akello had invited them for.

# Chapter Four

"Must I really go and tell Opuk about this? He does not look serious. I will wait. If he faints again then I'll definitely go to Opuk." Anyadwe thought as she approached the gate to her home. Before they entered the compound, they found some dried grasses, which seemed to have been pulled off a roof lying scattered on the sisal fence. She was still wondering what had happened at home when David who was ahead of her shouted, "Mama, mama, the roof of the granary has fallen down! Oh, look at the roof of the kitchen too, it's badly damaged". His mother walked in silence as if she had not heard what David shouted. Anyadwe walked on, put the gourd she was carrying on her head down near the granary and climbed up the open granary as if to check whether a thief was lying in it. She jumped down and said, "We must put up all these damaged right before the rain or else all we have in the granary will be spoiled. I am going to cut some bundles of grass, while you go and cut some reeds, good long ones in the forest, and prepare ropes for thatching too."

A strong whirlwind had swept across the village and it had inflicted casualties in almost all the homes it had passed through leaving every man, woman, and child busy that Sunday afternoon repairing the ruin before the rain. Anyadwe slid the door to the kitchen out of the way and they went in. The roof was badly ruffled above the hearth. The soot lay on the floor in a big heap. David took the broom, which was lying near their grinding stones and swept the soot out before he took a machete, his small spear, and left for the forest to cut the reeds and to prepare the rope, while his mother went to cut the grass. They came back, and in no time, they put back the roof of the granary, which was blown off by the whirlwind.

With the damaged roof of the kitchen also fixed, they started to cook their supper. They did not go to Opuk's home that day. Nevertheless, what happened to David two days later, forced her to take him to Opuk's home. They had just woken up on Wednesday morning, David was sitting on the stone in the compound waiting for his mother before they left for the garden when he collapsed as he did two days ago when they were coming from the church. When his mother walked out of the kitchen, she saw him lying sprawled on top of the stone. Hysterically, she ran to his aid.

"David, are you alright?" She asked holding him by his back to sit him up. David slowly opened his eyes and blinked three times before he stared at his mother before he answered. "Yes mama."

"How do you always feel before you collapse?"

"I fell dizzy as if I have been rotating round and round, I see trees dashing in front of me as I move with the dizziness everything becomes red later, and then after that, I don't know what happens but I always find you beside me asking me as you're doing now."

She smacked her lips, "I think we have to see Opuk today, this is becoming too much, can you stand up?"

"Yes Mama." David replied and got up.

"Can you walk?" His mother asked again holding him by the hand.

"I'm perfectly alright Mama" he replied.

In the afternoon, they reluctantly went to see Opuk. They found him seated near his usual trees where his gods stay making tether for tethering goats and sheep.

"May we come in?" Anyadwe asked.

Opuk lifted up his head and saw them.

"Oh, Mama Acellam, that's you, why not, you are welcome, come right in" he said with excitement and called his daughter Lanyero who did not go to the garden because she was feverish to bring them something to sit on. She brought them a skin of an antelope and dropped it next to her father, greeted them, and went back to lie in the sun where she had laid, covered with a blanket.

"She is sick, isn't she?" Anyadwe asked.

"Ah yes, she has been feeling hot, vomiting, sweating with diarrhoea, since Sunday, I've treated her and she's much improved."

"Diarrhoea always wastes people so much within a short time." Anyadwe said.

"Yes it does, it's a bad disease." Opuk agreed.

"How are you anyway?" Opuk enquired into her health.

"We are not very okay."

"What's the matter?" Opuk asked solicitously, left making the tether and peered at them looking from David to her.

Anyadwe didn't know where and how to start the story because she was certain, the coincidence was going to furnish him with better facts to argue the risks she faced if she should continue to deny her husband's ghosts the food he was demanding from her. She was without doubt Opuk was going to reject outright that David was becoming epileptic but to confirm his claim. Therefore, it was. After she explained what had happened to David on Sunday when they were returning from the church, and the Wednesday repetition, Opuk's response was stupendous. He flashed out like lightning.

"You woman", he boomed annoyed pointing his first finger of the right hand at her.

"I've already warned you several times, if anything happens in that home of yours do not fall back for my help, the burden will wholly be yours, I'm fed up to my teeth with your stubbornness. I'm …" Lajok, Opuk's wife, was returning from the garden carrying a bundle of firewood on her head, she dropped the bundle down causing startlement in all of them. She had also seen her husband pointing at Anyadwe.

"What are you people fighting over?" she said jokingly. She came smiling and knelt next to them on both knees, and sat on her heels before she greeted them.

"How are you?"

"We are fine thank you." Anyadwe replied.

"What fine!" Opuk interrupted, "while Acellam is fainting everyday like that and you shamelessly tell us that you are fine! You must be crazy with your white men's God or Christianity, whatever you call it." Anyadwe turned and looked at Opuk contemptuously.

Lajok became very inquisitive when she heard that. She shifted her position, sat down flat on her left buttocks, folded her legs backwards and supported her inclined weight with the left hand resting on the ground.

Anyadwe narrated the story to her again. She listened with great interest. Opuk, who had abandoned making the tether, sat with his head drooped down like a drunken man getting maudlin. Lajok, who was already indoctrinated by her husband's ideologies, was left with no choice except to agree with him.

"My dear friend" she addressed Anyadwe "my husband has been telling me everything that has been happening to you. I am not going to tell you to do what he has asked you to do. It is up to you to consent to it. However, my advice is this; custom is not going to start from you. It started long time back before any of us here was born.

We are not going to pick on these *Italiano* customs and forget ours. Decide and do whatever you want and I would like to appeal to Opuk not to squeeze this from you forcibly. It won't be of any use that way." Lajok advised.

After Lajok talked, everyone was quiet and meditative and Anyadwe, who was looking restless, broke the silence by asking Opuk to take charge, and to give the food to the spirit of Ogwok himself.

"Hmm Mama Acellam, I've already told you all I've to say. My nephew does not need food from me. He wants it from you; beside I neither have goats, cows nor sheep.

"I'll give you the animals you want and you'll do everything."

"Where will I do them?"

"Here."

"You are a mad woman."

"I'm not but . . ."

"Okay let me get you the medicine you want. You would better go away and leave me alone." Opuk said, and got up, rising steadily on his walking stick. He disappeared behind the trees and soon emerged with a climbing plant rolled into a heap in his hand. He sat down and began to give her the instructions on how to use the medicine, emphasizing the medication at each point in both words and action.

"All you have to do is pound the plant with all the leaves and the stems together, put the pounded plant in a small calabash; add a bit of water, squeeze out the extract, and give it to him to drink."

"All of it?"

"Yes, you'll dry the residue, grind it into powder and you can put it in his food, his porridge or he can just lick it. When this is finished you can come for more."

Anyadwe took the medicine, thanked Opuk and invited him to come to her home for more discussion, concerning the offertory of the sacrifices to the spirit of her husband. When they got home, Anyadwe was very pensive. David was wondering what was happening to his mother. She had hardly spoken a word since they returned from Opuk's home.

"What's the problem with you mama, has Opuk annoyed you very much?" David asked. "Not quite, but I'm thinking of giving him the goat and the bull and at the same time, I am also thinking of how I'll avoid participating in the ritual ceremony."

"How, Mama, last time you said if you gave in, you'll be required to participate fully as the wife of my father and the host of the ceremony, how are you going to avoid that?" David asked wondering who must have given a back stair influence to his mother.

"I'll fall sick that very day so that he believes it's the spirit of your father killing me. I will not be able to talk audibly. I will only whisper. I will keep shivering as someone who is chilled. I will not tell him of my sickness before the day of the ceremony otherwise he will postpone it until he thinks I would be well again and it is no use going on pretending indefinitely. For you, you will keep your mouth shut and pretend to be gloomy. Do you hear that?"

"Yes mama."

"Will you do it?"

"Yes mama but what if he postpones the ceremony because you will be ill?"

"I know he won't."

That night after supper, David had his first treatment for the suspected epilepsy.

He was seated by the bon fire he had built in the compound when his mother came out of the kitchen with the medicine in a small calabash, as Opuk had instructed her to do. Only the dark green extracted chlorophyll was in the calabash with some fragments of leaves and the stems floating on top of the green fluid. "Try the medicine, it isn't very nice." She warned and handed over the calabash to him. David took the calabash of medicine, looked at it the way a person who is not sure of committing suicide by poisoning himself would look at the glass of poison already in his hand. He drew the calabash slowly to his mouth and sipped the medicine. It was bitter, bitterer than concentrated bile. The bitterness made him shudder nearly pouring the medicine down. His mother who had sat watching him smiled and advised him to close his eyes and gulps the medicine at once. He did and squirmed as he threw down the calabash.

"The medicine is no good. How will I eat this in my food? This man must be crazy." David commented.

"I tasted the residue, it is completely tasteless, I think the bitterness is only in the extract."

"Let's hope so otherwise I'm through with it."

The following day in the evening, David was tying the goats and the sheep in their pen singing and hitting some of them with his fist unaware of anyone about when he suddenly saw Opuk and his mother at the entrance to the pen.

"Are they all in?" Anyadwe asked.

"Yes Mama." David answered surprised.

"So, Opuk you can go in and make your choice." Tall as he was, Opuk squatted and lowering himself on his walking stick and held on it with both hands as he entered the low roofed pen, and waded in, browsing among the animals like a scholar choosing a book on a library shelf. After he had touched the goat he wanted to be slaughtered for the ceremony, he crawled out of the pen. The bull was also chosen, after which they started to bargain for the day for the ceremony. Opuk had wanted next Sunday, but Anyadwe strongly objected it and suggested Tuesday. In compromise, Opuk accepted it.

## The Devout Woman

On Tuesday the following week before the arrival of the guests, Anyadwe made herself look more ill than a patient who had narrowly escaped from dangerous acute dysentery. She lay down on her mat near the granary looking pale and frail. Playing his part with artistic perfection to complete the set up, David sat on a piece of log near her looking very gloomy and miserable. Opuk, the chief celebrant of the ceremony, arrived first with his assistant, Tongpur, accompanied by their wives who were required to attend. Other people who were invited by Opuk also came including Kinyera, Anyadwe's family friend. They were all disappointed to find Anyadwe and David so helpless. They wanted the ceremony postponed but Anyadwe obstinately rejected it. Opuk readily seconded her. "We can't postpone this." he said. "It's the spirit causing the illness. If we postpone it again, we will worsen the situation. Secondly, we have come prepared with food commodities which depreciate very easily, I do not think we would start preparation again; we better go ahead and finish the ceremony today."

In a gloomy atmosphere, the offertory went on as dictated by Opuk despite Anyadwe pseudo illness. The goat and the bull were slaughtered and every drop of blood from them seemed to have been collected in two big calabashes by cutting the veins, and the arteries in the necks one after the other, and draining the blood from it completely into the calabash before another vein or an artery was ripped open. A small portion of the blood collected was later dished into smaller calabashes. The blood was to be for Ogwok's spirit to drink. A Small *Abila* of about a yard high and base diameter of about two feet was quickly built by Opuk and Tongpur near the grave of Ogwok, while the other went ahead skinning the goat and the bull. Everyone who came except David and his mother was busy doing something.

The meat was cooked in many big pots outside in the compound. When it was cooked, Opuk and Tongpur took portions of the goat's and the bull's meat in separate new well washed clay bowls, *kwon bel* was served in a calabash, the portion of the uncooked clotted blood in the smaller calabash with the clots submerged in the serum, the beer, in triple mouthed small clay pots, and some water in a tiny calabash, were put in the *Abila* the two men had built. Then, Opuk with his assistant Tongpur and their wives went out to collect the spirit of Ogwok from the big fig tree, which stood a little off the fence. Five or six minutes passed before they came back with Opuk in front being followed by Tongpur and the two ladies, shaking the maracas they had carried with them.

Opuk, the main celebrant kept on murmuring something under closed mouth. They walked passed the audience who were seated in the shadows in silence watching them escort the imaginary spirit of Ogwok into the small hut where his food, beer and water were already served. On reaching the *Abila* the three remained standing shaking their maracas while Opuk lowered himself on his walking stick and squatted at the entrance of the *Abila* built with three flat rocks and continued with shaking his maracas inviting the spirit of Ogwok to his meals in the *Abila*. They remained there shaking their maracas for a while then Opuk closed the entrance to the *Abila* using another flat rock. He got up, and they all walked away from the *Abila* to join the rest of the guests. It was believed that at that time Ogwok's spirit was already eating, so the feast was therefore opened to guests to begin tasting the soup and serving themselves lunch.

After their meal, Opuk blessed them. The blessing ceremony consisted of putting simsim oil on everyone's chest, back of the feet and hands, and sprinkling them with some cold water from the clay bowel using the leaves as the sign of peace.

The following day Anyadwe continued to be ill because most of the guests including Opuk spent the night at her home.

"How are you feeling now Mama Acellam?" Opuk enquired when they woke up in the morning, bending his head low down thinking that she was still inaudible like she was the previous day.

"I'm better today; my head isn't aching as much as it was yesterday." My voice too is coming back and the generalised pain of the body I had, has disappeared. I only have a bit of pain in my stomach. I think I'll be better by tomorrow," she said.

"Hmm, we are glad to hear you're improving, if we had postponed the ceremony yesterday, I'm sure you wouldn't have improved like this. I'll get you some medicine to clear your throat and the stomach ache." Opuk said. He got up and went to his "Pharmacy" which had an indefinite boundary, this time taking a bit long, indicating that he could not find the combination easily. While he was away, the two women had boiled the water and were ready to take Anyadwe for a bath.

Anyadwe lifted her head slowly from the pillow of an empty sack she had rolled into a bundle and stuck below her head, and struggled to sit up with both hands resting on the ground, her lips and eyes tightly closed together, she sat up holding her head as if she had migraine.

"Can you walk?" Tongupur asked.

"I'll try, I'm not sure." She said with a qualm as she struggled up on her feet like a toddling child. She staggered. After stabilising on her feet, the two women walked her to the bath shelter and bathed her. David sat on a stone and thought admiringly of his mother, "She's a smart tragedian actress, and she has convinced everyone that she's really ill, that's interesting. I wish they knew she was only being smart."

Opuk returned from his "Pharmacy" when Anyadwe was being bathed. His legs were wet up to the knees by the dew, which remained on the grass since the sun heat kissed the ground five hours ago.

"Where've they gone?" Opuk asked putting down the bundle of roots, leaves and some climbing plants on the mat where she was lying.

"To bathe her." Tongpur replied and continued.

"The sickness would've got serious if we postponed the ceremony yesterday. Look, she nearly fell down here in an attempt to get up. It's mainly on the head now." Tongpur remarked.

"She will be alright; the main root cause of the problem was solved yesterday as you rightly said. If she takes these herbs everything will be cleared and tomorrow she will be able to cook for herself." Opuk added professionally.

Anyadwe walked from the bath shelter staggering alone without any support from the two women, with droplets of water adhering on her hair some of which were trickling down her cheeks and neck, she came and sat on her mat, and began to wipe off the water on the face and neck, with her open palm.

"Ha, the warm water has relieved me of some of the headache; I am now a lot better", she said.

"Yes, warm water is good for headache. I always wash my head with warm water when I get one." Tongpur commented. Opuk explained to her how to use the medicine he had brought, repeating with concern each step to be followed.

"I'm sure you'll be alright soon." He assured her with a smile on his creased old face, and with the confidence of an experienced herbalist.

One month passed since the spectacular dramatic offertory of the sacrifice of the goat, and the bull, to the spirit of Ogwok. Anyadwe, and her son David, were happy about their achievement during the occasion. At the end, they were back to their normal routine labour in their gardens. One Friday morning, as they went to weed their cotton in the morning, David heard some reeds break among the shrub not very far away from them.

He ignored it at first and they continued to walk on. Before long it repeated, this time the *Twac* of the breaking reed was loud enough to be heard distinctively by anyone who was expecting something from that end. David could not conceal the excitement to himself alone any longer. He decided to let his mother know about it.

"Mama!"

"Yes!"

"Have you heard something breaking the reeds among that bush there?" I have heard it twice, it seems something is moving towards us or escaping away."

"No, David I haven't heard a thing." Immediately they stood upright swaying their heads from side to side in an attempt to catch that noise if it should happen again. Within a split of a second, the tree snapped again, this time stirring some guinea fowls, which were resting in the bush near them. Anyadwe looked round. Obviously, whatever it was, it was coming towards them. To cower would be a sell out risk if the animal approaching them were already aware of their presence there because an animal with a normal sense of smell would sort out anyone with its eyes closed from among any bush; a risk she later preferred. There were only two trees near them, the rest were towards the bush where the animal should be emerging any moment. The nearer one, behind which Anyadwe took cover, was a small tree not strong enough to bear any reasonable weight. However, it was better than standing in the open ground. She quickly took her son's hand and they ran behind the small tree, which was shaking, its branches in the wind in regret wishing it was old enough to help both of them up.

Seeing that they were too much exposed behind the tree, she thought of the other tree, which stood a few yards from where they were crouching from the approaching animal. "Go and climb that tree." Anyadwe ordered David.

"Which tree?" David asked in panic.

"That one." She pointed to the tree, which stood only a few yards away as straight as an electrical pole. The lowest branch, which was also dry and rotten at the base, was above five yards high. Desperately and helplessly, David ran with his hoe on his shoulder to the tree which towers many feet into the sky. Unlike the first tree, the one he was headed to seem to welcome him up, only if he could reach the safety it is to provide. He came and dropped his hoe down with the heart throbbing. No wonder David had asked his mother which tree he was to go and climb although that was the only one in the vicinity.

He knew he was very unlikely to make it but if he did, he would be floating in the atmosphere of safety where only God could reach him. All the same, in an emergency one almost tries to resort to all impossibilities to impunities. David gripped the tree with his hands and feet wrapped round it. He pushed himself upwards changing the position of his hands and feet as he dragged himself up like a tadpole learning to use the limbs for its locomotion over the water for the first time. He was happy at the progress he was making although it was being impeded by the smoothness of the bark of the tree. He was getting very tired to hook himself on the tree. He knew he could not hang on any more if he did not reach the dead branch soon. He went as far as the dead branch but as soon as he pushed his left hand to grip it, the branch parted from the trunk of the tree, the base gave him a knock on the shoulder as it flew down crashing down below.

His mother, who had already taken cover behind her tree, with her head resting on it, startled, and reeled round to see what had happened. She thought it was her son who had broken his neck but when she saw him stuck up the tree his face looking tired and gloomy, she relaxed a little and turned her attention to the approaching animal.

"Well, it's not him who has fallen." She thought.

Meanwhile, David was worried that he had attracted the attention of the animal to their direction. He cursed the branch for having broken off denying him the safety he was seeking.

"Dimmit" he whispered as he looked down and saw it lying a few yards below, scattered in a few fragments. Unable to hold grip on the tree any longer, because of the perspiration, which had started to ooze in his palms, and body as a whole, he began to glide downwards at sporadic jerk, but eventually, the downward journey became very easy and slow. He found himself where he had started, not on his feet but on his buttocks. He was tired and frightened stiff. He got up, his heart thumping violently almost splitting his chest open. His chest and stomach were full of whitish small marks with tiny bruises weeping blood. As he stood watching his mother crouching from the bending position to squatting, he saw what almost elated his heart, the tips of the horns first, then the head carrying the powerful horns, and then the dark buffalo hurled itself in the clear.

David was happy to see it because he mistook it for a cow.

"Mama, it's cow, it is coming towards you," he shouted. Nevertheless, the reaction he got from his mother warned him that it was a dangerous animal, even if it was a cow, it could be a mad one. His mother had signaled him to keep quiet by covering her mouth and waved him to hide behind the tree. Although he had not seen a buffalo, from the story his mother used to tell him about animals, made him aware that the animal he was seeing was not a cow but a buffalo. The description of the powerful horns and the solidity of the body built, left him in no doubt. He immediately hid himself away behind the tree, which had refused to welcome him up. He squatted down as his mother was doing and looked fixedly at his mother and the beast walking straight to where she was squatting. Its heavy footfalls could be heard and felt, where he was hiding so that he felt like sloughing off his own skin. His mother on the contrary was adjusting herself like a lion preparing to spring on its prey and bring it down with one horrible bite. David did not know whether to cry or scream. His heart was almost failing to cope with the rate of his blood flow. He unconsciously bit his finger hard nearly cracking the fingernails without feeling the pain. The buffalo came and stood almost a few yards only from his mother, and scratched the base of the left horn with the left hind hoof, as if to test if the base was strong enough to carry Anyadwe on it without snapping off. The animal moved on to an anthill near her and bent its weight on it rubbing its ribs on the anthill. After the beast was satisfied with its rubbing, it walked on, passed her about a yard when David saw his mother getting up with the hoe she was still holding in her hands. David wondered what she was going to do.

He saw her raising the hoe in the air as if she was going to chop a log of wood with an axe and landed it on the vertebrae bones nearer the hip joints of the buffalo with all the strength there was in her. The hoe found its slot between the joints of the vertebral bones and got stuck.

Apparently, the buffalo was not aware of their presence in the place and the wind was in their favour. The buffalo leaped forwards, ran a few yards in front with the hoe sticking at its back before it came back fully provoked scouring for them, prepared to tear anyone it would find in many pieces. At that time, Anyadwe had already deserted her hideout, came, took David by the hand and they ran towards home crouching. When they got home, they warned the entire village about the buffalo by making alarm. Most people had already gone to their gardens at that time, all of them were puzzled as to what was up as early as that in the morning, but, all the same, they answered the alarm and soon the whole village and beyond was full of noises of the responding rescue team on the move.

Kinyera, the native deputy chief game warden who was preparing to go for duty at Bulkur Game Park, was still at home. He was shocked when he heard the alarm originating from Anyadwe's home. He quickly threw away the dress he had already put on for his journey, changed in what he called his hunting dress, took his gun and quickly ran to help her. He found them standing on an anthill among their sisal plantation continuing with the sounding of the alarm.

"Anyadwe?" he called, panting for breath.

"So you've already come!" she said as she recognised his voice and turned to meet him. "What happened?" Chief Kiyera asked surprised to see her with a smile on her face.

"A buffalo", she said and explained to him all what happened.

"I thought it was a cow." David said.

"Oh, yes he shouted that it was a cow."

"They look like cows", Chief Kinyera agreed and looked at her, and rubbed his face without saying any more.

At that time, the mobilised rescue team had started to arrive carrying with them four spears and above each. In addition to their spears, every one of them was carrying a skinning knife with the hope that if the belligerent beast was killed the knives would be useful. Dogs, bitches were also brought, and there was a team of them groaning and snarling at each other in the compound. By about ten o'clock fifty spearmen had gathered at Anyadwe's home. Chief Kinyera, who had already taken charge of the operation, narrated the story to the spearmen. Immediately he finished, he led them away to the battlefield. When they got at the scene, everyone took cover while the dogs and bitches scattered randomly trying to locate the buffalo.

Overlooking their battleground was a small stream, around which the people of the village had carried out very intensive cultivation. They had planted all sorts of perennial crops, but mainly crowded the place with vegetables and sweet potatoes so that it was possible to see all movements on both banks of the stream from where they were.

Surrounding the gardens was a thin belt of thorn trees, which were gradually being replaced by food crops. Beyond that stream lived Oyat with his family. Alyeka, the wife of Oyat was deaf so that when talking to her one had to shout at the top of the voice. That day when the alarm for the buffalo was sounded Oyat was not at home. He had gone to see his brother who was sick at Binya, a place about fifty miles away from Coomit village. Alyeka did not hear the alarm although the whole village was under a sonic bombardment of the noise. They saw her come in her potatoes garden carrying a calabash on her head, dressed in her usual red frock. On reaching the garden, she put down the calabash she was carrying on her head, moved towards the thorn bush, broke a stick for digging the potatoes and came back to where she had put the calabash on one of the potato heaps.

The buffalo after searching for Anyadwe in vain, moved over in the thorn bush with the hoe fixed on its back. On reaching there, it kept on trying to remove the hoe stuck on its back by knocking it against the tree. "If I got that punk, I'd have scatter life out of him by now". It seemed to have thought as it struggled to get the hoe out. It was at about that time when it succeeded in knocking off the hoe from its back, that Alyeka snapped the stick near it, and walked back to where she had left the calabash. It saw her, red like a red hill, in the centre of the clear potatoes garden unaware of any danger probably admiring the potatoes she was digging. The buffalo calculated its steps and speed it needed to attack her. It did not want any error. It lumbered in the potatoes garden, charging Alyeka like a bull charging a bullfighter. In a second, she was tossed up flying in the air before she disappeared flat among the potatoes heaps.

The crowd on seeing that shouted simultaneously, "There it is, it has attacked that lady, come, hurry, help." They broke out running, tearing through the grass as if they were running on a clear football pitch, despite the fact that most of them were bare footed. Most dogs and bitches, did not follow the sequence of events, as a result they barked and ran aimlessly everywhere. Chief Kinyera was one of the first to arrive at the scene. The buffalo had concentrated on Alyeka, determined to dismantle her completely when Kinyera crouching like a skillful hunter, came and fell a short distance from the buffalo, lifted his gun up a little and fired; the bullets landed at the base of the horn. As it was lifting its head to see the new attacker, he released another bullet on the neck and almost immediately another one through the head. These made the buffalo leap from where it was burying Alyeka alive with its horn by scattering the potatoes heaps over her. When the buffalo left her, some men crawled to where she had laid half buried in a ditch between two potatoes heaps. The potatoes heaps impeded the buffalo from delivering its accurate blows, so that even if it wanted to gore her in many places, it was mainly digging the ground on her with a few cuts wherever the tip of the deadly powerful horns were able to touch her. However some men quickly pulled her out from the ditch as the buffalo fight was going on and carried her away to a clear ground.

Ongwec, a well-known runner in the village was among the men who uncovered her from her temporary grave. He unilaterally decided to run to the Mission and ask for help from the Priests to take her to Gulu hospital.

He left the buffalo fight waging on. Eventually it was knocked down dead. With the buffalo dead, no one bothered much about it, they all ran to see the condition of Alyeka.

They crowded round her where she was laid on a heap of grass prepared for her by the men who rescued her from the ditch. She had a deep cut on her stomach, a thin membrane over stomach prevented the contents from spilling out, and there were many minor cuts on the thighs and shoulders. Her red frock was torn in bits and pieces.

It was at that time that Ogwec returned with Padre Enriko carrying a gun. Dressed in his hunting outfit, they came straight to where there was a crown over Alyeka, lying writhing in pain on the grass.

"We must rush her to Gulu quickly." Padre Enriko said when he saw the wounds, and the blood she had lost which had clotted into a dark pool near her. The men lifted her and carried her away to Anyadwe's home where Padre Enriko had left his Jeep parked. When the patient and the escorts were gone, the rest returned to skin the buffalo. Anyadwe was the killer of the animal according to the Acholi hunting law. It rules out that anyone, who inflicts an injury on an animal first, no matter how small the wound, got the animal. The killer always took both hind legs, the ribs, head, skin and internal organs like the liver, heart and kidneys. The remaining parts were always shared among those who helped in the killing of the animal. Anyadwe, although she was declared the killer of the buffalo did not want to take the lion's share and make most men go back home empty handed. She took only one hind leg, plus the liver and the heart. The rest of the meat she gave away to be shared among the men particularly to the family of Oyat to whom she gave the whole of the other hind leg.

The head and skin, she gave to Opuk, although traditionally, according to hunting law, the killer never parts with the head and the skin of the animal.

On their way home, all the men were commending Anyadwe for her unique gallantry. "Even among us men, who would have dared to attack a buffalo with a hoe only? The best and the surest thing would have been to seek refuge on top of the nearest tree. Only a few months ago she killed a python which had caught and swallowed her goat, today she attacked a buffalo with a hoe, tomorrow she might kill an elephant," one man joked. However, Opuk had a different view of everything.

"Hmm, you people don't understand what is happening?" he said. All those who were there stopped and kept quiet to listen attentively to what the village head had to say.

Opuk cleared his throat and began to speak, "Hmm, if I were you, I would not esteem Mama Acellam for what she has done. Let us take the case of the Python. That was bad, because the goat, the python killed, was a scapegoat. The victim was to have been a human being.

"Sure? " the crowd asked.

"Yes!" Opuk answered with a nod of his head and the men started looking at each other.

"Tell us", they demanded.

"I hope you all heard about Ogwok, my nephew whose wife is this one you are esteeming for what looked very courageous acts; very rare to human beings, leave alone women." The crowd nodded approvingly.

"I'm telling you this because you are all mine." I have to tell you all that are going on in the village so that if you can correct it please do it.

My nephew you all know lived with his wife in Coomit here all their lives. His parents, sisters, and brothers all died and were buried here. Ogwok, my nephew, was very upright man in front of the gods before the *Italiano* came here." There were some murmurings among the crowd some jeered and said, "If that is what you're going to tell us then we'd better go home." While some kept quiet, but kept their ears open. "Ogwok, let me warn you all, denounced our ancestors' gods. He said they are no good, they are useless. The worst thing he did was he led the destruction of the *Abila*. Our sacred place of worship; where our gods stay. Who among you can tell me that Ogwok was justified in this act? I do not think so. As a result, the lion killed him.

## The Devout Woman

You all heard about it and you all put up a saying about it. Whenever anyone did anything audacious, you compared his or her audacity with that of Ogwok because he fought the lion with a knife and in the end, they killed each other. Can't you all see the abnormality? Well, to be short, the gods punished him. He had a punitive duel with the lion. He would have never died if he did not do what he did to the gods. Now he is dead. His brothers all died, his youngest brother ran away from home, and the only person who is looking after his home is mama Acellam. Ogwok's spirit became hungry, wondering in the wilderness looking for something to eat. No one except Anyadwe his wife is there to give him food. But she was reluctant to do this. He sent the python to kill his only son, Acellam, but the gods said no, you once punished us, and you see what it is to suffer. Your son will not die. They however, sympathised with him. To show his need to us, the python caught the biggest he-goat she had. In addition, of course, if the python went away I would not have known why the he-goat was killed.

Therefore, the gods anchored the python in one spot and gave courage to Mama Acellam. She easily killed the python and took away the goat. The gods still whispered to her to come to me first before she did anything with the carcass. She came to me and I went and found out why the he-goat was killed. I told her that the spirit of her husband was the one, which wanted food from her, because there is no other person to give him the food. She said no. What happened? The son started fainting every minute. She got worried just as much as I was. Later she accepted to give food to her husband's spirit. On the day of the ceremony which some of you attended, she nearly died. Some of you who came wanted us to postpone it, but she saw the risk she was in. Life is sweet. In addition, I too saw the risk she was in if we postponed the ceremony. We went ahead and did it. We gave food to Ogwok, and how long did she stay in bed? Not even one day more. The following day she was on her feet. Now, this buffalo story which looks so fascinating to all of you, it's nothing other than that the spirit of Ogwok is now happy, because he is now fed. He brought the buffalo right infront of her and she cut it with a hoe! Have you ever heard of such a thing? Old as I am, I have not. Why the buffalo did attacked Alyeka? I think you heard that Oyat destroyed his *Abila* last week. I have already seen, Alyeka is not going to die but it should be a warning to you. Who next we do not know. Mama Acellam would have killed the buffalo with the single blow but because the gods wanted to punish Oyat the buffalo did not die. Can you see why the buffalo went near the potatoes garden? Why Alyeka came out at that time to dig the potatoes? Where is Oyat? Therefore, you men of Coomit, watch your steps with these *Italiano*.

They are going to plunge you into big problems you will fail to intricate yourselves from. There were mixed feelings among the men. Some said he was right but the staunch Christians told him to go to hell with his elaborate diabolical explanation.

David and Anyadwe were walking home from church on the Sunday, which followed the Friday buffalo drama, when they met Padre Egidio, coming from Latinnyer, the sub-mission where he had been offering Mass. He stopped and they exchanged greetings before he said to Anyadwe, "I wanted to see you about David". He said and went on; "As you might know, he is eight years old now; I think he is old enough to receive confession and Holy Communion. We are going to enroll new catechumens next week on Sunday both here in Coomit and at Alworoda. I am thinking that David should be enrolled with them so that he starts reporting to the Mission every afternoon to learn the Daily prayers and the Catechism. When the rest will be preparing for Baptism, he will stop coming so long as he will have known all we will require of him, and next year when the new school term starts in February, I would like him to start primary one. What do you think about that?" Padre Egidio asked.

The information was a big surprise to Anyadwe. She was happy that David was going to be a better Christian if he should be able to confess and receive Holy Communion rather than, merely accompanying her to church every Saturday evenings, and Sunday mornings.

"I've no objection Father; I think your suggestion is alright. I agree with you, he is now old enough to confess and receive Holy Communion, but I have one fear, and that is, I might not be able to raise enough money for his school fees next year. My cotton doesn't seem to be doing well".

"You don't have to worry about his school fees, Ajulina; these are some of the secrets you've been walking over for many years waiting for the time to come. We have great sympathy for you. We do not only understand your problems, but admire, and very much appreciate your determination and effort, you are taking unilaterally, in spite of the many problems you're facing, to maintain yourself, and this boy", he said and patted David on the head. "We have decided to take care of his education as long as he will be interested in learning, we only pray that he shouldn't let us down. Will you, David?" Padre Egidio asked him.

"Everything will be okay, Ajuliana. You don't have to worry about his school fees." He repeated.

"Thank you very much Father. I just don't know what to say."

"You don't have to say anything Ajuliana, you go home and rest. Next Sunday, we shall enroll him and he'll start a different life." Good-bye.

"Good bye Father", they said, waved back to him and walked away.

The following Sunday David was enrolled with forty other catechumens. After their registration, Padre Egidio instructed them to start reporting to the Mission the following Monday at twelve noon promptly, because, their lessons were going to last from one o'clock until four o'clock when they would break off to enable them to return to their homes before dark.

At the beginning of the course, David found no difficulties at all in his lessons because most of the Daily Prayers which they were being taught, his mother had already taught him.

They did not know how to read nor write, therefore, their lessons were nothing but cram work. They had to learn everything by heart. One week before the course ended, Padre Egidio, satisfied with David's performance, withdrew him from the rest of the catechumens and began to instruct him on how to confess. It did not take him long to grasp and master the wording used during confession.

One Friday, on the last day of his schedule, he had his first rehearsal in confession; later Padre Egidio called him to his office for instruction. "David." He said, "I'm satisfied with your performance, you can now go home, practice continuously what you've learnt. Do not forget them. You can now begin to confess and receive Holy Communion. What you are left with is to receive the sacrament of confirmation next year when we will be confirming some Christians here. Now, you will stop coming to the Mission. Tell your mother that."

"Good bye David."

"Good bye Father." David left the Mission happy. Alone he started to run homeward singing some of his favourite church hymns.

At home, Anyadwe without salt, and washing soap left, had decided to go to the shop and purchase those commodities that afternoon. She took with her the calabash she always used for collecting vegetables from the garden, a bowl for carrying salt, and her one-shilling coin she got from selling a cock in the market, for buying the salt and the soap.

The time was about four o'clock when she finished picking the vegetable, packed them in the calabash and left the vegetable calabash in the garden under one of the trees before she continued through a footpath, which led from the garden to the main road. That was about the time David left the Mission for home. The clouds were rising from the Eastern horizon, their usual rain direction like cotton lint being hurled from the ginning machine with very light breeze blowing at non-specific direction, when Anyadwe crossed the road. She looked left and right, there was no human being. She continues to walk towards the shop. David continued running homeward singing mirthfully when he saw his mother coming "What are you doing here mama?" He asked.

"I am going to buy some salt for us because the one I bought last month is now finished and the rats have eaten up the soap I bought last week.

"Shall I come with you?"

"Yes, if you want, but if you feel you must go home then I'll get you home."

"I'll come with you."

"Okay, let's go, it's preparing to rain early today. I have already put the goats, sheep and the cows back into their pen and kraal respectively". Anyadwe said and they walked back to the trading centre.

"How was your lesson today, did you do the test you told me you'd do?" Anyadwe asked David.

"It wasn't quite a test; I had my first confession today. Padre Egidio told me to stop going to the Mission with effect from today, he said I can now confess and receive Holy Communion but ..."

"He said that, did he?" she asked with excitement, her eyes gleaming like those of an angel.

"Yes and the rest of my colleagues will continue for some time before they start to sleep in the Mission to prepare for their Baptism."

"Oh, so you've ended?" She asked with a relief.

They reached the shop and bought what they wanted and started immediately for home. The clouds, which were still as white as cotton lint a few minutes ago had already been transformed into dark thick clouds.

David and his mother were frightened of the approaching storm. They hurriedly walked home. David had run past the path leading to their garden when his mother called him back.

"David."

"Yes mama."

"Let's pass through the vegetable garden, I had picked and left some in the calabash in the garden". David came back and disappeared along the footpath. When they got to the garden, his mother picked up the calabash containing the vegetables, and put the bowl of salt in it. She gave David the bar and the cake of soap to carry. The wind grew stronger as the rain drew nearer. They had not gone the length of the garden when the rain rattled on the ground for a second or two before it was driven westwards.

"We had better hurry or we'll be drenched in the rain before we get home," Anyadwe remarked. As she said, another heavier spell came, and stayed on for a longer time than the first wave before it again stopped for a while.

It thundered then it continued into the real heavy down pour of rain as if the knobs were broken by the thunder to release the contents of the clouds. The wind grew stronger and heavier. David was in front with the soap in his hand giving a bit of foam. He was first to reach under the big fig tree near their home which seemed to have stood there from the time of Adam and Eve. Its branches had covered a wide space across the entire path. David ran and entered underneath it. Not much rain was dripping through.

"Mama, why don't we shelter here?" he suggested.

"How do you know it's going to cease raining soon? It is likely to go on raining for some time, so it will be useless to shelter here. After all, it is getting dark now. Let's go home." She replied.

They passed the brief shelter, which was provided to them by the branches of the tree only to find that the rain was heavier, and the wind stronger than before they entered underneath the tree. They reached home, entered into the kitchen, put whatever they were carrying in their hands down and began to wipe off the excess rainwater from their faces with their hands. David began to struggle to peel off his vest, which was glued on his skin by the rainwater as if it was a part of his skin. His mother was still rearranging the position of the salt near the hearth when they were blinded by a dazzling flash of lightning, which illuminated every inch of the kitchen as if the sun had fallen in their kitchen. Before they had time to organize themselves in the kitchen, they were deafened by a dry detonation sound of the lighting striking something not very far away from them. They moved hysterically in the hut like a group of rats, which suddenly discovered cat among them in the hole, thinking the blow was on their roof. It was repeated three consecutive times.

The detonation was so intense that they knew whatever was struck must have been fragmented badly. In the end, they found themselves holding each other. How they came to that position was a mystery to them. It left their ears whistling. Afterwards, the rain poured followed with hailstones as big as a child's fist, thudded on the roof then on the ground, and bounced away to rest. Soon white cold rocks scattered all over sowed the ground up. It went on like that for a long while before it switched on to a drizzle, which gradually passed away before it came to a halt. After the rain, in the dim evening light, they walked out to see what had been the victim in the rain. They were shocked to find that the gigantic fig tree under which David had wanted them to take shelter from the rain was struck down into a stump by the lightning. It was hard for them to believe it. With excitement, they went near to see the disaster.

Imagine, we took shelter here even for as long as five minutes only, as you had suggested, we would have been extremely lucky to be breathing now," Anyadwe said.

"Thank God we didn't." David remarked.

"Really, we must count ourselves very lucky; we would by now be dead, meat beyond recognition. Look at how this tree has been split!" As they talked, some of their immediate neighbours who, in spite of the dark, cold, and wet evening, came to witness what had happened joined them.

Everyone was shocked to see how that huge tree was fragmented. It was soon dark and not many people came to the scene. The following day Opuk was the first to arrive at the scene. He met David and his mother going to the garden.

"Good morning Mama Acellam."

"Good morning Opuk, you've come to see what happened yesterday?"

"Yes, I heard it, I was worried. I thought it had fixed a human being or some domestic animals!"

"No, but it would have struck us if we had sheltered under the tree as David had suggested."

"Struck you?"

"Yes."

"Where were you coming from at that time of the night?"

"We had gone to buy some soap and salt and it caught us on the way home."

"And you passed through the bush?"

"We followed the foot path through the garden to collect some vegetables I had picked and left in the garden before I went to the shop."

"You never shelter under trees or on rocks whenever it's raining because that is where spirits of dead people and gods stay.

Some of them are miserable. They have not been given food for years and when you shelter under trees or on the rocks where they are, they call the lightning to destroy you so that you join them.

"Now, where are you going?"

## The Devout Woman

"We going to the garden to weed the cotton."

"Where are you going to pass, where the tree has fallen?" Opuk asked

"Yes." Why? That's our path to the garden". Anyadwe replied.

"You don't pass near any place which has been struck by lightning before medicine for lightning is sprinkled at the spot. If you don't want your skin bleached."

"But we were there yesterday with other people, are we going to have our skin bleached?"

"Who are these?" They must all drink medicine for it before they lose their black skins.

"How soon should they drink the medicine?"

"Today; tell me their names and I'll visit them now and let them know about the danger they are in." Anyadwe told him the names of the people who were there with them the previous night.

"And you, you should drink yours now before I go to the others". Opuk stressed.

"Please we can't go back home now, will you leave it in our kitchen?"

We will drink it when we return from the garden. We must go and do some work first. It's getting late." Anyadwe protested took her hoe, put it on her shoulder and walked away. David followed her, leaving Opuk standing on the path perplexed.

## Chapter Five

It was the last day of the twelfth month of the year. Anyadwe was pushing in the twelfth last calf in the kraal; "It is nice the animals are multiplying well, David is starting school in a month's time, and with my work in the gardens, how are we going to manage it. I think it will be better for me to take these animals to my brother Kolo. He has sons who should be glad to help us look after them for us." Anyadwe thought as she put the twelfth last log, on top of the pile of logs closing the entrance to the kraal. "I am going to send Kinyera to call for him. If he comes, we will discuss about my idea and if he accepts to help us, then I will inform Opuk and Tongpur that I am moving the animals out."

The following day Anyadwe and David were going to their garden to pick their cotton, when they saw Opuk coming. First his white head and then the unique *Clack, clack* noise of the bangles around his ankles, told them that he was no other person but Opuk. His walking stick lay across his shoulders at the back of his neck. Both his hands held on it pressing it lightly on his neck his mushroom stool daggled below his left armpit, he walked with his head stooped as if he was tracking an animal.

"Good morning Opuk." Anyadwe greeted him.

"Good morning Mama Acellam. You are going to pick your cotton?"

"Yes."

"Aren't you too early? The dew might still be too much on the cotton. You will find sorting difficult when you pick cotton when it's still wet."

"I know, but it's better in the morning. In any case I don't think there is much dew now."

"I was coming to see you. I thought I would still get you at home."

"You were coming to see me?" Anyadwe asked.

"Yes."

"About?"

"I've been sent to you to find out if it's true that you want to move these animals from here to your brother. I have the presentiment that something is going to happen to them." Anyadwe was bewildered by the announcement from Opuk. She stared at him cynically. She did not know what to make of the old man who stood meekly in front of her with his walking stick still lying across his shoulders, his mushroom stool dangling at his left armpit.

"Is this really Opuk I am talking to, or is he one of those old prophets we hear about in the church. If he is Opuk, then the devil is at work through him." Anyadwe thought.

Anyadwe was always prejudiced, and biased about any Prodigy remark or act Opuk did, "Who sent you? And who told you that I am moving the animals?" Anyadwe asked.

"Mama Acellam, when will you talk sensibly? I did not expect that question from you." Opuk interjected.

"Do you know who I am? If you do, then you know who sent me and who told me that you are moving the animals. Who do you think told me that my nephew Ogwok was hungry, and needed food? Who is telling me that I must talk to you people of Coomit to refrain from disappointing your gods, the gods of your ancestors? The gods who kept your great grandfathers give you rain and sunshine at the right time; the gods who make your crops yield properly and the gods who give you children and keep them. Now, you have turned against them. You have thrown them out. No one among you now knows them. You have destroyed all their resting places and they are in the open, in the rain, in the sun, the wind blows on their faces day and night. Because you cynical sons and daughters of Coomit have preferred, the white men's God. Particularly you Mama Acellam, I have been asked to warn you that a dark future looms over you family. You are the most impudent of all the children of Coomit at present. You have spoiled our son Acellam in whom the gods had the confidence. You do not believe anything I tell you because you associate me with the devil. All my words and actions belong to the devil. Nevertheless, these are the words of the gods who keep you day and night. You have been given many warnings to enable you to change but you are not ready to accept our gods any more. Look, at how the lightening destroyed that tree which had stood over there. In addition, you had wanted to shelter under the tree. Did your gods not protect you by asking you to go home? Why was your hut not destroyed instead? Do you recall what I told you the day after that tree was struck, when I met you going to weed your cotton you are going to pick now? I told you, I thought the lighting had struck human beings. This was because I was told that you and your son were going to be fixed that way. Nevertheless, I interceded for you. It is up to you to defy the gods warning or accept them with apology, and here you still ask me who sent me after all these! What a head you have. You know me as gods' messenger since my nephew Ogwok brought you here.

All of you used to respect whatever I told you about our gods until these white men came, and confused you with their God and culture." Opuk concluded.

Anyadwe stood with the basket they were going to put the cotton in, balanced on her head, her arms folded over her breasts; she leered at the old man scornfully wishing God could send fire from heaven to burn him dead or to turn him to a pillar of salt.

"I have listened to what you have said. I wanted to see you and Tongpur later about the animals you talked about. However, as you claim you have already known about them, we could as well meet and discuss the matter today."

"Hmm, I will let Tongpur know. What time?"

"If you can, come in the evening. You should get us at home."

"Hmm," Opuk moaned and walked away.

In the evening, Opuk and Tongpur arrived as scheduled.

"Good evening Mama Acellam" Opuk greeted her.

"Good evening," she greeted them, and walked to where they were sitting in the compound. After some trivial conversation, Anyadwe opened up the crucial topic for the evening. She adjusted herself on the ground, cleared her throat, and said,

"Gentlemen. I am sorry for making you walk this evening against your wish I…

"It's alright with us, that is why we are called elders. In fact, if we don't solve problems in homes in this village, then we do not deserve our title." Opuk interrupted her.

"As I was saying, I am sure Opuk might have briefed you already why I am calling you here tonight," she said addressing herself to Tongpur.

"Yes he did," Tongpur replied.

"Well, if he has done so, then I would like to elucidate it a little more. About seven months ago, Padre Egidio told us that he would like David to start school this year.

Therefore, I thought, to make things easy for both of us, we should send these animals to my brother Kolo. He has two grown up sons who are now doing nothing most of the time.

If we sent these animals across, we will have just enough work for us to do, and those boys will have something to do. We are not giving the cows away, but they are only going to be kept for us. This is all I wanted to let you know. I talked to Kinyera about it, he has no objection." Anyadwe said and kept quiet.

"Have you talked to your brother about it already?" Tongpur asked.

"Not yet but I have sent Kinyera to him to go and ask him to come over so that we discuss the possibility of moving the animals."

"Well as far as I am concerned, I don't see anything wrong with it. Because, if David starts school this year, he will be out most of the time and you will be away in your garden for most of the time. Therefore, the care for the animals will be minimal. I don't see why you can not send them to your brother if he accepts to keep them for you," Tongpur said. Opuk croaked a dull laughter, which sounded as if he was suppressing a productive cough.

"Have you finished?" Opuk asked Tongpur.

"Yes I have." Tonpur agreed.

"Hmm, Tongpur, I must tell you that you are a child of I don't know how many years. Shall we say two, may be let us make you a little older and say five. Have you ever heard in your lifetime a woman who has refused to be inherited by the brothers of the deceased? I hadn't until when my nephew died and his widow talking to us now was left with a child you see sitting there," he said and pointed at David.

"Well after my nephew's death we gave his wife and the child to Otwol, the son of Birya, the brother of Gwaromoi. What did Mama Acellam say? You were there Tongpur; can I repeat it for you? She said, she would not, want any man. She only wanted Acellam alive and well. She said she is capable of keeping the animals. Didn't you say these words mama Acellam? Think over it yourself. Now you surprised me by saying that you want help from your brother. Have you asked for help from our clan and failed to get any?"

"Who is willing to help?" Anyadwe asked.

"Why did you refuse the help given to you earlier?" There was silence.

"Hmm, here we are"; Opuk went on. I Opuk very strongly object it. If these animals are to die let, them die here. The gods will not allow them to go. If you insist on taking them, you will see it for yourself. Even now I see them annoyed with your plan. I see a whirlwind, carrying away a big cow. I see blood on a rock, below it is dirty muddy water and a woman with a boy running away. I see another boy coming and the woman holding him frightened. I see a man, I see them walk back. I see them; they meet a young man carrying a spear. The old man and the young man on the rock, the water below is clear now. The blood on the rock has dried. I see them making alarm.

I see the woman and the son being questioned but the gods say they did not do it let them go. I see …

"Now, the thing is gentlemen", Anyadwe interrupted Opuk.

"Is there any other thing serious to be discussed? If there is nothing, we had better get along with other work. I must cook supper. Will you stay on for it? "

"I won't I am going home. Nevertheless, before I go, my warning to you Mama Acellam, when you defy it and you take these animals, you will be to blame for all the misfortune you are going to have on the way."

"Tongpur are you also going?" Anyadwe asked ignoring Opuk's warning.

"I think we should go together."

"Well in that case I will not hold you."

Good night to you gentlemen."

"Good night."

After four days, Kolo came to his sister's home to discuss with her and the elders about the message Kinyera had briefly told him. He stayed with them for five days holding discussion with the elders about the animals.

In the end, it was unanimously agreed that Anyadwe could move the animals to her brothers' home. Kolo accepted to help them to look after the animals, but he wanted to go back home to prepare the Kraal before they could move the animals. Two weeks later he came back accompanied by his two sons Karakak and Oru-Rac to assist him in driving the animals. Oru-Rac was two years younger than Karakak. When they arrived, David and his mother were busy collecting the crops from their gardens. They wanted every crop stored in the granaries before they left. Kolo and his children helped them with their fieldwork and in a matter of one week; every crop from the garden was stored. Chief Kinyera was requested by Anyadwe to take care of their home during their absence.

On the eve of their departure, Anyadwe prepared some foodstuff, which they were to carry with them on the long journey. The foodstuff consisted of roasted cassava and potatoes, groundnuts paste, and a gourd filled with honey. They woke up at the second cock crow and began to prepare for the journey.

It was a cool night only a light wind was blowing. An owl hooted for the first time on the gravetree, which stood on Ogwok's grave as if to warn him that the animals he left behind were shifting while the moon, like a gigantic red ball, hurled itself slowly over the eastern horizon thawing its cool rays across the earth like a motorcar crushing up a slope. Kolo and his two sons went and collected the cattle from their kraal and they were moving up and down in the compound mooing. The goats and sheep were also brought.

After their breakfast of cock meat with *kwonbell*, which Anyadwe prepared in the night, they started the long, long journey with the twenty heads of cattle, ten sheep and fifteen goats. Among the cattle, there was a cow in calf, and Kolo guessed it would calve down in transit.

David was entrusted with the bundle of roasted cassava and potatoes wrapped up in wet grass, while in the basket his mother carried on her head, were the two gourds of water and honey, and the clay bowl of the groundnut paste. For stability, Anyadwe had stuck some cloth in between the vessels to prevent them wobbling.

After sometime, they were away from home. The animals, by instinct, soon realized that they were moving. They started following the road, with their escorts walking behind them like raiders who had had successes in their profession. They kept whistling here and there to control the cattle or goats, which tried to stray in some gardens at the side of the road.

They had gone passed the sixth mile stone standing at the side of the road, which told them that they were only six miles from home, hardly one tenth of the total distance they were to cover. The moon had stolen its way through the sky and was poising at the position of the sun at ten o'clock.

The cocks were crowing everywhere warning their masters that they should be winding up their private activities because the sun was coming soon to lead them out to their daily tasks. The powerful, aggressive beam of sunrays coming to overshadow the cool, gentle moon rays, which had been guiding the nocturnal creatures along their ways only a few hours ago, reddened the Eastern horizon up. The cool, dry East-West wind was at its best, so that their eyes and noses started secreting water reflexively. In case of David, in his vest and the light pair of short he was in, he was chilled, he felt as if he was passing through aerosol of snow. His skin was more goosed than the goose skin. His teeth rattled against each other because of the cool wind, which made him stop from time to time to urinate while his team kept on driving the animals forward. He always found it hard to catch up with them running after them with the bundle of roasted cassava and potatoes on his head. He did not know how far he was going to survive the journey before he himself became a load for someone. After a short while, the sun was up above the horizon. The birds of all species sang melodiously in the air praising the Almighty God for the new day; eating some insects, which also came out with the hope of beginning the new day but ended up starting the food chain. The rest of David's colleagues were still looking fresh, strong, and energetic and above all, they looked still satisfied from the heavy night meal they had just had.

Contrary to their ability and state, David was already tired, and weak. It was not long before the strong sun, became hotter as the day wore out into the afternoon, heated up the cool morning wind. The sand on the road slowly but steadily took in the heat; by noon it was impossible to walk directly in the middle of the road bear-footed. All the other had sandals of some kind but David had none so he avoided blister forming quickly on his feet by walking on the short grass at the side of the road.

About past mid-day, all of them had absorbed enough heat, so that they needed a rest. The animals too, were very tired and hungry so that all of them preferred to walk at the side of the road, where they could pluck few leaves and grass to replace the cud they had been chewing for hours. David was very tired and weak. He wanted nothing more than a rest. His mother noticed the way he was dragging behind them and wondered if they could carry whatever he had on his head in their stomachs to relive him of his load.

"Karakak", she called, "Could you run and tell Kolo that we should rest a bit and have something to eat?"

"Yes aunt," he replied and broke into a run as if he was impatiently expecting such information to come through.

Kolo was informed. He suggested that they should go and rest in a plain, which was about five miles ahead of them and ten miles to reach his father-in-law's home where they were to spend the first night. "The plain is green most of the year round. There we shall let the animals feed for some time before we continue to my father-in-law's home." Kolo said and walked faster in front to catch up with Oru-Rac who was driving the cattle alone.

The position of the sun was indicating three o'clock. It was beginning to cool down a little and the wind was steadier. The information that they were soon resting after five miles, encouraged David to put in more effort to catch up with the rest.

The forest thinned out into a savannah with shrubs of different species of trees grouped up into their own clans with single ones dotted here and there giving a wide space of grassland between them.

They soon reached the plain, the grass there was burnt a few months back and the new grass growing up was about two feet tall. The luxuriance of the plain made it an immensely attractive resting place. When the animals reached the plain, without waiting to be driven in, they branched and soon began to eat the grass. They stood and watched them for a while, contented that they would not create any trouble, they walked to a big tree, which stood a little ahead in the plain. The tree had shed off all its old leaves, which were being replaced by young, greenish-yellow, oleaginous looking leaves most of them were already opened although not yet matured. A few were still in bud forms. The scattered shades it gave were not the type anyone would have rushed for if there were an alternative. As they were Hobson's choice for the scorching sun's heat, they took refuge in them by stamping on the grass before sitting down but soon repeated the process on other spots moving with the shades as they drifted away with the position of the sun. Their dried lunch was laid on the grass, which had already wilted in the hot sunshine. It was a self-service lunch. In a moment, all of them were quietly choking, with mouthful of either the roasted cassava or potatoes and groundnuts paste mixed with honey. They drank the water from the gourd to wash the solid lumps in their esophagus down their stomachs.

None of them paid much attention to the animals, as they were convinced they would not start trouble. But the cow in calf, Kolo predicted might calve down on the way came away from the rest, walked, passed them to a small tree which stood behind them and began to rub its ribs on it forward and backward making the tree swing under its weight. It also rubbed the bases of its horns on the tree before it resumed eating the grass around the place. They all saw it, but did not think it would stray away.

A small footpath led from the main road towards a little raised part of the plain behind them. The condition of the path indicated that either its users were not very many, or the occupants had long deserted the home at its end. Small grass with pointed tops grew right in the middle of the path. As they ate their lunch, an old man appeared from the direction of the main road following the footpath, walking towards them. He was a tall thickly built man, who although walked on a stick, walked upright without stooping on it. He had shaved off all the hair on his head except the goatee-beard, which he left intact. On the bearskin of his skull, he had smeared a red dye, which streaked, down his neck because of the sweat giving the picture of a man with a broken head. A skin around his waist, and the bangles on his wrists and ankles, completed his attire. When he reached near them, Kolo who wanted to give the animals some water to drink asked the old man where the well was; because, they had heard children laugh and splash water as if they were in a river somewhere beyond the raised ground in front of the old man. "Eh you there, good afternoon," Kolo greeted him. Nevertheless, the old man did not answer him nor did he turn to reply his greeting. He walked on. When he reached where the cow in calf was grazing, he stopped briefly, turned and looked at it admiringly.

Kolo thought that the old man probably did not hear him. He called him again this time nearly shouting at the top of his voice but the old man still kept quiet.

"He looks very sad and disappointed like some one coming or going to a funeral." Anyadwe commented.

"I think he is only deaf; he is an old man. Old age has all its problems which I wouldn't like to go through myself," Kolo retorted.

"He looks like a ghost," Oru-Rac commented. At this comment, although the old man was out of earshot turned and looked at him.

When the old man disappeared, a small whirlwind came from the direction from which he had come. It followed the path he walked through gathering strength as it whirled passed them towards the cow in calf, which was still grazing behind them. They did not reckon anything unusual about it as one saw a thousand of such winds in a day during the dry season. They were more concerned with their lunch other than the wind. Nevertheless, when they looked behind them after the wind had died down, the cow in calf had disappeared. Yet they took it for granted that it might have gone back among the other and was being obscured by them. However, the only person who seemed perturbed about the absence of the cow was Oru-Rac. After he had finished his dry lunch and had drunk water, he took his stick and went where it was; the tree on which it was rubbing its ribs was there minus the cow. He walked where the rest of the cattle were still grazing. All were there except the cow in calf. He came back more frightened than disappointed about his finding.

"Baba." he shouted, "the cow in calf is lost," he said.

"Nonsense," his father replied disbelievingly still munching the last piece of cassava in his mouth.

"How can a big cow like that one get lost in a plain like this where you are able to see a rat fifty yards away? What has picked it up?" It must be lying down somewhere near the others." Kolo said and got up, stretched, and walked away looking pleased with the lunch he had just had. Touched by the information about the disappearance of the cow, he started by checking for it among the others. It was not there. He searched around but he saw no cow with calf. Oru-Rac saw the embarrassing look in his father but declined to comment. The rest of the cattle immediately lay down to rest chewing their cud. The grasses were in fact short enough for a day-old calf lying down to be seen without difficulty. They walked as far as they rocky ground where the old man disappeared but they could not see the cow in calf. They searched every inch of the possible ground where the cow could have wondered but saw nothing. They only heard laughters of jubilation of adults and children coming in echo from beyond the rocky ground where the old man had vanished. They went and climbed the rocks in an attempt to see the laughing people, but the laughters repeated as if it was coming from behind them. That frightened them.

"Let's get out of here quickly," Oru-Rac said. It looks as if we have violated the roaming ground of ghosts." He added. As it was getting late, and they could not go on searching for the lost cow indefinitely, they came back and aroused the rest of the resting animals, collected their luggage and started to drive the animals to Kolo's father in-law, Okok, where they were to spend their first night.

When they were leaving the plain, the laughters came again in echoes above them.

"This is the power of the devils; I will never yield to it. The cow is gone. Let it get lost." Anyadwe said annoyed as they walked, away recalling what Opuk told them.

"I see whirlwind carrying a cow, a big one."

After a long exhausting drive, they got to the home of Okok late in the night. Although they reached late, they had no difficulty in waking Okok and the family, because of the sounds the animals made, and because of the habit of Okok's family sleeping in the open air in the compound during the hot dry season nights. They were welcomed and the animals were driven into their temporary accommodation where they went and soon laid down chewing their cud. They were tired and needed sleep more than anything else. After warm baths and late supper, they went to sleep.

The following day in the morning Kolo told Okok about the miraculous disappearance of the cow. He was surprised to learn that Kolo did not know that the plain was a haunting ground for the ghosts of dead people. "You're damn lucky in that you lost only one cow, and you're all sound and well. You would have disappeared all of you with all the animals. My uncle's daughter together with her son disappeared in that plain some years back and up to now no one knows their whereabouts. No one dares enter that plain my dear. The place looks an attractive resting place, but all what it is, is a deep, deep pit with a thin layer of beautiful vegetations to lure people to the trap. We have on several occasions met the ghosts of some of the old men we know, who died sometime back walking aimlessly on the road within the plain. We do not talk to them; they are inanimate although they look alive. If you observe their movements, you will find that they actually float a few inches off the ground. They do not walk on the ground as we do. Their eyes are dreaming and lifeless which do not roll in their sockets nor blink." Okok explained.

When David heard the explanations; he was terrified at the news.

"Mama" he whispered to his mother.

"Yes David," she replied.

"What do you think about Okok's explanation?"

"Nothing David, I wouldn't like to think nor believe such ghosts stories."

"But if these people have been meeting the ghosts of their dead people there then……"

"Then I should believe them? I think we have to accept the loss as unfortunate, disgraceful work of the devil trying unsuccessfully to pervert us from the right way of the Lord God and to accept him. Instead, I am ready to lose my life than bow to the devil or to his pomps. I encourage you my son not to be weak and yield to such heathens deities easily. True, there are devils all around us they are trying to show us their powers, which God left, to them when they fell away by working such devious miracles. Try to forget about all what happened." Anyadwe advised David.

They remained with Okok for two days. David's feet, which were forming blisters, were much improved. The animals too were much better for the last leg of their trip to take them to their new home. The moon was then appearing very late just a few hours before sunrise. Because of that, they did not see the need of waking up early. However, they started the journey a little after the third cock crow. With the help of the in-laws of Kolo, they drove the animals out with ease.

It was not long before the sun hauled itself over the Eastern horizon. The day was one of those unusual ones one encounters in the dry season. It was not a bright day. There were clouds hovering overhead occasionally obscuring the fierce heat of the sun from sticking the ground. The temperature was not very high as it should have been.

The usual strong dry wind was blowing steadily changing its direction at random.

Because of the cool weather, the journey was less tedious than the first part of it.

They were able to move fast, as a result, they completed the journey in ten hours. They got home at about three o'clock in the afternoon.

When they got home; the family of Kolo was still away in the field picking cotton. No sooner had they arrived, than Akongo, the daughter of Kolo brought a full basket of cotton home. Akongo was very afraid of domestic animals especially the cows. When she unexpectedly found the cattle, goats and sheep wondering everywhere in their compound she thought she had lost her way into a strange home, but when she quickly recalled that her father and her brothers had gone to transfer her aunt's animals to their home, she didn't retrace her path but came walking stealthily home, avoiding disturbing any of them. She came, stole herself into the hut like someone avoiding a cobra near the door, and emptied the cotton in the basket. As she emptied the cotton one of the young bull, which had passed its weaning age, was trying to breast feed when it was driven away by the mother. Disappointedly the bull walked away towards the door of the hut where Akongo was empting the cotton, stood against one of the pillars next to the doorway and began to rub its ribs on the pillar by moving forward and backward.

Akongo, after she had completed empting the basket, was walking outside happily singing one of the new popular songs in the village not aware of the presence of the bull at the door way. With the basket in her hand, she found herself face to face with bull at the doorway. Hysterically she screamed tried to run back inside the hut, but lost her way and banged her head hard against the door frame giving a low dull explosive sound you often hear when two rams fight *thub*. She fell down unconscious kicking her legs like an ewe being slaughtered. Anyadwe, Kolo, his sons and David ran to her aid. Anyadwe lifted her up on her laps and began to rub the swelling on her forehead exerting a slight pressure on it. "Is this some of the misfortune Opuk predicted?" Anyadwe thought as she rubbed the forehead of Akongo. After a short while, Akongo regained her consciousness and she began to cry holding the forehead she had crashed against the door frame.

When the rest were retrieving Akongo, Karakak had run to the garden to inform his mother about their arrival and the accident of his sister. A few minutes passed and he returned with his mother running in front of him. Her bare chest revealing two long pendulous breasts, boasting on her chest that they have nourished many souls, jumped on her chest up and down making pat-pat sounds which were amplified by the sweat on her body. She came and fell on her knees besides her sister-in-law.

"Akongo, why did you do this?" she asked. Hadn't you seen a cow before, see, you've almost broken your neck." Awilo the wife of Kolo continued talking regretfully to her daughter while tenderly touching the bulb on her forehead. "Let's put her down." She said and went inside the kitchen to bring a mat. Akongo was nursed, but was soon put behind the screen before warm welcome was extended to the new arrivals especially to Anyadwe and David.

On the sixth day, at about six o'clock in the morning Anyadwe and David left for their home accompanied by Kolo up to Okok's home. They spend a night with the Okoks before they continued to their home escorted by Okok's sons. It was not long before they reached the plain. The fear of meeting ghosts within the plain overshadowed the thoughts, which were pre-occupying their minds. A short walk from where the savannah gave way to the plain, they met a man walking towards them. David, who was walking a short distance behind his mother, ran and did not only catch up with her, but caught her hand. As the man walked passed them David scrutinised him to find out if he could be identified with the ghost of the plain, but he did not. He was a man who seemed scared of them as much as they were of him. After they had passed the man, they were flabbergasted to see what to them at first looked like a nightmare. On the rocky raise ground, where they went during their outwards journey to search for the lost cow, they saw a group of people seated on the rocks talking and laughing; they were all dressed in skins tied around their waists. They could hear them very distinctly as if they were talking over their heads but the language they were using was foreign to them. Their view was blurred because of the rain, which was falling between them. They could see in front of the crowd, sat a man who looked their chief holding a stick in his hand. When David saw them, he shouted to his mother, "Mama look over there" he said pointing at the group of people on the hill. Nevertheless, before David could say anymore, one of the men who were escorting them warned him to keep quiet.

"Shut up David, and don't point at them again." He warned.

Anyadwe saw them, crossed herself, and began to pray. The crowd on the rock seemed to have seen her praying, they all got up except the man with the stick who sat in front of them and roared, ho-ho-ho, the noise was a lot more than what you hear during a big football match when a popular team nets a goal. Then all of a sudden, disappeared as if the earth gave way and they all poured into the pit, leaving the man with the stick in his hand, whose view remained blurred, alone on his seat. Other stupendous things they saw as they came adjacent with the hill were, beside the man, there appeared the cow they had lost in the plain a few days back with the young calf it had calved down. Hysterically David shouted again; "Mama look up there. Our cow has calved down. Look the calf is there grazing near her," David said excitedly.

"Come on David, I warned you neither to talk nor to point at the hill." The man warned again. Nevertheless, David seemed to have gone off his head or has had the Holy Ghost, which gave him the courage to talk on.

"But that is our cow we lost and its calf sir."

"We can't get them back David," the man warned.

"Why?" David protested, with his eyes bulging out.

"Because they won't be there if we try to go near them." The man replied irritated.

"You don't seem to understand that you are going to plunge us in irreversible problem here." Anyadwe interrupted her prayer for a while and asked David to keep quiet when she noticed the angry scared look on the man's face.

They were nearly leaving the hill behind when the man who was sitting on the rock got up and stroke the ground in front of him with the stick in his hand. Then the cow, which was grazing up on the hill, started to run towards them with the calf in front.

"Look!" David broke out again.

"The cow and the calf are coming to us let's wait and you take them back to Kolo's home." He said with excitement.

"Come on David, you shut up' the man repeated. "You're brewing for us big problems." "But don't you see that the cow and the calf are coming?" David asked.

"That isn't normal happening David" another man intervened. The cow and the calf were only few yards from them when the man on the hill whose view remained blurred stroke the ground again. Suddenly a swarm of bees sprang from nowhere surrounded them and began to sting them everywhere on their bodies. To safeguard her son from the bees, Anyadwe broke a branch of a tree growing at the side of the road and used it for driving the bees away from David, but to her surprise, she was unable to hit a bee. It seemed the bees were able to dodge the leaves each time she stokes. They continued with their unsuccessful flee from the swarm of bees with David crying. From behind them, they heard the man on the hill laugh triumphantly, and the shouting men soon joined him again. The cow and the calf, which were following them, had gone back on the hill only their silhouettes could be seen. As they continued fleeing, the two men who escorted them ran faster leaving Anyadwe and David behind. They never thought they would survive the bees' stings. The bees chased them until they crossed the two miles wide plain. Immediately they were out of the plain, the swarm of bees suddenly disappeared and they were left tired and breathless like asthmatic patients. It looked a nightmare than reality. When they tried to search for the bees stings on their bodies, as they expected numerous of them, they were astonished not to find any. They also, expected severely inflamed skins, but not a single hair on their body was ruffled. Their skins were as smooth as if nothing had happened to them. None of them could believe what happened to them. Definitely, something had happened. They were not dreaming.

It was about eleventh o'clock when they were through with the plain drama. The two men who escorted them left them a mile away from the plain boarder and returned home through a footpath avoiding the plain although the path was longer than the direct road through the plain. "We don't want to run again; this time, they may escort us with lions instead of bees," one of them said.

The weather was boiling hot and windy, the sky was clear and blue it was difficult to walk in the middle of the road bare footed. Notwithstanding the heat, they did not have heavy load to carry to hamper their movement; as a result, they walked fast.

After some miles walk, David found that, his mouth and throat were dried making breathing difficult. He desired immensely for a drop of water on his tongue to quench his thirst.

"Mama"

"Yes, David!"

"I'm dying of thirst; I badly need some water to drink."

"Where can we get some my dear son? I don't know this place myself. To make it worse there is no any home near the road around here to show human existence. Let us rest in the shadow in front may be it will do you some good. We should have brought some water with us to use in these empty gourds."

"You'd have probably lost it in the exercise we had in the plain." David reminded his mother. As they prepared to sit down in the shadow for a rest, they saw two young girls in their teens crossing the road carrying calabashes full of water some of which was spilling down from the vessels. They were talking and giggling as they ran. Almost immediately the girls crossed the road in haste, two young boys about their ages also lumbered across the road in hot pursuit.

"Eh! You, Eh! You", Anyadwe shouted to the girls who were about to disappear along a footpath in front. When the boys heard her shout, they thought she was the mother of the girls, and therefore the shouting was directed at them. Therefore, they fled back. The two girls stopped to wait for Anyadwe who went running towards them with David dragging behind her.

"We need some water my dears; we're very thirsty, please help us," she pleaded.

One of the girls gave them a drink.

"What is your name?" Anyadwe asked the girl who gave them water.

"Acan," the girl replied.

"Who are your parents?"

"My father is Acoko and my mother is Kertoo." Acan replied. Anyadwe later asked her where the well was. She directed her to the wells and Anyadwe thanked her for her help.

"I think we should go and fill one of these empty gourds with some water at the well. You never know we might need some more on the way. The journey is still long." Anyadwe said. Acan had told them that the wells were across the road. The first one below the rock was for bathing and the second one below the anthill, which flows into the first one, was the one they used for drinking.

"Shall I go and bathe in the first well Mama, while you go and fetch water for us to drink in the second?" David asked his mother as they crossed the road and disappeared along the footpath leading to the wells.

"Sure, why not, if you like. I'll wait for you; it will make you feel better." They walked and soon got to the path leading to the first well. It was a little off the main path.

"That could be the well, go and bathe but be quick," his mother said and continued to the second well to fill the gourd. David jumped along the path leading to the well running while pulling off his vest. When he got to the well, he was stunned at what he found there. The water below the flat raised rock was not cleared; it appeared as if someone deliberately walked through the water to mix it with the mud below. On the rock, fresh blood as red as it was in the owner's veins few minutes ago, was still flowing slowly towards the water below like a meandering river seeking a new course the sea. David moved near to see the blood, wondering what short of blood it was.

"Has someone got hurt on the rock?" He thought as he moved nearer. When he got to the sport, what he saw made his heart skip a beat or two.

A tuft of human hair with some flesh adhering on the rock formed the source of the blood making its way down the water. As if he was being guided to it, he turned left and there it was. Under the shrubs on the rock, he saw a body of a young boy pushed up behind the climbing plants. Some dried leaves were sprinkled on him for camouflage. The broken head lay facing him. Blood still dripped from the wound, indicated that the murder was freshly accomplished. Astounded by his finding, David was too frightened to scream, his heart thumping in his chest; he forgot all about bathing but put back his vest and ran as fast as he could to his mother, fearing he might be the next victim, if the murderer was within the place.

"Mama, Mama, Mama! …," David cried out almost out of breath.

"What is the matter?" his mother asked as she stood up from where she had knelt drawing water in the gourd and stared at him surprised, her eyes nearly popping out of their sockets. "What is wrong David?" she asked again and held him by the hand. David with trembling voice told his mother about the body he saw under the shrubs.

"I think the other boy killed his friend," Anyadwe said indifferently.

"Which boy?"

"One of the two boys we got chasing Acan and her friend."

"How do you know?"

"I got one of them here washing his hands. When he saw me, he startled like a fugitive and broke into a run. I thought it was odd for him to behave like that as if he was expecting trouble from me."

"But they ran from us all the same from the road," David reminded his mother.

"Well that's true but there was no cause for him to continue running from me here again. Besides, if he's a boy from this place he should have noticed that I'm not the mother of Acan at the close distance he saw me."

"And we aren't sure if the body I saw on the rock belongs to the other boy."

"Your argument could be right David," his mother admitted.

"What're we going to do mama?" Should we go and report about this to Acoko?"

"No, I don't think we should implicate ourselves into this matter. If we do, we are going to be held up here to vindicate the case. They will of course appreciate our reports but how can they be sure that we did not do it ourselves. I know if the news licks out, the two girls will probably inform them that the deceased was in the company of the fugitive I got here, that is if they are the two boys, we saw on the road, so it will be up to him to prove that he did not touch his friend. "

"Let's get away from here quickly then", David said.

"Not in panic David, otherwise if we meet an observant person on the way he'll suspect why we are so nervous, so be yourself when we …" As they talked, a man who was coming from the road carrying a basket in his hand coughed. He looked a stranger or a resident who was returning from a journey.

"Good afternoon," he greeted them as he approached them.

"Good afternoon," they replied.

"Is this the path leading to the home of Nekimwodi?" The man asked.

"Sorry sir, we wouldn't know if it is, because we're also strangers in this place." Anyadwe replied him, politely.

"Where are you coming from?" the man asked her.

"Opokopwac."

"Is that where your home is?"

"No, we went there for a visit. My brother lives there with his family."

"Where is your home or rather where are you going?"

"Coomit."

"What about you? where is your home?" Anyadwe asked.

"I'm from Alworotto and I am called Toolit. I've come to follow my daughter who has eloped with the son of Nekimwodi.I met some men on the way; they told me that his home is about this place passing through a rocky bathing place."

"I am Ajulina Anyadwe this is my son David Acellam. I think the place you are looking for could be ahead or you have left it behind as you can see that this place is not rocky."Anyadwe said pretending to be ignorant of the place.

"I'm sorry we aren't going to be of any help to you. We came here because we needed some water. We met two girls who live across the road, they told us about this well but they did not tell us about any other well. May be you could find out where you are going from their homes. Anyadwe advised.

"Yes, I think that is wise. I should do that, before I spend all my life roaming like a nomad in this bush trying to find my way. May be that is where I'm even going." Toolit said. They walked back towards the road together, but when they were about to get to the road, they met a young man following the same path. When he got near them, he stepped a little off in the grass to make way for them to pass. When she was adjacent to the boy, Anyadwe who was in front stopped and greeted him. He replied in a gentle voice.

"Might you know the home of ...?"

"Nekimwodi," Toolit completed it for her.

"Yes, I'll be going there but now I am going to deliver funeral message of my dead aunt to several homes. I think we shall walk together if you do not mind." The boy suggested.

"Oh! We are sorry to hear that please accept our condolence." Anyadwe told the boy.

"Of course I will come with you." Toolit replied.

"I am sorry your visit is not going to be a happy one," Anyadwe said addressing herself to Toolit.

"Okay my dear, thank you very much for your short company. We might meet sometime in Coomit. I've some relatives there." Toolit said.

"You'll be most welcome. My home is next to that of Chief Kinyera." Anyadwe said and they departed. When they reached the main road David told his mother, "you handled Toolit very carefully."

"I think I did. As I was telling you before he came, you do not need to be nervous when anything should stir up. I know if they are going to pass that way, Toolit seems to be a man who knows all the gravels on his way.

If they should brew trouble for us after finding that body, you remain calm.

It seemed the conversation I have had with him has convinced him that we do not know anything about the bathing well leave alone that dead body. Your part in the game will be silence and remaining calm. Do you understand that?"

"Yes Mama." There was a pause before David talked.

"If it's one of those two boys we got on the road who killed his friend, why do you think he did it?" His mother giggled at his question first and said, "I wish I knew the answer to your question David, but my guesses are; it could be that they were merely playing on the rock with wet feet and that fugitive might have pushed his friend accidentally and he fell and crashed his head on the rock or they might have fought because of those girls."

"But they were two and the girls were two as well."

"Acan is more charming than the other one, isn't she?" His mother pointed. David did not comment. They walked on, they were some eight miles away from the scene ; the sun was beginning to set when they heard alarms which had started hours after them caught up with them and spread through the villages. They realised that the dead body was at last found, possibly by Toolit.

## The Devout Woman

"Won't they come after us?" David asked.

"Only if the body was discovered by Toolit and that boy and if they made us suspects. I am not sure if Toolit will have that in mind. Just keep on walking as I told you with your mind on the rule; silence and calmness, I mean."

In spite of his mother's warning, David walked like someone who was aware of a lion tailing him.

He looked back after almost every one minute to see if the spearmen were coming after them, but instead they met with spearmen in groups of six and above running towards the place where the alarm originated. The men stopped them to enquire if they had any knowledge about the alarm, but Anyadwe answered them making her voice sound ignorant, surprised, and concerned about the alarm, as any other woman would have done when she found herself caught up in such a situation.

"We don't know, we've also just started hearing the alarms originating from behind us," she told them.

The sun went down; the alarms eventually died away with the setting sun indicating that all those who responded to the alarm must have reached the place of the trouble. Yet no one came after them. It was about seven o'clock David was beginning to brighten up confidently that it was too late for them to be at their heels, when he looked behind, and saw about a dozen spear-men running after them.

"Mama, Mama! Do you see them?"

"Yes."

"They are coming after us."

"Let them come. Do not worry. They could be those we met going back home. If it should turn out that, they are after us, then remember what I told you. I will do the talking while you remain quiet and calm. If they should ask you any questions repeat what I'll have said as we were together all the time, do you hear that?"

"Yes Mama."

"Eh! You there, the men who were running after them shouted."

They heard it and stopped. The men came and surrounded them.

Anyadwe showed signs of bewilderment and amazement as an innocent suspect would show when apprehended by the security men.

"What's the matter?" She asked puzzled. One of the men surrounding them probably, their leader, cleared his voice and said:

"You don't have to worry woman. We would like some information from you. We believe you will help us to find out who has committed a murder a few hours ago".

"Murder! how do we come into that?" Anyadwe asked.

"You've heard the alarms which were made a few hours ago?"

"Yes, we did", she answered politely.

"A body of a young boy in the village was found by a man who is a visitor of Nekimwodi."

"Toolit," Anyadwe mentioned the name.

"Yes, with the grandson of Nekimwodi," the man added. What we are after is, we would like to know from you whether you saw anyone around that place when you went to fetch some water. Toolit claimed that you were the only two people he got at the well. Apparently, the murder was committed about that time. Because they found that, the pool of blood, which flowed from the head of the deceased, was just clotting and the one on the rock where the murder was committed had dried because of the heat on the rock. We do not mean to say that you are the one who did it because we understand that you are coming from Opokopwac, and you are going to Coomit. Is that right?"

"Yes sir." Anyadwe replied with all the confidence she had in her.

"So you see why I said your co-operation is very vital to us. If you saw anyone in that place, try to describe him or her as vividly as you can remember him or her. There are not very many people around that place you can almost count them on your fingers and they fortunately all have different identifying features on them", the man said putting more courage in her.

"Well, gentlemen", Anyadwe started. I wish the information I am going to give you would be of help to you. First, I must tell you that we did not see any dead body. If we did, we would have most certainly reported the finding to the home of Acoko or told Toolit about it. Its true Toolit got us at the well.

"Which well is this you're talking about?" Anather young spearman interrupted her.

"I thought Toolit told you where he got us. I didn't know there were two wells about that place, we fetch the water in the well under the anthill," Anyadwe answered.

"Yes he told us that, he said, he got you almost leaving, and he walked back with you until you met the grandson of Nekimwodi." The man who spoke first agreed with her.

"Anyway, as I was saying, we didn't see any dead body," Anyadwe said and went through the whole story for them but she was carefully to exclude David. In the end, she asked them to go and ask Acan, the daughter of Acoko and Kertoo to give them more information concerning the two boys and to verify her statement. Although a few of the men wanted them to be dragged back the majority of them including the man who spoke first were satisfied with her explanation and her address of location if they should want her again.

The man thanked her for the information she gave them and exonerated them. David was relieved when they were left to continue with their walk, but it soon became dark. The stars dimly lighted the night. Anyadwe was quiet most of the way because she was thinking about what Opuk told her and Tongpur before they took the animals out. "I see blood on a rock, below it, is dirty muddy water. I see a dead body under the shrubs on the rock, and a woman with a boy at well. I see the boy running away. I see another boy coming and the woman holding him frightened. I see a man. I see them walk back. I see them. They meet a young man carrying a spear. The old man and the young man go back. I see the woman and the boy walk away. I see the old man, and young man on the rock. The water below is clear now. The blood on the rock has dried. I see them making alarms. I see the woman and the son being questioned. Nevertheless, the gods say they did not do it let them go. I see many things."

"It's true he told us what really happened, but I know the devil is trying to win me over by talking and showing a lot of wonders through him. I will never yield to his words. Instead, I will pray to the Blessed Virgin Mary the mother of Christ to make him change and accept the true God who made him, the God who created him; the God who is making him breathe. Lord, have mercy on Opuk and make him accept you, as all of us have accepted you," she said and made a sign of the crossed. A few hours walk brought them to their village market, which was only two miles from their home. "We are back home," Anyadwe announced as they approached the bridge which lay between their home and the market. David was happy to return home at last. It was about ten o'clock at night.

## Chapter Six

The following day, they woke up very late in the morning and stayed at home to rest. During her resting hours, Anyadwe found herself thinking admiringly about Opuk. "He is a bigot polytheist pagan; nevertheless he is working all these things to help the people who were suffering. They were sick, they were dying and he healed them. Won't God give him his due for that benevolence he has shown to His subjects? The trouble with him is, he strongly believes that there is no God beside our traditional gods we used to worship. He is stuck to his belief like a skin on flesh; if he could only accept the Christian God and continue to prophecies I would believe him. Look how he has cured David. I am sure without that medicine he would still be fainting repeatedly. Alternatively, could it be he is cured because, as he put it, the spirit of my husband has now been fed and he is now happy with me. However, how do spirits eat and drink? The Priests tell us in the mission that after death our souls go straight to heaven to meet God or they go to hell to suffer. In heaven, there is neither pain nor suffering but enjoyment forever and ever but in hell, there is that dangerous fire. You burn in the fire of hell day and night, forever and ever. Can you imagine? Moreover the fire is supposed to be hotter than any fire on earth. So if the allegation of Opuk is true that the spirit of my husband was really suffering, was hungry and needed something to eat then it means he is in hell! Nevertheless, Father Egidio assured me that on the day he died in Gulu, he was anointed with the last sacrament of the dying and indeed, he died a happy man; a man who was pure at heart and free from sin. I do not believe Opuk. He is lying. My husband should be with God in heaven.

Could it be he committed a sin he forgot to confess or hid from the Priests? And is Opuk right?" To brush off the thoughts about Opuk, Anyadwe decided that they should go to the mission for confession and benediction, to refuel her soul with the grace of resistance against the devil. Because she did not know whether to take Opuk for a man of God or just a soothsayer, a seer, a man in the devil's grip.

After the prayers and Benediction Padre Egidio asked Anyadwe and David to come with him to the Presbytery. They went and when they got there, Padre Egidio said: "I wanted to remind you that the school term is about to start. It is only next week on Monday, so we have to start organizing something for David. Have you done anything for him as yet?" Padre Egidio asked Anyadwe as they all sat down on a form at the veranda.

"No, I was just thinking of making for him some new khaki uniform this week before I contact you to know when the school starts."

"Okay wait a minute, I come back." He excused himself got up, entered his sleeping room, and soon came out with a receipt. He went and sat next to Anyadwe and gave the receipt to her.

"This receipt, I have given you, is to show that he has already paid school fees. You will keep it safely at home. On Monday next week, when he comes to school, he will come with it first to me before I take him to the headmaster for introduction. Because, you know, all the pupils pay their fees directly to him, who issues the receipts for the fees received, and registers them according to their classes." Anyadwe received the receipts, folded it into a tiny little piece of paper and cupped her hands over it.

"Take this money to pay for the uniforms. Paul Lugeny is not a bad tailor. I have been making some of my pair of shorts from him, and he charges reasonable price too," he said and pulled out a ten shillings note from his purse and gave it to her. She accepted the money and thanked him for it. After that they wished him good evening before they left for their home.

On their way home, they passed through Paul Lugeny's shop. They got him very busy sewing the uniforms of very many pupils ordered through him. The rattling noise of his sewing machine could be heard from far away, and from morning to late in the night. He was happy to see them come in. He lifted his eyes up only for a second or two before he buried his head back on the machine adjusting the cloth on the machine while he operated the wheel with his feet.

"Good evening Anyadwe how are you and your son? You are welcome. Have you brought new work? I like people who bring me work, work is what I need," he said with his eyes down on his job.

"More and more work, means more and more money", Anyadwe replied.

"Yes, that is the idea."

"Well here is some more". We want a pair of uniform for him. Could you measure him?

"Oh yes, I will do that." He said and got up from the stool and took a tape measure to measure David.

"Are you paying something now for my labour and material? I always deal fast with those who give me fat money too; I mean those who need quick service give in quick money. First come, first served only work with me when I have only these people with sticky fingers on my register," he said and laughed again.

"Nice work is always accomplished by nice money."

"How much will you take?"

"Eight shillings will do."

"Thank you sir," Anyadwe said and produced the ten shillings note.

"Good." Lugeny remarked, got up from his stool, went, and put the money in a small wooden box with a slit hole on top he used for a safe. He took the two shillings balance and gave them to her.

"When should we check on you?"

"Um-um, what is the day today?"

"Saturday", Anyadwe said. He flipped back pages of his register where he enters his clients and their particulars to see how many people had paid in full.

Try me on Wednesday evening he said, and closed the register.

"Okay we will see you tomorrow in church then". Good evening Lugeny."

"Good evening Ajulina."

The week ended like a flash of lightening to David. On Sunday evening the eve of the Monday he should begin school, he had built the fire in the compound and sat on one of the firewood looking gloomy and sick like a chick suffering from coccidiosis. He thought of the daily getting up early and running to school instead of sitting home with his mother. He thought of the bullies, and the beatings at school by the teachers, and he became more and more worried the more he thought about them. He was never hit nor manhandled by his mother. It was then that he realised how much his mother loved him.

"David" his mother called him.

"Yes Mama."

"Come and carry the water out let us go to eat, I'll carry the food." She ordered. David went and took the water obediently and left for the fireplace followed by his mother almost immediately with the supper. While eating she kept on talking to him about the benefit of education and how to behave at school.

## The Devout Woman

"You are not going to remain with your catechumen's knowledge when you crammed the catechism by heart from cover to cover and recited all the daily prayers that exist in the Church without knowing how they are written and read. By going to school, you are going to know how to read and write. What I strongly advise you against are, rudeness to your teachers, and whoever is going to be in authority, even your fellow pupils, playing or sleeping in the classroom when the lesson is going on, you must always finish the work given to you in the class. When you do not understand anything do not be shy, ask the teacher for assistance and explanation, that is why he is called a teacher. He is being paid for that. If he is a good teacher he will always love to help you no matter how many times you ask him. My final advice or should I call it a warning this time is, the school is a mixed school as you have been seeing on Sundays. There will be girls studying with you in the same class. Do not have immoral games with them. There will be some older boys who will like such games. Please avoid their company. I trust you will be alright in that," she finally said as David cleaned the last remains of food at the side of the bowl with his fingers.

"Have you understood all I have said?" She asked him.

"Yes Mama," he replied subserviently.

"I will be very disappointed if you break any of them. I am sure the priests will be more disappointed because they are the ones paying your school fees. So please I appeal to you to behave yourself and be a good lad at school." Anyadwe concluded.

As she did, David said, "Opuk is coming Mama." When he heard the bangles on his ankles clacking as he walked in.

"Why is he out late tonight?"

"I don't know."

"I hope he's not coming to bore me with his nonsense."

"May I come in?" Opuk sought for permission to enter the home.

"Come in," Anyadwe welcomed him. Opuk walked in, pounding his long walking stick on the ground as he walked. He held his mushroom stool by the string in his left hand. He came and put the mushroom stool near Anyadwe and lowered himself sliding his hand on the walking stick and sat on it. He laid the walking stick near him before he collected the skin tied around his waist in front of him to cover his nakedness.

"Good evening Opuk."

"Good evening Mama Acellam. How are you here?"

"We are fine thank you. You are out late tonight."

"Hum I am. I have in fact come to see you on an urgent matter."

Anyadwe's heart skipped a beat and blood started racing around her body.

She felt her armpit moistening with sweat. She did not know what to tell him.

She almost told him to get up and go away. However, she kept quiet and waited.

"Urgent matter?" she asked.

"Yes. Don't let Acellam go to school tomorrow."

"Why? He is to go and start school. Everything for him is ready, why shouldn't he go to school tomorrow?"

"Are you asking me why I am saying he should not go to school tomorrow or you are obstinately telling me that you will let him go to school in-spite of what I have been told?

"David is going to school tomorrow that is all I know" Anyadwe stressed.

"I see. So you are determined to disobey the gods."

"I am very tired Opuk I want to go to sleep. As a matter of fact you nearly got us in bed."

"You mean now? It's only seven p.m," Opuk commented.

"There is no time for sleeping depending on when you have the sleep you sleep."

"I know you are avoiding me. But let me warn you woman, the gods have lost patience with you and …"

"Let them loose it. I am not worried."

"You are not?" Anyadwe kept quiet.

"I have seen trouble. What did I tell you when you stubbornly took the animals to your brothers? And what did you tell me when you came back? Not what I told you before you went? Now I am rushing here to save the life of our son Acellam. You want to throw me out. If anything happens to this boy tomorrow at school, I myself will hang you. I will kill you. If the gods will spare you, I will do it," Opuk said viciously while waging his finger at her.

"In fact Opuk I will be happy to die in your hands because I refused to accept your gods. David goes to school tomorrow. If he is going to die, let him die, because no one is immortal here. We will all die." Opuk sighed, and took his walking stick collected his stool without saying another word and walked away very annoyed.

When Opuk left, Anyadwe was put on the fence. She did not know what to do in spite of the irrational statement she made that if David was to die let him die. Surely, this man always told the future. Now he is telling me that I should not let David go to school tomorrow! Supposing he goes and he is killed as, he has predicted what is going to happen? The whole clan will certainly blame me for his death. He will definitely herald that he had warned me, but I obstinately defied his warning. David is dear to me, very dear indeed. Nevertheless, should I really yield to Opuk's gods this time for his sake? What will I tell Padre Egidio tomorrow if he does not go to school? Shall

I lie he was sick? In addition, yield to the devil with his pumps? No, I will not do that we shall all go tomorrow. If he gets killed let them kill me because of my love for the Lord Jesus Christ who died for us sinners. Meanwhile where he set David was nearly falling asleep. He stirred and said Mama what is wrong?

"Nothing"

"Why are you quiet?"

"I hate Opuk. He always tricks me."

"Shall I go to school tomorrow?" David asked concerned.

"Of course; do not be scared for nothing. I have warned you to be ready to die for Christ and never to believe in these heathen stories about gods."

The following day Monday David woke up earlier than usual. The day was one of those odd days in the dry season, which makes everyone begin to worry about the busy period of the rainy seasons. It was about six a.m. The morning was not going to be fine. There were thick black nimbus clouds rising from the Southeast, their usual rain direction. Soft low thunder could be heard coming from the direction several miles away.

Small current of wind blew from the direction of the thunder carrying with it some stratus cloud, which drifted passed overhead.

"Is it going to rain?" Anyadwe asked David who was already at the door way.

"It looks like it." He replied.

David got out and spent his time envying the birds, which had already started the day by singing happily in the forest flying and singing melodiously praising the Creator.

"How I wish I was one of them, David thought while urinating, I wouldn't be thinking of going to school but fly around romancing like those doves are doing. Knocking off insects which cropped my way and sink them down by esophagus like those sparrows. They are so content with life. God feeds them from morning to dusk and not a cent do they pay for all these!" he finished urinating and went back inside. The rain started drizzling but soon cleared away before it was seven a.m leaving only the cirrus cloud drifting about. After breakfast, he dressed up in his new uniforms, and was ready to go to start school first day, first term, and first year. He said good-bye to his mother and walked away.

When he got to the road, he looked left and right. There was no one on the road. David thought he was the last pupil to school that morning.

"First day I started, I start with late coming! What a beginning?" He thought and broke out running. When he reached a corner in front of him, he saw two children about his age. The boy, who was holding the hand of the girl, was older than he was. The girl was crying with tears streaming down her cheeks. David guessed they were also going to school because of the uniform they had on. He walked and passed them without talking to them before he started running again leaving them behind. He ran until he reached the school. David went straight to the presbytery and sat on the waiting bench waiting for Padre Egidio, who was in the church saying the morning mass. After the Mass Padre Egidio walked out of the vestry, locked the door, and came walking towards David.

"Good morning David", he said. David got up as Padre Egidio approached him.

"Good morning Father", he replied.

"How are you this morning?"

"I am fine thank you Father."

"How is your mother?"

"She is fine Father."

"Come and sit down here and wait for me. I will be back soon". He said and pulled an office chair for him to sit on.

"You are forty five minutes earlier", he said and walked out of the room to join Padre Enriko, and Bro. Albertini who were already at table in their dining hall for breakfast.

David sat in the office, which was not elegantly furnished. Beside the table and the office chair on which he sat, there were eight more similar chairs lined up against the walls, four on each side of the opposite walls facing each other. The tenth one was Padre Egidio's personal chair. It was similar to the other nine except that it had side arms for supporting his adipose arms. There was a simple bookshelf, which covered the whole length of the wall up to the doorframe. About six feet long, and five feet high, it contained four horizontal shelves, which were packed with religious books of various size so that they gave the atmosphere of an office of a Professor of Theology. Behind him was a framed photograph of the Sacred Heart of Jesus. A papyrus mat, covering the entire floor serving as the carpet, completed the luxury of the office.

After about thirty minutes, David heard the door squeak and open instantly and Padre Egidio entered in the office,

"Are you alright?" Padre Egidio asked him, and came near him raffled his kinky hair before he went and sat in his chair.

"Yes Father. I am alright." David replied.

As they talked, the school gong, around, thin, steel sheet, with a central round hole, suspended by tough wires on the slopping end of one of the poles, in front of Primary four-class room rang. Padre Egidio pulled out his pocket watch and looked at it.

"They are ten minutes ahead of time." Padre Egidio said and got up from his chair. "Let us go to school and I introduce you to the Headmaster." He said and they walked out of the office. They passed groups of old boys and girls playing happily with each other in the compound.

A few colonies of new pupils stood deserted under trees, near classrooms, and in the compound looking as strange as new herds of cattle being introduced on a farm. A short man about a foot taller than David walked to meet them and opened a door situated between classes five and six and led them in as he charted with Padre Egidio. When the two men had finished their conversation on administration, Padre Egidio brought David on the scene.

"By the way Kul, this is the young boy David Acellam I told you about, the one the Mission is going to take care of his education as long as he will be interested in learning at school. He lost his father about eight years ago. You must have heard of Gitano Ogwok who fought a lion with a machete and at the end they killed each other?"

"Yes I did," Kul confirmed with a precise nod.

"Well that was him. He was very helpful to me when I came here and took over from Padre Santonino. It was he who first assisted Padre Santonino here, and when I came, he did the same to me. Without him, we would have found our work difficult here. This Mission and the school would have probably not been standing as they are now. He taught us Acholi language and took us out in the villages so that we were able to meet and preach to the people. He became even more helpful to us when we opened up the work on this school. He worked harder than most of the people who had their children at school here, although David was not yet born. His death was a great loss to us particularly to Brothers Albertini with whom he worked hand in hand. Since then he does not have anyone as industrious and reliant as him. Because of these facts, we have decided to educate his only child David. It's all up to him to learn while we take care of his needs. If he will say no more of books before he reaches the end, then we cannot do anything to help him.

"That's right Father," Kul answered pathetically while looking at David. It was then that David realised that the short man was the headmaster of the school.

"Will you register him in his class register?"

"Yes father. But what number are we going to use for his school fees receipt?"

"He has one. David, will you give him the receipt?"

"Yes Father," David said and gave the receipt to Kul.

Kul copied down David's receipt number and gave it back to him. So when it will be time, we shall start by morning prayers first then you will come back to clean up the classes and their surroundings. Tomorrow we should be in a cleaner home than this jungle," Padre Egidio said and walked out of the office still holding David by the hand while Kul walked out, stood on the dais infront of his office and stared after them meditatively. The number of the pupils had increased three fold. As they walked towards the church, they met the teachers coming to school. Padre Egidio waved to them and they waved back to him.

After morning prayers, Padre Egidio took David and the two pupils he by-passed on his way to school to weed a flower bed near the church. It was there that they knew each other. The boy was called Olel, a second year pupil. He was one of the well-behaved lads in school; as a result, he was an elite of the school authorities, especially Padre Egidio. The girl was his sister Latigi coming to start school for the first time with David.

The rest of the pupils went back to the school marching according to their classes to the assembly ground in front of Kul's office.

After the assembly, every pupil was busy tiding up the school compound and the classes while David, and his friends Olel and Latigi weeded the flower bed. They became good friends as if they had known each other for months. They co-operated in their work and finished it before time. Padre Egidio, who was expecting them to weed the flower bed in two days, was amazed to find that they had completed the work in time, yet they did it marvelously.

"Oh dear, this is a beautiful work. I didn't expect you to finish weeding the garden today in such a short time." He said when he came to see how they were working. He hugged them one at a time wishing he had more than two hands to enable him to embrace them all at once.

"You must be tired." Padre Egidio asked them affirmatively.

"Yes we are." David replied.

"You can return your tools to the store and rest but don't go home as yet, wait for your friends. You will go after the assembly, may be the headmaster would like to ask you to bring something tomorrow for the school." Padre Egidio said and walked with them to the store of Brother Albertini from where they had taken their tools.

Olel knew well about the rough behaviours of the pupils at the well where they washed their legs after work. He advised Latigi and David, to go with him to wash up before everyone else was released to go down the well.

"Let's go to wash our legs before it's time," Olel suggested.

"Why? It's not yet time; Padre Egidio said that we should wait for the rest of the pupils here." David protested.

"I thought he said that we shouldn't go home as yet but wait here for other to hear whatever the headmaster has to tell us for tomorrow. We will not have space at the well if we wait here until everyone is set free to go and wash. There are going to be a lot of bullies there mainly the older pupils and moreover they will keep us out of the well until they have finished washing themselves. By then, the water will be nothing but mud. You'll see if we don't go now," Olel warned. They heeded to his warning and ran to the well as quickly as they could, hurriedly washed up, and got out of the well to dry themselves. Hardly five minutes had elapsed, when they heard the school gong ringing, followed by the whistle of Kul indicating that it was time, and everybody had to stop work.

"Let's get out of here quickly. Do not let them get us here. They are going to storm this place like a heard of elephants. If they get us here they are going to bully us". Olel said and began to run back taking his sister by the hand. David followed them. They ran. Immediately they crossed the main road, they heard them shouting, imitating the blearing horns of motorcars, while running towards the well, their footfalls could be heard several yards away.

"Let's go in the opposite direction, let them not meet us. They are going to run us down knowing that we have been to the well before them. You follow me don't run now," Olel advised them and they walked towards the shops. The other pupils came charging behind them like devils released from hell for an ice-cube. They kicked and trapped one another from behind, so that, they younger boys and girls were left regretting why they have ever come to school.

"Didn't I tell you? Have you seen what they do to younger pupils? They are merciless. They only care for their brothers or sisters or if they know you well otherwise they make you walking ground." Olel said. The warning from Olel was no fun to David. It worried him and he began to wonder how he was going to complete the six years at school with the rough companies thronged around him every day with no one to scare them from him. After about one hour's stay at the well, the pupils returned to school and assembled in front of Kul's office for the announcement. Taking his stand on the dais, Kul announced that all the male pupils in the school except those in the first three lower classes should bring with them a pole and a hoe each for digging the holes for rebuilding the urinary shelters for both the girls and the boys. The boys in the first three classes were to bring with them six good reeds each while all the girls were to bring with them knives for cutting the grass. With his new friends, Olel and his sister Latigi, David walked back home after the school was closed by the Headmaster at two o'clock. Soon most of the pupil branched off to Bulkur. A short walk brought Olel and his sister to their path and David was left walking alone on the road. As he briskly walked home, a girl came running after him.

"Eh, you, wait for me." The girl shouted. David looked at her and stopped to wait for her.

## The Devout Woman

"Good afternoon," the girl greeted David.

"Good afternoon," David replied her greeting.

"I'm Ventorina Ayot. What is your name?"

"David Acellam is my name." He said.

"Where is your home?" Ayot asked.

"Just on that slope in front of us."

"Are you the son of Anthony Kinyera?"

"No, he is our neighbor."

"Who is your father?"

"I've none. I live with my mother only. My father died many years back. I didn't even see him."

"I'm sorry about that David."

"That is life my dear, you live today, tomorrow you are a big sausage for maggots."

"Who is your mother?" I know Anyadwe who lives near Kinyera. She is a good friend of my mother. My mother told me that her husband was killed by a lion, could she be your mother?"

"Oh yes, she is my mother."

"I see, we occasionally met in the market and walked home together. Your mother is a very nice, friendly lady."

"Thank you for your compliments."

"Your father was a brave man. The day my mother told me about his dreadful story, I passed a sleepless night. I was very frightened. I could not imagine a man wrestling with a lion like that. I thought my mother was telling me one of the fairy tales. I must admit he died a heroic death.

"I hope you will be as brave and strong like him." She said.

"Where is your home?" David asked Ayot ignoring her remark.

"Our home is not very far away from yours. We live inland about two miles from the main road at Lamin'acwang.

You know, I am also fatherless as you are, but a lion did not kill mine. He was called Ogwang. Not much is known about him. Even my mother seems to know very little about him. He was a poor man. He died when I was four.

"Are you staying only two of you also?"

"No, we are staying with a horrible uncle, Erokulano Olwit."

"Why do you call him horrible?"

"It is because I don't have any word in my vocabulary at the moment, stronger than that." "You hate him?"

"Yes, I do."

"Does your mother hate him as you do?"

"Perhaps, worse"

"And why are you staying with the man you hate?"

"It is a difficult story to talk about. The thing is David, when my father died; this uncle of mine inherited my father's properties by right according to our tradition. Of course, that included my mother and me. That was the beginning of the problems. He has complicated our lives. I have two brothers with whom I share mother now.

These boys are the sons of Olwit; Kwerowat and Lebmon. Olwit's wife, I mean, the co-wife of my mother, has two daughters and those are all she got for Olwit. Olwit hates me. He openly denounces me that he has nothing to do with me because I am not his daughter, that is true anyway, but he has anchored on my mother because of his two sons. I bet he would have said the same to my mother if it were not because of those vulgar boys. Yet, even if Olwit loves his sons, his wife, with her two daughters, hate the boys including my mother and me, because Olwit adores her, his dialogue with the sons is not very cordial. Odd enough the two boys have been indoctrinated to hate me by their father. They do not like me. My mother loves them because they are her sons. I do not blame her for that. She has been trying to bring us together but the boys will not listen.

They are spoilt children anyway. They drink alcohol like the bottles, which keep the liquid. On top of that, they smoke opium to inebriate them whenever they are without money. They smoke cigarettes and only sleep takes it from their lips. They do all sorts of things, boys of their ages should not do. None of them is thinking about school. In fact, only my mother is interested in my education, my uncle and his sons say I am wasting money for their liquor and that I am merely on a course for prostitution. For the last two years my mother has been struggling alone to pay my school fees, buy my uniforms, and care for herself, and the very annoying thing is that, the little money she tries to keep, these bunch of drunkards steal it from her or force her to give it to them. So, most of the time, we go working for the actual material from the shopkeepers, things like soap, salt, etcetera etcetera. We have been living very rough lives.

One never knows how hostile life can be to lose father and to be inherited by an inhuman man like Olwit. I think I would have been happier if I was living with my mother in a lonely place somewhere," she said with a lump in her throat. "I don't know why I told you this story, I've never told it to anyone. You must be very lucky to have heard my problems, or must I say I am very lucky to have met you to talk out my problems. Even now I feel relieved after I've told you all these."

"I think you told me because you found out that we are in the same boat." They soon got to David's home and he excused himself.

"I know your home because of your mother. Will you wait for me tomorrow in the morning so that we walk to school together? " I'll try to be early." Ayot said.

"If you promise I'll wait for you."

"I promise", she said and walked away and David walked home feeling more worried about Ayot than for himself.

"It's no use to be born if people lead miserable lives like this. Look at this girl, innocent as she looks her happiness exists when she is out of that home and yet the reverse is true for children of people with blue blood." David thought as he entered their fence.

When he got home, his mother was not there. He knew she had gone to the garden to hoe down the old cotton stalks to prepare the garden for sowing millet at the beginning of the rainy season. After his lunch, he took his hoe and the *machete* for cutting the reeds and followed his mother in the garden. He got her very busy cutting the old cotton stalks. He joined her in the work and told his mother all what happened at school that day.

After their work, she went home while David remained behind to cut his reeds. He quickly got six tall nice ones, which he brought home with him.

Meanwhile as Anyadwe walked home, she thought.

"So, you see, if I yielded to Opuk's warning that David should not go to school, I would have annoyed God. I would have yielded to the devil with his pomps. Thank you my mother, the Blessed Virgin Mary, for the courage you gave me.

The following day, David left for school with his bundle of reeds properly tied up for him by his mother. Ayot arrived early at the junction as she had promised him. The early morning dew had moistened her legs and had plastered a few fragments of grass on them. She stood waiting for him with her knife for cutting grass at school held behind her.

"Good morning Ayot."

"Good morning David." They exchanged greeting and continued to walk to school chatting.

A good number of pupils turned up punctually that day bringing with them whatever they were asked to bring so that work on the urinary shelters started early. The pupils in primary one and two swept and arranged the desks in all the classes from Primary one to six. David and his friends Olel and Latigi worked together with a few other pupils, arranged desks in class five and six. They were not dirtied by the work they did so they did not go to the well to wash themselves when they finish their work. The other pupils who had been toiling in the hot sun, cutting grass, carrying rocks, and building the urinary shelters, needed proper baths.

Beside the well, which the school used more often, there was a dam built next to the well by blocking river Lukwor where it constricted after leaving a large expanded body of water behind about two hundred yards wide by three-hundred yards long.

The dam in those days was the relaxing site for the British colonialists residing in Gulu. During the weekends, they came to Coomit dam with their families in their cars carrying canoes in which they always spent most of their time on water in the dam. If they were not rowing in their canoes, some of them remained fishing using hooks, while others roamed the forested eastern bank of the dam in search of animals. Nevertheless, their women and children most of the time sat in the shades which they improvised with their tents. The local people were allowed to use the dam from Monday to Friday only. But the porter who unloaded and loaded their kits upon arrival and departure, were allowed to keep watch around the dam without touching the water.

River Lukwor is very near the school. The slopes of the western bank flattened out into a semi-plateau, the site that Ogwok and Padre Santonino chose for the mission of Coomit. Labourers were employed to slash all around the dam. There were rocks all along the Lukwor dam, which provided standing ground for those who would rather bath than swim. While tall trees and grass, strewn the eastern hills ending into a thick forest where the animals and the birds the colonialists hunted lived.

The school was built at the edge of the Western slope, which fell away on a steady gradient down into the sparkling water below. In the bright early mornings, the water in the river sparkled like a large sheet of glass reflecting a dazzling sun light to the school. The well, which the school used more often, lay between the school and the dam.

That Tuesday afternoon, when the girls finished cutting grass, they needed a bath badly because of the itching they got from the grass. So they ran to the dam to have either a swim or a bath before the boys were released.

They went, striped themselves of their uniforms, plunged into the water, and began to swim. Those who knew no swimming stood on the rocks at the side of the dam to bathe. They were shouting happily splashing water on each other not knowing that what they were doing was having a stimulating impact on the boys whom they left at school finishing their work. The boys could see them like black dots in the dam and at the bank. Although far, the scene was informative enough to them. Their shrilling screams and laughters crept up the slope to the school and stroke the boys' ears invitingly so that they were at the get-set-position waiting for the whistle and the bell to tell them to stop work and they rush down to the dam.

After what seemed to be an endless wait for them, the gong rang and the whistle went indicating that they should stop work. In tumults, they left whatever they were doing as if they suddenly became red hot in their hands and started running down the slope like a heard of thirsty elephants. With their warning, hooting sounds of motor cars, they flew down the slope. None of them wanted to remain behind. Barefooted as they were, they ran on the short grass growing near the river, stumbling and falling occascarionally as they ran.

The girls were warned of their coming. Those who were near the bank rushed for their uniforms and were soon dressed up before the boys arrived. They warned their friends who were competing in diving and swimming far away in the centre of the dam to come back and dress up before the boys got them naked.

They tried but the boys were too fast for them. In no time, the place was crowded with panting boys, laughing happily at the girls arrested in the dam.

They remained in the water-submerged neck down with their heads only above water pleading to the boys to allow them out of water to get dressed but none of them seemed to want to miss the fun. One old boy, of class six stripped himself naked in spite of the girls near him, dived in the water, and started swimming towards the girls. The girls screamed and dived as the boy got near them, but the boy continued swimming. After some minutes under water, one of the girls resurfaced and found herself face to face with the boy. She was still wiping water from her face with both palms when the boy grasped her young germinating breasts. She screamed alerting her brother's attention to what the boy was doing to her. The boy, who was fondling the breasts of the girl in the water, had his sister in the dam too. She was just about to get out walking in the shallow water covering her nakedness with her palms. In retaliation, the brother of the girl whose breasts were being caressed in the water ran to the girl and pulled out her hands to expose her nakedness. She also screamed. The boy in the water identified the scream of his sister and swam back like an angry crocodile rescuing her young one. In a moment, a huge fight broke out in which one boy was savagely hit on the head with the rock and he fell down dead.

The incident worried David. He did not know why his mother would never heed to Opuk's warning. He did not know whether his mother really wanted him alive. He began to think of many events Opuk predicted and they happened.

"Why does Mama not see these? I am going to talk to her about this." David thought as he walked home worried. Anyadwe was frightened at the news David told her. She spent her time in prayer so that such things should not happen to her dear son.

## Chapter Seven

The boy killed at the dam was the son of the brother of Fedelis Otwol the cousin of Ogwok to whom Anyadwe was given by the elders when Ogwok died. Fedelis Otwol was one of the first few people of Coomit to receive the Christian faith. A short stout, barrel-chested man, Otwol was a zealous believer in the Christian God. He was unmarried before Ogwok died. Nevertheless, he was betrothed to a girl and preparation was underway to take the dowry to the parents of the girl. When Ogwok died, the elders of the clan wanted Otwol to inherit Anyadwe and stop his planned marriage. But Anyadwe rejected the suggestion of the elders. Otwol was very disappointed but later he went ahead with his arrangement for his planned marriage. Before he completed everything, one day, he went to the forest to cut trees to build his hut as a part of the preparation for the marriage. A new woman is better welcomed in a new hut. He went and never came back. He was not seen for a day or two. Search for him was mounted everywhere but without success. For one full month, they searched for him. Some rumored that he committed suicide because Anyadwe rejected him to inherit her, while many believed a wild animal ate him. However, none of those guesses was true.

When Otwol left home to go and cut poles for his hut in the forest, he found an old man sitting on a log in the forest. He thought he knew him. They exchanged greetings and the old man asked him; "You are looking for something?"

"Ah yes, I want to find some poles for building my hut."

## The Devout Woman

"I see, they are not very many here. People have felled all good ones here," the old man said. Otwol looked at the man surprised.

He could not conceal his desire to know who he was.

"*Muzee*,(swhilli word meaning old or important person male or female) if I may ask, I seem to know you. Who are you?" Otwol asked. I am sorry *muzee*, but it looks I saw you sometime somewhere", Otwol added.

"Yes you saw me a long time ago."

"I must have, because your face is familiar to me."

"You ever heard of Balmoi?" The old man asked.

"Balmoi! Of course I have. You? Balmoi my grandfather? Otwol said trembling with fear." Otwol said and collapsed down like a rotten mushroom.

"Don't be afraid my son, he said and touched him on the shoulder and picked him up.

"Okay now you know me. I will take you where you will get good poles for your hut. Come with me," Balmoi said.

Balmoi had died from snakebite. A snake bit him one night as he slept in his hut. Birya the son of Balmoi and the father of Otwol killed the cobra. Otwol was five years old when his grandfather died. His name was Opira, but later changed by his father Birya to Otwol, literally meaning snake. Otwol followed his grandfather. They walked and walked, crossed rivers and streams, climbed hills and hills, before they got to a place where there were tall nice trees and a hut just newly built. There was no one around nor any domestic animals or birds to show human existence.

"Here we are my son; let's rest first before you cut down your trees," his grandfather said. Otwol sat outside resting on a log while his grandfather went in, and came out with something in a broken pot and asked him to eat it.

"What is this?" Otwol asked his grandfather.

"Dried flies, and don't ask your grandfather such questions. Eat whatever I give you. It won't kill you." Otwol, with difficulty took one fly from the broken pot and tested it. It was nasty. He had never eaten any nasty food like that in his life. He nauseated and gave the broken pot with its content back to his grandfather.

"I'm sorry I can't eat it Baba."

"It won't kill you; eat it. It will give you strength to walk back with your poles."

"But I have never eaten anything like that Baba. You will excuse me. I am not despising your cooking."

"Okay son. You can leave it. I am going to take you back. However, before you go I want you to spend a night here because I am going go give you something very important. I want to make you a snake-charmer," Otwol fidgeted at that information.

"How, Baba?"

"I will give you the medicine which will enable you to be, and to command them from anywhere wherever you will be. They will never kill you. Their poison will be like water to you. The ceremony will be conducted by me now," he said and snapped his fingers. Immediately three huge cobras appeared with their mouths opened and their fangs jutted out. Their eyes glowed with ferocity. Otwol jumped up yelling for help. His grandfather only croaked a laugh and asked him to sit down. He sat down trembling and the snakes immediately hooked themselves onto his leg, stomach and neck. Whether it was because of the horror of the sights of the snakes or their poisons, Otwol fainted. What happened there after he did not know; nevertheless, when he came around, he found deep tattooed marks on the back of his hands, feet, neck, and elbows. They seemed to have been axed. They were paining him severely.

"I had to make you sleep, because without that I would not have tattooed you and applied the medicine against the snake venom." His grandfather said as Otwol writhed with the excruciating pain.

"How will I go home? The pain is too much for me, I am going to die."

"No my son, you won't die the gods will take care of you. I will give you medicine to kill the pain". *Muzee* said and disappeared in the hut and reappeared with another huge cobra following him. "Don't be afraid my son; she will give you the pain killer." He said. The cobra came and hooked its fangs in the wounds one at a time and the pain left him and he became even more courageous to see the snakes near him. He felt he loved the the cobra. He wanted to carry it. He asked his grandfather to bring more of them near him. He snapped his hand and not only cobras came but snakes of all kind rattlesnakes, black mambas, vipers, Boas etc came, wriggling near him. He found that he loved them. He picked them one by one and talked to them and they did whatever he told them.

They bit him but he felt no pain. "Okay my son; the gods have given you the power over them. Control them. Do not hit or kill any of them. The medicine I am going to show to you is for you to go and help your brothers with. Any of them who will be bitten by the snake you give this medicine to him or her to drink, or you tattoo the site of the bite, and you let the patient dip the affected area in water containing the pounded medicine. In this way, the poison is extracted out in the water. Alternatively, you could combine both treatments.

You are not going to show this medicine to any other person except to the person who will thank you first for any good work you will have done to him or her."

Balmoi said and led him to a creeping plant and said, "This is the herb." When Balmoi said this, he disappeared. Otwol found himself alone with the snakes, the herbs, his axe, and the spear. The hut also disappeared. He was in the jungle alone.

"Baba, Baba," he shouted. "Where are you?" There was no answer only the forest echoed his calling. Otwol uprooted the plant looked at it and pocketed it. He took his axe, spear, and walked away tracing his way back without the pole.

He got home late in the evening seven months after he disappeared. When Otwol came back, everyone was amazed to see him. They could not believe it was he. They thought it was his ghost, which came to them.They all ran away from him. Only Anyadwe could not accept that it was his ghost. She believed Otwol was lost and he has come back. She was not frightened to see Otwol.

It took the people of Coomit a complete one week to acknowledge his humanity.

Otwol stayed alone first wondering how he was going to exhibit the new power he had just acquired over the snakes. He knew that if people have to know that he was a snake charmer they would even be more scared of him than they were when he first returned.

Otwol's love for snakes increased with time so that more often he walked with them in his pockets. The people eventually got to know that Otwol had acquired a unique ability during the period he had been away. Everyone dissociated from him, so he was most of the time alone.Even Angwec, the girl he wanted to marry before his disappearance, refused him when he wanted to renew his plan to marry her.

With all the frustration Otwol went to consult with Opuk seeking for help. Otwol explained to Opuk the problem he was in. Opuk listened to his explanation attentively. He sighed and lifted his head, "Hmm", Opuk groaned wrathfully.

"This is yet another problem facing Coomit village. Of course, this morning when I woke up, the gods told me that there is a young man coming to me with this complaint. They said you have caused hardship to them in the past. You disobeyed them, and you followed the white men's God. You, together with your cousin Ogwok, destroyed all the *Abilla* in your homes, their resting places, and you sent them out in the rain, in the sun, to be drenched and scorched, respectively. You despised them that they were not worth to be your gods, the gods of your grandfathers, the gods who made you, and is keeping you now. The gods who is giving you everything including the wife, you are crying for now. Do you think if the gods do not whisper good words in the heart of that woman to go back to you, will she really reconsider? I do not think so. Even now I see that she will not come back to you. The gods have already told me, that you are not getting the woman back. She has divorced you for good, and never will you see her in your home again. Look, even if he was dead, your grandfather Balmoi appeared to you. He was the one who pleaded to the gods for mercy; you would have been dead by now like your cousin Ogwok. He took you in the wilderness where the gods gave you that power over the snakes. They wanted to show you how good it is to be loyal to them, the gods of your grandfather. Now you are the King of snakes. No snake can bite you and kill you. Meanwhile you can use them to do anything you want. If you never disappointed our gods before, you would be happy with your wife Angwec now. I am sorry my son Otwol, your future is very dark. Your wife has gone for good and she will rather die than come back to you." Opuk warned Otwol.

"How have you known all what happened to me?" Otwol asked.

This is the problem with you misguided sons and daughters of Coomit.

You knew me in the past as the messenger of the gods; all of you ask me the same silly question. How have you known this? Who told you this? How foolish you are."

"Is there nothing you can do to help me now?" Otwol asked desperately.

"I don't think. I, as the servant of the gods, cannot unbind what the gods have bound."

Otwol was skeptical about Opuk's warning but insisted in wining back Angwec.

After six months, Angwec showed no sign of accepting Otwol. He was annoyed and sent a snake, which bit her, and she died.

Anyadwe was worried when she heard the news about the death of Angwec and the circumstances, which led to it. She wondered if Otwol would turn on to her to try to intimidate her with his snakes in order to make her yield to the last proposal of the elders to make him inherit her. She waited in prayers begging the Blessed Virgin Mary not to let such thing happen to her. Days, weeks and months passed without any incident.

David and Ayot had become good friends because of the proximity of their homes and because the two children go to school together. One Saturday, Ayot came to David so that they went together in the forest to collect some firewood. In the forest, they located a log of wood, which was easy to split. Nearly the whole length of the log was hollow according to the "dong, dong, dong, ding" sounds it gave when David tapped on it with the back of the axe. David split it into thin long pieces while Ayot sat on another thicker solid log twisting the rope for tying the split wood. David did not break through the tunnel in the log. Soon the pieces were enough for Ayot to carry, and she bundled them up together including the axe, using the rope she had made. With the bundle tied, David helped her with it on to the *otac (a* round grass head pad used as a cushion between the items to be carried on the head) on her head. David decided to carry the remaining log home for their bonfire in the compound. They started to walk home with Ayot in front. As they walked, before they got home, David sensed some movement in the log, which never repeated again before he dropped the log down. He escorted Ayot and soon came back to make the fire in the compound. He forgot to check on what he thought moved in the log. The fire he had built in the compound was burning angrily giving pop-s-s sounds hauling, some small lumps of fire a few feet away from the heap.

After their supper, they sat near the fire talking, while warming themselves. The moon was nearly as bright as the sun. David sat on the smooth side of the log a little towards the tunnel while his mother sat on a mat in front of him. As they talked, David thought he saw something with the corner of his eye, poking its head out of the tunnel in the log he was sitting on. His mother, who should have had a better view of the object, had a common cold, and by the time David thought he saw something with the corner of his eyes, she was sneezing, and had turned her head away from the fire. David's suspicion was removed when a big dull orange moth came flying from behind him, crushed on the log he was sitting and started fluttering on the ground moving towards the tunnel of the log. David turned and saw it pouring the Powdery stuff from its wing, and at the same time blowing a lot of dust. He picked it up with two sticks, threw it away in the grass without killing it, came back, and sat where he had sat before. Hardly three minutes had passed since he regained his seat, when his mother jumped from where she was sitting, grabbed him and carried him on her chest, and ran with him for about two yards before she put him down on his feet.

A gigantic snake was out of the tunnel of the wood; only the tip of its tail filling the bore of the log, still remained inside the log. They did not know what to do at first as they fled in panic from the snake. The snake, as if it was sent to hunt them down, saw them and started chasing them. David sent a whistle like scream and started crying, while Anyadwe silently took him by the hand and run away towards the gate. She did not cry or scream, probably she feared that she would show to her son that she was frightened, and therefore helpless or may be she was thinking of a way of challenging the snake or both.

The latter seemed to have been the case. When they got to a young mango tree growing in the compound, they hid behind it and she whispered to David: "You keep here so that it assumes we are all here. I'm going in to get the machete and spears, we must kill this snake," she said and dodged in the shadow of the tree, slipped behind another pawpaw tree the shadow of which was very long lying almost across the compound. She soon reached the line of the pillars of her husband's hut and began to steal her way into the hut avoiding the snake as much as possible. It looked as if the snake was meant for Anyadwe. It did not seem to bother about David although it saw him; it did not attack him but remained standing on its belly with the head up in the air, apparently in search of Anyadwe. Anyadwe stealthily crept along the pillars towards the door. She was about to reach the last pillar next to the door, when a loose earth suddenly rolled away from under her feet, bringing her on her back. She quickly got up, and entered the hut. However, the snake had seen her. It immediately started after her. David yelled and screamed running after it beating a stick on the ground to attract the attention of the snake away from his mother, but it was in vain. The snake continued towards the hut where Anyadwe was. It was at that split of a second that Kinyera and some of their immediate neighbours who had heard David screamed earlier came to their rescue. They did not need to ask what the matter was. The snake was there.

In the hut, Anyadwe had got the machete and two spears presumably one was for David and she was on her way out for war with the snake, stripping the machete off it's sheath, when the *bang* of Kinyera's gun exploding in the-still night frightened her, and she dropped down her weapons as if they were the one which exploded in her hands. She knew with his accuracy of shooting, he had done it for her. She would have returned the weapons back to their positions before she got outside, but unconsciously collected them from the floor and walked out with her hands full of spears and the machete.

"It's over Anyadwe," Kinyera said after he had cut off the head of the snake with his gun.

"Oh, thank you very much. I didn't know how I was going to start the attack although you see me armed up to my teeth."

"It is not easy to fight a snake of this size with a spear and machete."

"I know, but what else could we have done, than to try killing it with these?" Anyadwe asked while showing them the weapons in her hand.

"I think we have to clear this forest. There are many dangerous snakes in it. How did this one come in?" Kinyera asked.

David narrated to them how he brought the log home and how he thought he sensed some movements in the log when he was carrying it. They went to check in the log incase there were some more snakes still left. They did not find any, except the nest, and the slough, it had just shed looking new and its replica. With the bright moonlight, the men dragged the snake outside the fenced and buried it.

This event gave Anyadwe a twist in the stomach that night. "Was it the beginning of Otwol's terrorism with his snakes or is it coincidence which has nothing to do with him?" Anyadwe thought as she pulled her covering sheet over her head, wondering if she would sleep a wink.

The following day, Sunday, David and his mother woke up looking tired and exhausted because they did not have enough sleep. They were doing their Sunday morning routine before going to church, when they saw Kinyera walking in being followed by Otwol. Otwol, with his small snake like eyes, looked nervous as if he was frightened of something. The two men walked home to Anyadwe, and they exchanged greeting.

"I m sorry Anyadwe, if we've disturbed your work." Kinyera said apologetically and went on. "Otwol came to me this morning enquiring why I fired the shot last night. I told him what happened. He is worried that we killed the snake. He fears that, as the snake was a very big one, very many of the grandchildren are going to come here to mourn their grandparent where the blood has poured. He has the power of preventing this from happening. He's going to tell you how to go about it." Kinyera said and kept quiet. When Kinyera was introducing the subject, Otwol became very attentive to what he was saying nodding his head approvingly at every word he said. Otwol coughed and cleared his throat like a politician preparing for a television interview and said, "Yes Mama Acellam as you might know, all creatures mourn their dead ones of the same family, and snakes, are not exceptional. Snakes have very high sense of smell for their blood and I am sure if you ignore my advice, you are going to prove it yourself. I will be very surprised if you stay in this home up to dark. I am not scaring you, I am telling you the truth, and I want to help you. All I want is a cock, spotted black and white. I will mix its blood with some herbs and sprinkle the mixture on the spot where the snake was killed. The mixture of the cock's blood and the herbs will destroy the smell of the snake's blood. Therefore, no other snake will come here," Otwol explained. Aware of Anyadwe's hatred for such diabolical functions, Kinyera asked Otwol if it would be all right if he gave the cock himself.

"It's alright, all I need is a spoted black and white cock." he told him.

"Are you going to do it right now?" Kinyera asked again.

"Well if everything is ready, why not? The sooner I do it the better for them."

Kinyera immediately left for his home to collect the cock Otwol demanded.

It was then that Ayot arrived at David's home on her way to church. The time was about nine o'clock. David and his mother were ready dressed. After a while, Kinyera returned with the species of the cock Otwol had asked for.

"Are you going somewhere?" Otwol asked.

"Today is Sunday. She is taking the children to church. I think we don't need her around do we?"

"Oh, no it's alright she can go. I could even do this alone now that the cock is here. For me, I don't know when I last went to church," Otwol said.

In fact, Otwol knew when he last went to church. It was on a Sunday when he had just returned from his seven months long trip, during which he became a snake charmer that he went to church with one in his pocket. As they knelt praying, the snake slipped out of his pocket and on the floor. Those who knelt behind him saw the snake come out of his pocket. They were frightened and began to run away from the church.

The commotion took those who did not see the snake unaware but they did not have to wait to see, nor for God to help them out of the tumult. They abandoned the prayers, and ran for their lives. Although he did not run, the priest, who was saying the mass was startled and frightened. He just managed to control himself. That was the last time Otwol saw the inside of the church.

"May be one thing she could do for me is to show me where the snake was buried before they go to church," Otwol said pulling out some roots of a plant out of his pocket. As he did, a small snake came out of his pocket and started wriggling towards the place where the big snake was shot.

"Do you see what I told you," Otwol said, got up and followed the snake. When it got to the spot, it remained motionless. Otwol followed it, came and stood near it. Immediately another snake bigger than the one on the ground spilt out of his pocket, followed his leg and foot until it got on the ground to join the smaller one. The rest stood yards away watching Otwol and the snakes. Otwol went and crushed the roots he had brought on a stone leaving the two snakes lying on one spot looking sick as if they were having stiffened back bones. After he had crushed the roots, he went and got the cock and the knife from Kinyera. He ripped of all the blood vessels on the neck leaving only the bones and set the cock free, so that it started jumping up and down fluttering, and throwing its blood in all directions. The snakes, which were looking dead, were enlivened by the noise the cock was making. They all ran to Otwol for refuge like frightened puppies.

He picked them up, rolled them into coils on his arms and slipped them back into his pockets, and sprinkled the medicine on the spot, and the surrounding areas.

"It's okay here now. Let's go to where you buried the snake," he said to Kinyera. Kinyera looking confident and fearless of the snake in

Otwol's pockets came and joined him. Otwol took up the dead cock with its legs, and they walked away to the grave of the snake.

A month since David brought the snake home; he and his mother were going to market their cotton at the ginnery when they met Otwol returning from there. Otwol walked with his head bent down looking sad as if all the miseries of the world were on his head.

"Good afternoon Otwol." Anyadwe greeted him.

"Oh, Anyadwe that's you! Good afternoon. How are you?"

"I'm fine thank you, what about you?"

"I'm also fine but a bit tired."

"By the way Otwol, thank you very much for what you did for us. We have not had time to come to your home to thank you because we were busy."

"It's all right Anyadwe, that's my work. I help people but most people have misunderstood me to be a wizard, a snake charmer, a man to be isolated and not fit to live in this community. My own people have thrown me out. They would not shake hands with me because they believed I am a wizard. Well I do not mind. I do not hate them. If it is my fate, I will stay alone. Do you know the funny side of it, these very people who hate me, always rush to me for help whenever, they are bitten by snakes.

How many have I saved from deadly snakebites, people who were at the point of death? They come to me crying, their tears running down their cheeks like streams of water, but when I help them, who remembers me as you have done today? You are the first. I am extremely surprised." He said looking dejected and walked about five yards backwards with Anyadwe as if he wanted to escort her back to the ginnery then stopped at the side of the road, and picked a leaf from a creeping plant and came back with it to Anyadwe who was following him slowly. "Do you know this plant?" He asked giving the leaf to her. She took it in one hand while the other had held on the sack of cotton on her head, and scrutinised it. Although the leaf was familiar, she did not know the name of the plant nor its use.

"If you don't mind, put down your sack. I would like to show you the plant. It might be useful for you in future. But please promise me that you'll not let anyone else beside you know about it."

"What is the medicine used for?" She asked worried.

"It is a cure for snake bites and not for snake charming." So will you now promise me that you won't tell anyone else about the plant? Since you now know the use of the plant." Otwol asked.

"I promise," Anyadwe agreed.

"If you tell anyone, the medicine will be ineffective in your hand," he warned, and continued, "This is the best medicine against snakebites in the whole world. There is no medicine better than this. He said and bit on it and began to chew it. "You can burn the leaves in the compound and all the snakes around the home will run away. You can administer the medicine in three ways; orally and intradermally or both.

Nevertheless, its efficacy is high with oral treatment, in which you give the extract of the pounded plant to the patient to drink, while for intradermal treatment, you suspend the pounded plant in a big calabash containing water and tattoo the area around the site bitten and the patient dips it in water containing the medicine for a long time. The medicine will extract the venom out into the water in the container and the patient recovers instantly. Therefore, you see what it means to be grateful to some one who has done something good to you. I have not shown it to anyone except you. So do not show anyone, but you may help anyone in trouble with it."Anyadwe thanked Otwol, who later helped her with her sack of cotton onto her head. He wished her good-bye and a happy stay, while she wished him good-bye and a safe journey to Wipolo.

Although Otwol assured her that the medicine would not transform her into a snake's handler, she was very afraid of it. She would not have touched the plant again had it not been for their neighbour's child who was bitten by a snake late one night. The parents of the child did not know any Acholi medicine against snakebite nor could they walk to the Mission in the night. They went round at that late hour of the night arousing everyone in neighbourhood they thought might have Acholi medicine against snakebites, but, to their disappointment, all those whom they visited did not know anything. Anyadwe, because of her bigotry to Christianity, was the last person in their minds to be contacted. As they passed through her home, with the child on the back of his father, left with only a few hours to live, the mother of the child desperately suggested to her husband that they should try her in case she had something.

"Why don't we try Anyadwe, she might be having something?" The woman suggested.

"I doubt very much. I don't think she knows anything traditional," the husband answered despairingly and stood away while his wife went to rap on the door. Anyadwe woke up, lit her small lamp and asked who she was, and what she wanted at that time of the night. The woman introduced herself as Dul and explained the problem they were in. Anyadwe opened the door for them. David also woke up. Without hesitation, Anyadwe took a hoe and the small lamp with her, and went behind their sisal plantation where she had seen the plant earlier. David, Dul, her husband and their dying son were left sitting in the kitchen lit only by fire burning in the hearth. Shortly, she returned with the plant Otwol showed her, she quickly pounded it, and in a small calabash containing a small amount of water, she added the pounded plant, squeezed out the extract and gave it to the dying boy to drink. They all sat watching anxiously how the boy would react to the medicine. The grandeur of the medicine was absolute, the boy who was dying, came round like a rising moon. In a short time, he started playing with his mother's hand. It was at that time that Anyadwe acknowledged the genuineness of Otwol's medicine.

Two days to the end of the year, Anyadwe was thinking of passing her gratitude to Otwol through Kinyera when they heard that Fedelis Otwol had been dead exactly one month since he left Coomit village.

# Chapter Eight

The first day at the beginning of the school year after the long Christmas holidays was always difficult and uninteresting for most pupils. To make the beginning of the year even less interesting, it consisted of nothing other than the routine tiding up of the school compound, the classrooms, the presbyter, and the teacher's compound. Because of that, very few pupils, particularly those in the upper classes turned up to school punctually while most pupils never came at all.

David was still turning lazily on his sleeping skin, looking up at the sooty roof of their kitchen thinking of their boring walk to and from the school every morning when his mother entered the kitchen with the small calabash they used as their mug for drinking water, in her hand. Her face was wet with water, and plenty of droplets, which adhered on her face, gave her the face of chicken pox patient. She wiped the droplets of water with her finger and splashed it off on the floor.

"David."

"Yes Mama."

"I thought you are beginning school today? Isn't that what you told me yesterday?" "Yes, I'm going Mama."

"When are you going? The sun is already high up in the sky. Aren't you going to be late? Come on do not start being lazy. Get up and wash yourself. I'm getting your breakfast ready."

"But you see …"

"What?" His mother interrupted him.

"I'm waiting for Ayot."

"You don't wait for her in your sleeping skin there, do you?" David got up meekly, put away his beddings, and walked out of the kitchen. It was about nine in the morning. The sun was high up in the sky. He came back in the kitchen, fetched some water and went to wash himself behind the kitchen. As he bathed, he heard his mother talk to Ayot. He came back in the kitchen, and dressed up in his Khaki uniforms. After their breakfast, David and Ayot left for school. As soon as they got to school; the school gong rang for the third time and Kul, the Headmaster who was in his office walked out on the dais in front of his office, and blew the whistle. The pupils came and stood in lines according to their classes, before he began his welcome address. After which they went through their routine tiding up of the school compound and the classroom before the regular classes started two days later.

The rainy season came early that year. Grasses sprang from the ground as if they were escaping from suffocation. Trees, threw new young, greenish-yellow budded leaves, which soon became green oleaginous leaves, covering the trees with green hats making the short neck hebivours envious of giraffes, which fed luxuriously above them. Swarms of bees buzzed over-head migrated from hive to hive and later returned to collect nectar from the beautiful attractive flowers. Butterflies as if in competition with the bees, fluttered sparingly in the sun from one tree to the next sucking the nectar from the flowers. In the forests, the mushrooms cracked the ground with their clubbed heads, which triggered open in the sun as umbrellas while the rivers and the streams, angrily busted their banks in an attempt to give more space for the excess load the rainwater had given them. All creatures which hibernated because of the ephemeral drought swung back to lives vehemently.

The peasant farmers on the one hand prepared their implements for the beginning of the assiduous period of the year while the ploughing oxen instinctively looked sulkily at the yoke being prepared for them wishing the rainy season should never have come at all. One Saturday when everything was happy with the return of the rain season, Ayot came to David and asked him to escort her into the forest to collect some mushrooms. They went, and not very long after they got to the forest, they found a place where the mushrooms were spawning as if they were sown there. They soon filled their baskets and were about to return home when David remembered that he had no firewood at home for that evening. He asked Ayot to carry the two baskets of mushrooms while he collected the firewood. Since David transported the snake home in the log of wood, he was particularly careful about hollow logs. He always checked, and made sure that the log he carried home did not have a crevice on it. He had been lucky with his picks for over a year. He checked thoroughly for holes in the logs and the snakes only, but this was not absolute for all hazards tree barks could provide. When he gave his basket to Ayot, he went for a log small enough to be carried home with ease. The dried bark on it, had cracks in some parts. To ascertain that there was no snake under the barks, he knocked on it. It made a compact sound indicating little air space beneath the bark. To convince himself that there was no snake underneath the cracks, he forced the barks away from the log; no snake came out but a tarantula darted out, ran and immediately disappeared into a hole in the ground near them, which was excavated by field mice. Where it had been underneath the bark, the eggs had just hatched into hundreds of nymphs scrambling over each other in a white opaque circular cocoon, which he managed to peel off with difficulties from it gluing material on the log. Suspicious that more tarantulas could be hiding under the bark, he continued forcing most of the loosely attached barks off the log but what came out again was neither a snake nor a tarantula.

It was a creature, which neither of them had seen before. It darted out off one of the cracks on the bark, ran as fast as the tarantula and took refuge in another hole next to the one in which the tarantula had disappeared. It resembled the tarantula but was about the size of a gecko, with four pairs of segmented legs welded on its stout elliptical thorax, yet jointed to another funny-segmented tail with a pin like structure at the end. It ran with its segmented tail turned upwards.

"What a funny creature?" Ayot commented.

"I haven't seen anything like it before."

"I haven't either." David replied.

"It looks like a dragonfly."

"Yes it does; a dragonfly without wings."

"Strange," David said with a shrug.

"That's the wonder of the Almighty God; he has to create all these creatures for a purpose." Ayot said.

After David had rolled the log again, and again, tapping all the parts, and was certain there was no living creature underneath the bark on the log he heaved it on his shoulder including the barks he had peeled off. When they got home, Anyadwe was busy outside the kitchen peeling sweet potatoes for supper.

"Where did you get these nice mushrooms?" She asked as she helped Ayot with the baskets and examined the mushrooms they had collected.

"We got them near our simsim garden." David replied.

"Were they many?"

"Plenty Mama"

"No wonder you came back so soon. They are very nice and clean, insects and worms have not spoiled them. How about going back for some more tomorrow, do you mind?"

"No, not me," David replied.

"Will you come, Ayot?" He sked her.

"Yes, why not," Ayot agreed.

"We shall dry as much as possible for the future," Anyadwe said.

After a brief rest, Ayot proceeded to her home. David escorted her as usual. When he came back, he started to build the fire in the compound as he always did every evening. The log including the barks he had brought with him and the other wood started to burn. His mother having washed the sweet potatoes packed them in the cooking pot and took them into the kitchen to cook. The weather was not fine that evening. The setting sun with its neon rays illuminated the thick white clouds above it yellowish red. While in the East it was raining miles away, the thundering could be heard faintly.

"Is it about to rain?" Anyadwe enquired from the kitchen.

"Not very soon, Mama," David replied.

"Why do you waste the firewood then? You could preserve it for another evening", his mother advised.

"I've already lit it."

"The rain will put it out anyway."

"Let me enjoy it within this short time before it starts pouring." David said and squatted near the fire spreading his palms over the fire.

As he did, one of the strange creatures they had seen in the forest, which apparently wasn't disturbed when he thought he had made a thorough and complete check of the log, squeezed it's way out from one of the cracks and tumbled down in the clean compound before it started running at breakneck speed escaping into the grass at the side of the compound, with it's tail turned upward, the pin like organ at the tip of the tail, was held up like a needle on a syringe ready for injection. The creature was expelled from its hide out by the combination of smoke and heat creeping between the wood and the bark. David saw it, ran after it, and grasped the creature with the intention of taking it to his mother for identification but he did not hold it for long. The creature coiled its tail, drilled his thumb with the pin like organ, and pumped into him all the venom it had. The venom ran through him like an injection of hot pepper. He screamed, and quickly smashed it on the ground dislocating all the limbs. It remained on the ground at one sport rolling itself from side to side unable to move. David ran to his mother crying shaking his hand in the air in futile attempt to shake off the pain, which had already started to mount in him.

"What is it David?" his mother asked as she jumped out of the kitchen nearly knocking him down at the doorway.

"Something bit me on my thumb."

"Where is it? Don't you know snakes?" His mother asked panting.

"It isn't snake", he said amid crying. I smashed it down there. It's dead." Anyadwe ran to the place David was pointing, while he followed slowly crying because of the pain. Because the compound was clean, it didn't take her long to spot the dark brown, creature lying in the compound.

"It's a scorpion! You have been stung by a scorpion!" she yelled. "My God, what are we going to do?" she cried deliriously.

"Does it kill Mama?" David asked sobbing.

"No it doesn't. But the pain is very severe and persistent."

The information worried, and sickened him. The pain radiated all over his body and he continued to cry. His mother forgot all about the supper she was making.

As if to barricade all helps from reaching them, the rain soon began to pour.

Anyadwe looked at the rain disdainfully and said. "If it wasn't because of this damn rain, I would have taken you to Mission in the night, perhaps the sisters have some medicine if not an antidote for this," she said and walked towards the door. She kept staring at the rain with contempt contemplating what she should do to help her son David.

The rain kept on pouring down as the evening wore out into pitch-dark night. Not a thing could be seen outside without the flashes of the lightning.

The night was sleepless for both of them. David writhed on his sleeping skin tormented by the pain of the scorpion sting while his mother sat up on her sleeping mat, resting her back on the wall, watched him sympathetically with slow warm tears streaking downs her cheeks. The rain continued to pour profusely until the second cockcrow when it switched on to a drizzle from seven to eight o'clock in the morning. David thought he was going to die. He cried until he could cry no more and wrung his hands in agony.

After the rain, they left for the Mission with small droplets of rain falling on them as they walked on the wet and muddy road to the Mission. Puddles, of rainwater stood in most parts of the road while some flowed into the gutters along the side of the road, and eventually into the main gutters, which drained the road.

The absence of any fresh footprints on the road that Sunday morning told them that they were the first people out that morning. They got to the Sisters' Quarters and found their house girl washing the cookeries and the cutleries in two big Aluminum sculleries. One scullery was for washing the dirty utensils while the second scullery contained clean water for rinsing them before they were wiped dry with a cloth. The girl was surprised to see them in the Mission at that hour of the morning.

"Hey, good morning Anyadwe," she greeted them while wiping the bundle of spoons and forks with the cloth in her hand.

"Good morning, Alunya, but David is not all right." Anyadwe said.

"No, he doesn't look all right."

Are the sisters up yet?"

"Yes, Sister Veronica is in the kitchen. You can go and see her." Anyadwe went to the door of the kitchen and tapped lightly on it as if she was afraid she would make a hole in it. Sister Veronica who was frying eggs did not hear the feeble knock, which was muffled by noise of the eggs being fried. It was not until the noise from the pan died down that she heard the third soft knock on the door repeated. At first she ignored the noise, but when a second thought struck her that it could be Alunya coming in with her hands full of the utensils, the pain of loosing all the plates at the door made her spin on her heels and quickly walked to the door and jerked it open. It was not Alunya she saw but Anyadwe. "Oh, Ajulina it's you! Good morning. You…, what is the mater with David he's weeping", Sr. Veronica said looking above Anyadew shoulders at David who was standing behind his mother. Anyadwe went ahead and explained David's problems to Sr. Veronica.

Sr. Veronica stood in the doorway wringing her hands together as she listened to Anyadwe explanation how David was stung by the scorpion.

"He hadn't seen a scorpion before?" Sr.Veronica asked.

"No, not until yesterday."

"I'm afraid; I don't know what we can do for him because we do not have an antidote against scorpion venom. Perhaps what we are going to do for him is to give him anti histamine tablets and sedate him until the pain dies away by itself. It's a pity your son is very unfortunate, he's always bringing one thing or another back home with the fire wood". The Sister remarked and immediately took them to treatment room and showed them the form, which was in front of the table while she sat on the chair behind the table. She pulled the clinical thermometer out of a glass container containing spirit plugged with cotton wool, and wiped off the spirit adhering on the bulb of the thermometer, checked the mercury level in the stem, and shook it violently about four times in the air, and rechecked the level of the mercury in the stem again, before she inserted the bulb of the thermometer below David's tongue, and asked him to close his mouth. While he remained with the thermometer in his mouth, she went and prepared his injection. She soon returned with a kidney shaped plastic dish containing the syringe, loaded with the medicine to be squirted into his muscle.

She pulled the thermometer out of the mouth and read his temperature as 40 degrees centigrade. "Come and lie here." Sr.Veronica said inviting him to the bed.

Under normal circumstances, David would have yelled a protest, and resisted to move at the sight of the syringe and the needle, but that day he got up meekly and timidly mounted the smartly made bed with his dirty feet full of mud they had been walking through on their way to the Mission.

"Shouldn't we remove the bed sheets before he lies down?" His mother said aware of his dirty feet.

"Why?" It is okay, they will be washed. Lie on your stomach and unbutton your pair of shorts David". Sr.Veronica ordered. David followed the Sister's instruction and lay on the bed. He felt her jerking his pair of shorts down his thighs exposing his buttocks. She sorted an area a little above his left buttock, wiped it with cotton wool soaked in spirit and almost instantly, he felt the sting of the needle entering his meat.

He heaved from the bed as the needle tore into his muscle and he felt the pressure of the medicine in the syringe jetting into his muscles.

"Don't move, lie still and relax your muscles," Sr.Veronica warned as she continued squirting the medicine out of the syringe in him. David had stiffened himself, and he was as hard as a lump of frozen meat. She pulled out the needle when the entire drug had been injected in him, rubbed the spot with her open palm and asked him to fasten his buttons. Finally, she gave him two small greenish-blue tablets and two white ones to swallow. "You look after him until he falls asleep. I must go for my breakfast now. I am late for everything. We should be sweeping the church now but we have not done it. I'm sure Padre Egidio must be wondering what is happening." She said and glanced at her wrist watch while walking out of the room.

Anyadwe sat on one of the forms pushed against the walls facing her son, folded her arms on her breasts, and stared at David writhing on the bed from the new additional pain of the injection he had just had. David did not know how long he stayed awake before he fell asleep. He vaguely remembered seeing Padre Egidio in the treatment room consoling his mother, before he passed off into a deep sleep. As he slept, his mother left him alone, closed the door gently behind her, and walked out of the room. It was the first time David ever slept on a bed. The sedation, the insomnia he had the previous night, coupled with the comfort of the bed, kept David in a deep semiconscious slumber. At one time, as he slept, he rolled off the bed and fell on the cemented floor. He opened his eyes for only one second before he fell back into a tranquil sleep on the floor and summed up all what happened to be one of those violent dreams.

After Anyadwe returned home from the Mission alone that Sunday, she was worried about her son whom she had left in the Mission. She had no strength to cook. The potatoes she had cooked the previous night were still packed full in the pot. She looked at them without interest and walked out of the kitchen and sat by the door, and began to think of the many misfortunes her son had been gone through. "Why?" she asked herself. This old witch doctor Opuk tells me that we are going to lead miserable lives. If we are going to suffer for the love of Christ, I will not be afraid. We shall suffer until we die in the hand of the Lord. What is the use of being happy on earth here, the temporary home, and miss heaven the everlasting home. There is no use. I know the devil is trying his best to enter my home. I am confident, with the help of my mother, the Blessed Virgin Mary, I will win I ..."

"May I come in?" The voice she abhorred and yet knew quite well interrupted the thoughts she was enjoying. Anyadwe knew Opuk had a good Acholi antidote for scorpion venom, but because she feared that if she had taken David to him first, he would have bored her with all the nonsense about heathen deities and ghosts stories, she never wanted to hear, so she decided to seek his help as the last resort.

"Come in." She said and looked away. Opuk came, put his mushroom stool near her, and sat down inclining his walking stick on one of the pillars of the hut.

"How are you?" Opuk asked her.

"I'm fine." Anyadwe replied curtly.

"Is Acellam alright?"

"No."

"Yes, that is why I've come. Mama Acellam, let me tell you one thing today. I am not going to get tired of you, because the gods still believe there is plenty of room to bring you back. They want …"

"You shut up I am …"

"You shut up yourself. Let me talk" Opuk barked. "How do I always know what is happening in your home before I am told by you? Who do you think tells me?" He asked. Anyadwe was tempted to tell him the devil, but she kept quiet. When Opuk did not get any answer from her, he coughed and said, "Hmm, my dear woman, it is the gods, the gods of our ancestors, the gods who are keeping all of us including you. The gods who see us in our sleep, and everything we do, day and night, are the ones who are telling me all these, and you are just", he paused, sighed and went on "I don't know how to describe you.

Just ask yourself, why your home is always the centre of trouble. Acellam brought a snake home only a year ago. That snake was sent to kill you. The gods wanted you dead."

"Why didn't they do it?" She asked.

"Because I pleaded for your life," Anyadwe stared at him and sneered.

"Thank you for that. Go on and tell me more." She said contemptuously.

"Yes, the snake was to kill you. I pleaded for you. They said okay, we leave her, but tell her she must apologize to us otherwise, we shall make her son suffer. You very well know that scorpion do not sting people without any fault. If you didn't know, let me tell you today, scorpion always sting people from homes where there are taboo; people who have defied the words of the gods. This is what has happened to your son. Tell me Mama Acellam, you have been in Coomit here for almost thirty years, there are not many scorpions here these days and your son Acellam is the first to get stung after so many years; why is this? You must examine yourself and change. Look, all your so-called Christians, the people who have decided to follow these *Italiano* have not completely forgotten our gods, and they are doing fairly well. Not many problems at their home, but yours, snake, scorpion, buffalo, python all sorts of things. You even know I have the antidote against scorpion venom and yet you could not come to me, instead you went straight to your white men. I get sick talking to you. Let me ask you one question, supposing these white men did not come with their God, which would you, be following now? Not our gods, the gods you Anyadwe adored before these *Italiano* came and confused you.

Ogwok himself was always the first in front of *Abila* offering sacrifices to our gods, he was loved by the gods but he suddenly turned against them when these white men came and you saw what happened. In addition, you, he said pointing his finger at Anyadwe, "the gods are still kind to you. They are forgiving you everyday, but you obstinately refused to listen to them even once. I leave everything to you. I must go," Opuk said annoyed, took his stool, and the walking stick, and left.

David was astonished, when he woke up on Monday morning. He noticed that he was sleeping on the mattress made for him on the cemented floor while the bed stood without him and the mattress. David did not know what happened. He tried to recall how he came to be there but he could not make out whether he fell off the bed or was transferred on the floor for fear that he would fall off bed. He vaguely recalled what he thought was a violent dream. "Could it be that it was a reality? Well whatever the case, it has happened, I'll hear from those who witnessed it," he thought and got up from the mattress,

## The Devout Woman

stretched himself, walked towards the window, pulled the bolt open, and pushed the wooden shutter outwards. It swung on its hinges and crushed on the wall outside. It was not a fine morning. It was one of those gloomy mornings in the rainy season when you open the door to the greeting of the nimbus clouds telling you to go back inside, and continue with your sleep while they pour down the rain. The sedation made him sleep for the whole of Sunday. The scorpion pain had almost disappeared with the exception of slight irritation at the site of the sting. David felt hungry when he thought of the potatoes his mother had been cooking for their supper before the scorpion stung him and his stomach rumbled at the desire of the food.

The hunger worsens as the cool breeze carrying the sweet smell of the food the Sisters were preparing hit his nose invitingly. He did not know what to do. He was certain he was not going to withstand staying at school until late in the evening on an empty stomach, furthermore, all his books were at home. "I'll ask the Headmaster to allow me to go home first." David thought. As he thought, he heard a knock on the door and he spun round to see who was coming in. The door opened and Sr. Veronica came in.

"Good morning Sister," David greeted her.

"Good morning David, how are you?" the sister asked.

"I am better," David replied.

"I'm pleased to hear that." Come out and wash your face. When you finished washing your face will you return here?"

"Yes sister." David said and went to a tap below a huge cemented tank built by Brother Albertini near the church in which all the water from the roof of the church was trapped by gutters put at the lower ends of the corrugated iron sheets. He turned the tap on and washed his face, arms, legs rinsed his mouth and went back to the treatment room as the Sister instructed him. Alone, he lugged the mattress back on the bed, spread the sordid bed sheet he had dirtied with his feet and sat on the bed. He looked at the drugs' 'cupboards thinking, why

Sr.Veronica had asked him to go back there instead of telling him to go home. "Does she want to sedate me again on an empty stomach? What will become of me? I don't want to be drugged again," David continued to think. However, it was not the drug he was scared of that he was asked to come back for.

He heard another knock on the door, and it opened instantly and Alunya, the sisters' house-girl walked in with a tray lay with different types of food.

David wetted his lips with his tongue and adjusted his buttocks on the bed disbelieving what he was seeing. "Could this tray be for me?" He thought. A tea pot full of tea, an empty tea cup covered mouth down in a saucer, a sugar bowl, with a tea spoon stuck in the sugar in the bowl, a bowl of porridge, half lemon, five sweets, six biscuits, a table spoon, and an egg rolling on the tray from corner to corner wherever there was a passage, completed the assembly of the tray. Alunya put the tray on the table and asked him to move on the form annexed to it. It then occurred to him that the tray was meant for him. Alunya poured the tea in the cup, she had then stood open in the saucer, put in two and half teaspoons full of sugar and stirred it until the sugar dissolved.

"I think you'll be all right after these." She said smiling to David who was not interested in her sneer or her comments but on the tea, she was serving. "When you finish this cup, you may pour the second cup and put in two and half tea spoonful of sugar and do as I've done. Is that all right?"

"Yes," David replied obsequiously but with an aversion to her slowness, and looked at her with dismissal eyes. Alunya took the half lemon and squeezed it in the porridge. She put about six teaspoons full of sugar, stirred it with the tablespoon and the porridge began to steam.

"It's alright now you can go ahead but be careful with the cup and the rest of the utensils." She warned and walked out with the empty lemon peel in her hand, closing the door behind her.

# Chapter Nine

At the beginning of the ninth month that year, a bright dazzling star with what looked like a long tail appeared in the west surrounded by galaxies of smaller stars. Everyone was bewildered. They did not know what was going to happen. The Christians fell on their knees yapping prayers to God day and night asking for forgiveness for the sins they had committed against him. They were obsessed that the end of the world was in sight. Especially, when they recalled some of the preaching from the Priests, in which they had said, when you begin to see signs and wonders in the sky above and on earth you should know that the end of the world is near. They had never seen those stars since they were born and their sudden appearance worried the Christians a lot. Even the priests themselves did not know the explanation as to why those stars appeared. "They could be new planets." Padre Egidio one day tried to explain to console the fear stricken Christians. Anyadwe was not satisfied with Padre Egidios' explanation. She spent most of her time praying and fasting to prepare herself for heaven. She urged her son to do the same.

The panic in Opuk was different from those in the Christians. Opuk did not worry about the end of the world nor did he believe there would be one. He believed that when one dies, then that is the end of the world for him. "There is nothing like the end of the world," Opuk said. His concern about the stars was that, the gods were very annoyed with the people of Coomit, because they had all turned away from their gods; the gods who gave them rain and sun at the right time; the gods who had given them their lives; the gods of their ancestors. The people of Coomit had fallen into oblivion of them.

They no longer gave the gods food after their yearly harvests as they used to do instead; they took their harvest to the Christian church. They had destroyed their *Abila*, the traditional sacred resting places for the gods, at a very fast rate.Opuk blamed all those on Ogwok, the pioneer of Christianity in Coomit. He blamed Anyadwe for perpetuating Ogwok's work and to encourage people to defy the warning of the gods. He said, because of that, that year was going to be a bad one for the people of Coomit. You must repent to your gods. Come back to them and you will be happy and healthy as you have always been. Don't you see the illness you are going through now that you have turned away from the gods of your ancestors? Scorpions have started stinging you. Did you ever hear of that when you were obedient to your gods? No, no scorpion in Coomit stung even one person. Now all of you, who have turned away from your gods, are being stung day and night. The first of course was the son of your ringleader Mama Acellam. The gods tell me she has a very dirty home. They want to kill her but I am begging them to spare her life. I have tried to make her understand the danger she is in, but she is determined to go ahead and defy the gods' warning. There you are, you see up there in the sky. Have you ever seen those stars? You foolishly believe what Mama Acellam tells you that the end of the world is near. What a lie. There is nothing like that. When you die, that is the end of the world for you, and your spirit goes to wonder in the wildness. That is all there is to a man. Enjoy yourself with your gods when you are still alive, listen to them and adore them you will be all right. Now what I have been sent to tell you are these, there are going to be many deaths in Coomit this year. A woman is going to be killed; this is shown by that big star with the long tail you see there.

Many children will die because of either snakebites, or accidents. To avoid all these happenings, you sons and daughters of Coomit why don't you turn back to your gods and give them the sacrifices they want, and be at peace with them? They will forgive you, and those stars will disappear. Otherwise, the stars will stay on, until the wishes of the gods are accomplished," Opuk went on preaching these words from home to home until the end of the year.

When the school closed for Christmas that year, after they had all been given their yearly report cards, and certificates, David and his friend Ayot ran home jumping happily at their successful results. Anyadwe was pleased to hear the good news that they had all passed their final examination well. She was especially happy to hear that Ayot had not only passed the examination but also won the first bursary award of the school to go and study in St.Theresa Junior Girls School in Gulu. She facetiously hugged her and encouraged her to work hard in her new school in future. David and Ayot happily spent the day playing, until darkness took them unaware and Ayot spend the night at David's home. The following day, when the excitement about their successes was beginning to die down, David escorted Ayot to their home and they found her mother lying on a sack in the compound. Her back was turned towards the Saturday morning sun. As soon as they saw her, they knew that something was wrong. They rushed to her as the excitement of meeting her happy, disappeared from them. Where she lay, a long walking stick lay on the ground near her head. She was holding a bundle of cassava leaves in her hands, which she was using to drive away flies from her legs, back, and head.

There were criss-cross lines of wounds left by the whip, which had been used for scourging her all over her body. It looked as if she was flogged with hot rods. Black blood dried randomly on her body where the cruel whip had peeled off her flesh. The head had three big deep cuts, on the foreheads, the side and the back. Her swollen lower lip, which had been cut by her lower incisors and canines teeth, oozed blood, mixed with plasma and saliva, which she kept spitting on the ground near her. The offensive smell of the spittle attracted more and more flies at the scene. Ayot knew at once that Olwit or his sons must have battered her mother.

"Why don't we let Padre Egidio know about this?" David suggested to Ayot.

"Do you think he will come?" Ayot asked.

"Why not, I'm sure he will. I don't see why he shouldn't come to see someone dying."

"What are-you-talking-about?" the mother of Ayot drawled.

"We're going to call Padre Egidio to come and treat you." Ayot said.

"No-don't bother-yourselves dears, I want-to-die-like this. They have beaten me-for-nothing; they should-be-the-ones thinking of taking me-to the-hospital," she drawled emotionally like a record player playing on a flat battery and began to sob painfully.

"What are you saying Mama?" Ayot snapped in. "Why do you think they have beaten you like that if they want you alive? Stop talking like that Mama. Do you want to leave me alone in these animosities and tortures? I will not live even for one day longer if you do that. If you think of me then forget what you are harbouring in your head". Ayot said and broke down sobbing covering her face in both hands.

"Come on Ayot," David whispered.

"Let's go don't waste time, she is only upset now. I know she will receive the treatment. Moreover if the Priest comes, he will encourage her to bear her agonies patiently." David said and dragged her away by the hand. Ayot followed him and they were soon running to the Mission leaving her mother lying in the compound.

The heat of the afternoon sun at the beginning of the dry season when occasionally the weather is cooled by the sporadic rain was beginning to intensify, so that one desires nothing more than a siesta after a sizeable delicious lunch. That was in fact what the Priests and the Brothers were about to be going for. They had just finished their lunch, walked out of their dining room, and every one of them was digging in his pocket for the key to his room to go and stretch up on the bed when David and Ayot arrived in the Presbyter. Padre Egidio, who probably didn't need his bed badly that afternoon, sat at the verandah chewing on a match stick, holding his breviary in his hand. He had just opened it and was turning the pages with strips of cloth when he saw David and Ayot come. They went knelt down and greeted him.

"God afternoon Father," they greeted.

"Good afternoon. How are you?" He said removing the matchstick from his mouth.

"What is wrong? Is your mother sick?" He enquired addressing himself to David.

"No, but her mother is."

"What is wrong with her?" Padre Egidio said shifting his gaze from David to Ayot expecting the explanation from her.

"She-she- was beaten …"

"Badly beaten, her body is full of sores. The lip is badly cut while the head is broken in three places, the front, the side, and the back." David interrupted Ayot when he saw that she was nervously beginning to explain the condition of her mother to Padre Egidio.

"Who beat her?"

"Must be Olwit and the children," David replied.

"Erukulano Olwit?"

"Yes Father."

"You'll like me to come over and see her don't you?" Padre Egidio asked affirmatively.

"Yes father." They replied. Padre Egidio went into his room, changed into a white short-sleeved shirt and a baggy black pair of trousers held in position by a black suspender looped over his shoulders and took a box of their first aids kits. He went into their garage, pulled out their bicycle, and rode it to where David and Ayot were standing.

"I'm sorry I shall not be able to lift both of you. I will take only Ayot and you will come on foot David, Padre Egidio said and gave the first aid box to Ayot to carry. Ayot sat on the pillion of the bicycle and they rode off while David ran after them.

Anyadwe was expecting David back home for lunch, but she did not see him at their usual lunchtime. She had her lunch and was thinking of going to pick cotton, when she saw him running in through the gate sweating and looking very tired and depressed.

His mother thought it was strange.

"Where are you coming from?" she asked.

"From the Mission," David replied.

"Why? What did you go to do there? I thought you were with Ayot?"

"I was with her, yes but we went to call the Priest to come and treat her mother."

"To treat her mother! What is the matter with her? Come in and have some lunch". Anyadwe invited David in realising that he ought to be hungry.

"Let me cool down first, it's too hot." David said and pushed the collar of his shirt away from the back of his neck to avoid the excess sweat and fanned his sweaty face with his hands.

"What is wrong with her?" Anyadwe repeated her question.

"Oh Mama, she was savagely beaten by the brutal Olwit and the sons. She didn't tell us why, but all we gather from her was that they beat her for no reason at all".

"When did they beat her?"

## The Devout Woman

"Last night. She was badly beaten Mama. Her head is about the size of football with three deep cuts on the forehead, the side of the head near the left ear, and at the back of the head. The lower lip was nearly chopped by the teeth and it is swollen as if it was stung, by a swarm of bees. The body is covered with criss-cross wounds left by the whip, which whipped her. She is looking awfully bad."

Anyadwe sighed and said, "My goodness."

Did you get the Priest?" she asked.

"Yes we did. Padre Egidio has gone with Ayot on his bicycle and I came after them running."

"Well done David, you did a good thing. Thank you very much for that. I was thinking of going to the garden to pick some cotton, but now I think I will put it off until tomorrow. I ought to go and see her now."

"Shall I come with you?"

"You have lunch first then we can go if you would like to come."

David and his mother got to Lawino's home and found that Padre Egidio had bandaged her and had left for the Mission. With the help of her daughter, she had transferred her sack in the shadow of their granary where she was lying. Ayot was in the kitchen preparing porridge for her. Anyadwe came and sat near her on the sack and when she saw the head swathed in bandages, the yellowish ointment of iodine on the body, and the plaster covering the open wounds on the chest, back, neck, legs, and the arms, she could not say a word but only wept.

"You're welcome Anyadwe." Lawino said forcing herself to sit on the sack.

"You lie down." Anyadwe said in a sobbing voice holding her down and asked. "Why did they beat you like this?"

Ayot heard them talk. She came out and greeted Mama Acellam and she went through the story, which she had heard her mother struggle to tell to Padre Egidio. She did not want her mother to go through the same pain narrating the story again. Anyadwe was equally grateful that she had already known the story, so she focused her attention on her and asked Lawino no more question.

"They beat her," Ayot began. "Because Opuk told Olwit that you are spoiling my mother by indoctrinating her with the Christian God. He went on to say that if my mother does not stop walking with you, Olwit's home is going to suffer like yours. Many bad things will happen to his children as it is happening to David. Scorpions will sting them. Snakes will bite them. He warned him that lighting might strike his home soon.

Opuk added that he has seen a bad future for us before the end of this year. He said he has pleaded to the gods for mercy but they have refused and it looks, according to him as he puts it, that the long tailed star with those galaxies are indicating our misfortune. That is, my mother and I. Of course when Opuk said this Olwit confirmed that something must be done immediately to stop my mother from associating with you. He said that my mother was giving me away in marriage to David and that you have already confused my mother that there is nothing neither good nor genuine about our gods, customs, and traditions. He concluded that we are not to follow the white men's God, customs, and tradition. When he talked, again Opuk said that he had wanted people of Coomit to boycott the *Italiano* in this place, because they could not have stayed where they are not accepted. He said the gods were pleased with Olwit and his wife. Because, even if they were confused by Ogwok in the past, they have not forgotten the gods of our ancestors. They have their *Abila* intact where they give the gods food and other sacrifices, which is very good. When Opuk left Olwit and his sons went out and drank some alcohol and the three of them came straight to my mother here. The first question they asked her was where I was. She told them that I was not back at home, but she was sure I was safe at your home. The information sheared them off their little reasoning abilities and they indicted my mother that she was giving me away to David in marriage. They warned her that if she does not stop her plan they'd kill both David and me. My mother was refuting their allegation that she was giving me as a wife to David when the brutal Olwit gave her a blow on her mouth, which caused her to cut her lip with her teeth, and the boys began to whip her, kicked her, clubbed her and she dropped down unconscious.

It was by sheer mercy of God that you see her lying in front of you there breathing.

She was dead," Ayot said and broke into tears. There was an interlude of weeping, and sobbing from all of them as the mother of Ayot continued to writhe with the throbbing pains in the head. Her swollen lips could not allow her to talk and the burning pain on her skin induced by the ointment Padre Egidio had just applied put her in a hell of a world.

One and half months had passed; the mother of Ayot was slowly recovering from the injuries inflicted on her by Olwit and the sons. She was able to walk without the aid of the stick. All the wounds on the body and the head had healed.

It was in the month of February in the new year, a busy month for parents to sell their cotton, buy school uniforms for their children and pay their school fees, preparing them for new academic year, when Ayot and her convalescing mother, took two bags of cotton to the ginnery to sell to get money for buying her beddings and uniforms for her new year in the junior secondary education in St.Theresa in Gulu. Anyadwe and David also came later to the ginnery with their two bags of cotton to sell for buying his uniforms, in Primary five Coomit school. Ayot and her mother welcomed them and helped them to sell their cotton before they walked back home.

When Ayot and the mother got home, Ayot began to clean some millet to be ground for *kwon* for their late lunch while her mother cut and washed some smoked buffalo meat to be cooked for the meal. Lawino made the fire, put the meat in the cooking pot and put it on the fire to cook, and then she went to the granary, fetched a bowl full of simsim, came with it into the kitchen and roasted it in a saucepan before she winnowed it and left the cleaned simsim in a tin plate for Ayot to grind.

There was hardly any water left in the pot for the evening. Therefore, as Ayot ground the millet, she went to the well to draw water. A little while after she had gone, Ayot had finished grinding the millet, collected the flour she had ground and swept the grinning stone clean. She then took the simsim her mother had cleaned and started to grind it on the grinding stone for simsim paste. No sooner had she done any work on the simsim than the older son of Olwit, her half brother, Opota entered the kitchen. He was carrying a bow and five arrows in his left hand, his right hand held a small axe hooked by the blade on his right shoulder. About five feet tall, dark in complexion, Opata came in wearing a pair of rubber sandals made from motor tyres. The sandals were covered with lots of black ashes from burnt grass adhering on them. He wore a dirty rugged pair of shorts patched with cloths of different colours. There were plenty of whitish criss-cross streaks running randomly on his bare chest, arms, and legs forming a disorganised network design on any uncovered part of his body. Ayot lifted up her head to see who was entering the kitchen without permission. When she saw that he was Opata, she ignored him and continued with her work. She did not look at him again partly because of the immodest way in which he was dressed. His rugged pair of shorts was a little low down his waist so that his pubic hair was showing, bad omen for a young girl of her modesty to see. Opata came and stood right in front of her. The dried meat her mother had put on fire had started throwing out a nice appetising scent.

"Ayot," he called her standing in front of her swaying backwards and forwards.

"Umm!"

"Why do you answer me with a closed mouth like that?"

"So what?"

"Don't think I've come here because of the meat you're cooking". He said sniffing in a lung full of the scent of the meat while staggering from side to side with the alcohol in his head.

"Where has your mother gone?" he asked.

"Why? what do you want from her, the woman you nearly killed?"

"Answer my question Ayot."

"As who? Do not bother me. If you want my mother, you go and sit outside and wait for her there. Your smell is offensive. It's suffocating me."

"You haven't given me anything to sit on. Where do I sit?"

"There are logs and stones outside, do I have to come and offer you which one to sit on?"

"I'm not going outside I'm sitting right here." Opata said, dropped himself on the floor carelessly and sat with his back resting against the wall, his knees drawn up, his feet stood on the floor so that his penis showed distinctly like a black rubber tube jutting out from the hem of his tattered pair of short. Ayot saw it and regarded him as one of the lunatic who walk naked and are capable of doing anything. Opata's bow and arrows laid on the floor at his left hand while the small axe rested on his right.

"Eh! Ayot, is it true that you're going to St.Theresa Girls School in Gulu next week?"

We have warned you several times that your so-called education is merely training you to be a prostitute, nothing more than that. You and your mother, who happened to be my mother by mistake, are all floogies." He said pointing his finger at Ayot. The malicious onslaught afflicted her.

"How dare you talk about my mother like that?" Ayot said exasperated, stopped grinding and gave him an angry stare.

"Well, if we are it's none of your business. Why don't you stop poking your noses in our affairs then? After all, it is our bodies not yours. Why don't we use them the way we chose?"

"It is our business Ayot, particularly in your case, we want you to get married this year and bring us the cows for our marriages. You are already old enough. A girl, who sees the women's monthly thing, should be old enough to get married. I want to get married and so is my brother."

"That is your funeral, none of our business. If you knew we were very significant in your future lives, why have you been very hostile to us? You have been torturing us at your will, you've even forgotten that only about three months ago you nearly killed my mother, and now you even still called us prostitutes, I think I'd rather go and roam the street than get proper marriage, and you use the cows for your marriages." There was a pause between them, and the boy was nearly falling asleep, or at least he closed his eyes and pretended that he was falling asleep. Then he suddenly opened his eyes, sighed and blew the alcohol-laden breath towards Ayot. She fanned her hand in front of her nose in an attempt to prevent inhaling the alcohol vapour but the boy took no notice of what she was doing.

"Did you sell your cotton today?" He asked Ayot.

"What about it? Why do you want to know? What good is it to you anyway?"

"Ayot don't be a fool, I want to know how much you have got?"

"None of your business"

""Phew, I see, you've learnt a lot of rudeness and disrespect for men, that's very untraditional."

"I'm, glad you've realised it, although too late."

"Ayot, I'm going to sink one of the arrows in you right now, if you keep on answering me like that."

"Why don't you do it? You've got them heaped up near you there." The boy took one of the arrows from the floor and the bow, stuck the etched end of the arrow on the string on the bow and pulled it but held hard on the arrows, and called Ayot to see, warning her that he was going to release it. Ayot did not bother to look at him, but continued with her grinding. "It's your hand operating it, why do you have to ask for permission from me?" Opota relaxed the bowstring. He pulled on it again, his hand maintaining grip on the arrow pressing it on the bow and relaxed the bowstring again. He repeated the joking process thrice not knowing that he was sweating lightly on the hand gripping the arrow on the bow, and that the fingers were loosing control of the string and the arrow. When he pulled on the bowstring for the fourth time, he lost control of the arrow and it flew from the bow in his hand whizzing towards Ayot. He jumped after it, trying to catch the arrow amid air, but he was too slow. The double rows spiked poisoned arrow had reached the target. It penetrated just over her left breast, and the tip of the blade showed an inch at her back.

Ayot stooped down clasped over the wound on her breast where the handle of the arrow was showing about seven inches and began to cry in agony. Thin jets of blood shot out from around the arrow handle. Her fingers became soaked with bright red blood within a second.

"I didn't mean to do it." Opata cried and bent over her. Hysterically, Opota tried to pull the arrow out, but the spike held in the muscles of Ayot as it could neither be pushed backward nor forward. Once an arrow of such make penetrates the target and is stuck, only surgery can get it out. Almost immediately, after Opota shot Ayot, her mother returned from the well. When Opota heard her footfall, he became wild and jumped up like a sanguinary murderer, grasped his bow and the remaining arrows, fitted one of the arrows on the bowstring and pulled the string while aiming at the mother of Ayot who was lowering water pot from her head. She heard the arrow striking the water pot and a jet of water spurted out from the hole dug on the pot by the arrow. She knew that they were under attack. She dropped the water pot down and it fell and broke into fragments, spilling the water all over the place. Instead of running away, she forced her way in the kitchen when she heard her dying daughter groaning in an agony. Opota was very unsteady then in his shooting, he ejected the third arrow, and it zipped through the air, caught Lawino on the arm and went through. She felt the sting but did not retreat. Opota grabbed the two remaining arrows and the bow, on his left hand, the axe on his right hand and sneaked his way out as Lawino forced her way in. Lawino came and took Ayot on her lap, the arrow that Opota shot her with stuck out on her chest, as blood continued to jet from the wound.

Ayot held on her chest with her slender fingers, which were smeared with bright red blood beginning to clot on them.

"Why did he shoot you?" Lawino asked Ayot.

"I - I don't know." Ayot said battling with death.

"Did he just come in and shoot you?" Lawino asked beginning to feel strange on the arm.

"No he-wanted-to-know-how- much-money-we-got-today. Then said he-was-going-to-shoot me, and-he-did. Good-bye-Mama." Ayot said and dropped her head on the arm of her mother, which had already started paining her, she closed her eyes, and she died.

"Oh no, Ayot my daughter," Lawino screamed. She was mad with rage. She ran out of the kitchen crying and making alarms. She threw herself down and began to roll on the ground. It was not long before the poison began to work on Lawino. Few people had gathered to witness what had happened.But, before she could explain anything to those men, she collapsed and died with the words; my own son has killed us for money.

As Opota ran out of the hut, he had carried the arrows with their poisoned blades, facing him. He escaped into the bush along the path Ayot and her mother used to use when going to the well. A few yards from home, some creeping plant growing at the side of the path entangled his feet and he fell down on the poisoned blades of the two arrows. One got him right over the diaphragm and the other through the peritoneum. The bow flew away from his hand and fell across the path in front of him. The axe, as if to finish him up, fell with the handle resting at the back of his head.

Twongwok, the brother-in-law of Olwit lived beyond the well Ayot and her mother used to fetch their drinking water. He had come to the well for a bath a little after Lawino had left the well. He had finished bathing and was beginning to go back to his home when he heard the alarm originating from the home of Olwit. He rushed home to collect his spears and left immediately for the scene. A few yards from Olwit's home, along the path he was following, he found the body of Opota. He took the bow, which lay across the path, came and turned Opota on his side. He was dead. Fresh blood still oozed from the wounds with the broken rudiments of the arrows handle sticking out. The blood from the two wounds had soaked in the sand where he laid gave the place the look of slaughtering ground.

Anyadwe and David had just finished their late lunch. David was sitting in the shadow of their granary resting while his mother was having a nap in the kitchen. David heard the alarm, which Lawino started spreading in the village from home to home. He got up and walked to his mother.

"Mama, Mama!"

"Yes." She answered startled from her sleep, stretched her arms and quickly wiped away some saliva, which had spilt at the corner of her mouth during the sleep.

"There is something wrong somewhere," David said.

"Why?"

"People are making alarms all over the village."

"Oh yes I can hear now. What could the matter be?"

"I don't know. I've been hearing it for some time now."

"Well, what can we do? We just have got to sit and wait". She said, and they went out stood side by side in the compound and listened to the ululation of the alarms spreading throughout the village.

The sun was almost setting when men who had responded to the alarm, started coming back. Anyadwe and David were sitting in the compound when the gloomy men walking back in silence told them solemnly that Ayot and Lawino were dead. They were shocked to hear the news. They could not believe the story nor accept that it was true. Anyadwe cried and cried.

When Ayot and her mother were murdered by Opota, who later killed himself the big star plus a few smaller ones, which used to dazzle in the west disappeared. Everyone saw it, and they began to argue over Opuk's prophesy.

"Did he not tell us that they were symbolising bad omen? He told us that they would stay on until the wishes of the gods were accomplished. And did Lawino, Ayot and Opota not die to accomplish the wishes of the gods. Lawino was one of those who never listened to Opuk's words. Opuk said there were going to be many deaths in this village. A woman was to die and her children too. Has it not happened? He even said that they were going to kill themselves and some will die of snakebite probably that is why some of those stars are persisting. Now, who are going to be the victims" We must listen to Opuk as we used to do. He is right, we have ignored our gods. The gods who gave us our lives, the gods who feed us, and give us rain, and sunshine, we have ignored them. We must turn to them now. We must apologize to them by offering sacrifices as we used to do. Those of you who have destroyed your *Abila*, the sacred places of our gods, must rebuild them to avoid all this suffering and deaths we are facing. If we do this, we might save the lives of those who are to die because of snake bites and the remaining stars will disappear." A good number of Christians in the village found themselves in a dilemma. They did not know which way to go; the Christian God or the traditional gods with Opuk as the high priest. In the end, they decided to follow both. Few persons including Anyadwe and David were never shaken by the observation. They called all those vain works of the devil. They spent their time in prayers to God to help bring back the Christians who were led astray by Opuk.

Two months passed, one evening Anyadwe and David had gone to recite a rosary on the tombs of Ayot and Lawino. They had spent a long time there, which made them get home late. As they came in their compound, they saw with the dim evening light, the silhouettes of two men sitting on the stone, which they always used for washing their feet.

"I wonder who those are." Anyadwe said.

"I wouldn't know Mama," David answered. When they got nearer, Oru-rac, got up and walked to meet them smiling.

"Hello dear Oru-rac, so it is you!" Anyadwe said as she shook hands with Oru-rac and they walked back to meet Karakak who had remained seated on the stone with hunched back looking too tired to stand up on his feet any more.

"When did you arrive?" Anyadwe asked.

"We've just arrived."

"Sure! So we have not kept you waiting outside too long?"

"No," Oru-rac replied.

"How are your parents? Were they alright?" Anyadwe asked.

"Yes, they were fine and they send you greetings," Karakak answered.

"Thank you very much for their greetings." Anyadwe said and told David who had stood near them in silence, to go and light the lamp in the kitchen. David walked away quickly, went inside the kitchen, and after a short while there was light. Anyadwe invited them into the kitchen after she put down a mat for them to sit on. They went in, and Oru-rac continued to ask David about his school life since he started school five years ago. David was also delighted to talk to them about his five years experience at school. After their baths and supper, they slept immediately.

One of Anyadwe's old granaries had broken down so that the contents were showing outside. The chicken took advantage of this and spent most of their times round the granary extracting out the millet and the sorghum from holes around it. Anyadwe and David had started to build a new one for themselves but since none of them was adroit in the art, they started something similar to the actual granary they wanted to build.

When Oru-rac and Karakak woke up the following day in the morning, they saw the work and decided to build a better granary for Anyadwe. They dismantled the work they had done and got more reeds from the forest and in four days, a big strong granary was hoisted up on a table-like framework. The new roof for the granary, grass thatched was hoisted in position on the new granary after two days. Since the whirlwind had destroyed the roof of the other granary, and their kitchen some years back, no decent repairs had been done on them. Oru-rac and Karakak decided to mend those damages on the kitchen and the granary before they went back. They went to the forest where they always collected the reeds for their work. Because of the abundance of good reeds in the forest, they cut enough for themselves to carry home soonest. That day, when they had finished cutting reeds, Oru-rac and David sat down on the heaps of reeds they had cut, while Karakak moved a little away from them to prepare the rope for tying the reeds. After he had finished making the ropes, he collected them and was coming back to the place where Oru-rac and David were sitting waiting for him when they heard him scream. He kicked his leg in the air as if he had stepped on a trap. The shrillness of the scream startled Oru-rac and David. They turned to look at him. They did not need to ask what the matter was, because they saw it clearly. A rattle snake had intercepted him. It had hooked itself on his ankle.

He kicked again but the hideous creature never unlocked its fangs from his ankles, instead, it started coiling on his leg. Oru-rac took the Machete, which they had been using for cutting the reeds, lying at his side and ran with it to rescue his brother from the snake. He slashed the snake into pieces before it pulled its fangs from Karakak's leg after it had pumped all its poison into him. David lost no time. He ran home to his mother who was at home at that time preparing lunch

"Mama, Mama." David said as he ran into the kitchen almost losing his way at the doorway.

"What is the matter David?" She responded jumping up from the grinding stone where she was grinding simsim.

"A snake has bitten Karakak; a very big one, it couldn't leave him. Oru-rac had to cut it with the Machete before it left him …" David narrated the story panting. But before he finished, Anyadwe was already at the doorway running outside towards the forest.

"Come on David, let's go. Show me where you have left them."

She said while running as fast as she could. When David and his mother reached where Karakak and Oru-rac were they found that Oru-rac had tightly tied the leg of Karakak above the calf with some of the rope he had prepared for bundling the reeds. The lower part of the leg was soggy with the blood, which made the leg look like that of an elephantiasis patient. Anyadwe carried Karakak home on her back, while David and Oru-rac collected the reeds they had cut. When she got home with Karakak, she put him down on a mat outside the hut, and hurriedly went into the kitchen took a hoe and ran out into the near by bush to dig the medicine for snakebite. She came back, pounded it, and put it in water in the calabash before giving it to him to drink. He drank it but soon began to complain of nausea and immediately he began to vomit. He vomited blood, mixed with bile. "This is strange," Anyadwe thought. Because her first client she treated on the antidote did not react that way. The observation perturbed her. She held Karakak by the chest while one hand held on his back and watched him sympathetically as he ejaculated his stomach contents. Karakak kept on vomiting while getting weaker and weaker every minute he shot out blood from his stomach. David and Oru-rac feared he might die soon.

"Otwol had warned me not to tell anyone about this antidote, if I do then it would cease to be medicine in my hand. To the best of my knowledge, I haven't told anyone about it or was it because I used it to help Dul's child? Nevertheless, he advised me to use it to help anyone bitten by the snake. I don't see the reason why it should fail toady," she continued to think. "Perhaps I must drain out the blood from the site where he was bitten." Anyadwe said. She put Karakak on the mat and went inside the kitchen and soon returned with a razor and a big calabash full of water. She put some of the antidote in the water and stirred it. Then she tattooed the site where the snake had bitten with the razor, and dipped the leg in the water solution of the antidote. Dark blood oozed out of the cuts into the water in the calabash. She kept Karakak's leg in the water until bright red blood issued. She was getting happy that the medicine has worked afterall. However, after a short while, Karakak began to convulse violently in Anyadwe's hands and he stretched, shuddered dropped his head backward on her hands, hissed out the last pocket of air from his body through his nose, and went into a permanent sleep.

Anyadwe broke into a torrential cry. Oru-rac and David too broke out crying bitterly. Anthony Kinyera and a few of their neighbours, including Dul, whose child she had helped one night with the antidote against snake bite, were some of the few people to respond to their startling cries.

"What happened to him?" Kinyera asked when he saw Karakak lying dead across the thighs of Anyadwe.

"He was bitten by a snake today."

"I thought you've an excellent antidote against snake bites?" Dul asked.

"I'm unable to explain what went wrong with everything today. I think God has decided it that way. I gave him the medicine all right but he could not improve." More and more people came to sympathize with them. Before sunset, Karakak's body was shrouded up in a white sheet ready for burial.

Opuk was one of those who came to the funeral of Karakak at Anyadwe's home. He took the advantage of crowds to address them about the risk they were facing if they did not turn back to their gods. Taking his position in Anyadwe's compound that day, Opuk sat on his mushroom stool, his walking stick laid near his feet. His knees drown up near his face; he pivoted his elbows on them and clasped his head with his palms. He stared morosely on the ground between his feet. The men and the women all sat in front of him attentively, waiting to hear his opening speech analysing his view about the death of Karakak. After a spell, of silence, Opuk cleared his throat and swallowed something which made his Adam's apple swung up and down.

"Hmm", Opuk began as usual and continued, "I don't know where to start my address from today. Because I feel, I am repeating myself to you impudent children of Coomit each time I talk to you. I have talked to you on the same subject repeatedly, and you continuously repeat the same mistake, the same fault, the same contempt, to our gods, our traditions, and our customs. I have been going throughout the village from home to home. I walked on my feet, until they are all soared to warn you all about these. I always got to my home tired like a ploughing ox. Why? Because, I want you to repent to your gods; more so, you are dear people to me. I love you all. I do not want you to die, before your times have come simply because you have defied the gods' rule. I do not want our young boys and girls to be killed as you are seeing these days. Who will continue our clans if they all perish? We old men and women are now useless as stones. We have given birth to them. They must also leave their off- spring before they die. Now, because of your obstinacy, the gods are snatching our sons and daughters every day. I warned you about the stars, didn't I? I told you a woman was going to die, some children of her own were going to die with her, and some children are going to die from snake bites, I told you all these, didn't I?" Opuk asked.

"Yes you did," the crowd answered.

"Yes I did, and what did you do when I called on you to repent to your gods, adore them and offer sacrifices to them those who apologised to the gods, got blessing, but those die hard impudent children are continuing to get punishment from the gods, and this was the cause of the death of Lawino and her children and this one we have gathered here for. Look around the home and see if you will get any *Abila*, we rebuilt one in this home when we gave food to the spirit of Ogwok. Where is it now? It has been destroyed again. What do they do with their harvest every year? They take them to the Mission to be offered to the white men's God. Do they get any protection, blessing, from that so called Christian God? Do they? No. Their children are dying, they are not happy. I warned you about the scorpion. I warned you about the stars. Few of the stars are gone plus the big one. Have I lied to you? I call upon you all, if you want us to stop this incessant mourning in Coomit, we must all combine forces, don't leave it to me alone, to convince some of our children who are being led astray by the few to follow the imaginary God of the white men. You have your gods, why do you send them away from your home by destroying their shelters. You starve them, you show contempt for them; you do all the worst things you can to anger them. They have condoned you enough. I am getting older and older everyday, I will not be able to intercede with the gods for you any more. The young men who should be preparing to take over from me, are either dying or turning away from the gods of our fathers, and are being brain washed to follow the Christian God. It's all up to you." Opuk said and began to sob; he sobbed bitterly. All those who were there felt that they have ignored their gods and Opuk was right.

"Why? Did he not warn us about the scorpion?

Did he not prophesy correctly about the stars? Of course, Lawino and her children died. The son killed them. What happened to the stars? The big star plus some of the small ones disappeared. Now this boy, did he not die because of snakebite? This must be the work of the gods. We must stop disappointing the gods," the crowd argued.

Anyadwe never paid any attention to whatever was being said. She sat at the far end of the crowd. With her head in her palm, she recited her rosary asking the Blessed Virgin Mary to pray to the Lord Jesus to forgive those who were critisising the Almighty God the Creator. She prayed to the saints the angels to guide the soul of Karakak to the eternal life. She continued to weep for his loss. Sorrows gripped her heart about the Christians who were reverting to the devil and his pomps. She recalled what Padre Romano told them when he preached to them during the inauguration of the chapel in Latinnyer.

"You must not be afraid to identify yourself as a Christian in all places. You must not be ashamed when they call you, your Christian name, during persecution," and here are Christians reverting to paganism because of a little suffering. She closed her eyes and whispered "Lord Jesus Christ, Mary helper of Christians, I love you, give me grace to bear my troubles.

# Chapter Ten

The gossiping about Karakak's death went on until the end of that year. "The gods were angry with Anyadwe; she has perpetuated Christianity and has fallen into oblivion of our gods. She has a very good antidote for snakebites. Did she not help the child of Dul with it and yet she could not help Karakak? Look, more stars have disappeared since the death of Karakak. The prophesies of Opuk are correct. We must listen to him. If we do not make appeasement with the gods, rebuild our *Abila* the sacred place of our gods, and offer our sacrifices to them, those remaining stars with claim more lives. So why don't we save the lives in danger by doing what Opuk is telling us," the people of Coomit argued.

On the first day of the first month every year, the people of Coomit used to bring small amount of the seeds from their previous year harvests they intended to plant in their gardens to Opuk to sacrifice to the gods, while the bulk of the seeds, they put in front of their *Abila* in their homes, in order that the gods blessed them before planting. The people of Coomit had fallen into oblivion of these ceremonies since the birth of Christianity in Coomit. However, at the beginning of that year, because of the few strange visiting stars, which had remained in the sky, the people were frightened. Nearly everyone wanted peace with the gods to avoid deaths in his or her home. Opuk had said, unless the wishes of the gods were accomplished, the strange stars would not disappear.

"Obviously the remaining stars are still demanding human lives or peace with the gods before they disappeared." They argued. As a result, many people took their sacrifices to Opuk, but Anyadwe, Kinyera and a few others did not take theirs.

Whenever they took their seeds to Opuk, they were always told the summary of the events of the year. When the rain would come, the misfortune that would befall the village in general, or the success they were going to achieve and so on. That year, when he had received their sacrifice, Opuk prophesied that the new year was going to be a bad one for Coomit, because there were still some people at large who have not heeded to the gods' warning.

"Hmm I see the sun burning. It will burn us for a long time this year. I see the animals and human beings dying because of lack of food to eat and water to drink. The rain will come very late this year and it will claim many lives of both animals and human beings. Still, there will be no food for people to eat and we will continue to suffer. Convince the die-hard-defiant to repent before it's too late. The good news for you is, I see one of the white men. I see him clearly. He is being lowered in his grave. Opuk would say and croak an ugly mirthful laughter."

Indeed the rainy season which normally begins in March after the five months dry season from October to February, came late that year as Opuk prophesied. It was nearly the end of October in the new year and there was no single drop of rain. The sky was clear and blue, without a single cloud to be seen drifting about to raise any hope for the rain. The sun stroke the ground with all its fury. The east-west wind was strong and dry like the Solano wind in the desert. It swept the sand from the bare compounds and heaped them near the huts, and at the edges of the compounds. The ground was boiling hot. It was difficult to walk bare footed in the compound in the afternoon. Young children crossed the compound jumping and crying as if they were walking on lumps of fire.

The trees started shedding their leaves off prematurely. The birds were not happy because of lack of foods, so that they were forced to migrate before they starved to death. They could hardly be seen anywhere. They sang pathetically far away in the forest with leafless trees, more often around the streams, with trickle of water struggling to move over the mud at the bottoms of the rivers and streams. The hippopotamus and the crocodiles did not have homes. They nearly forgot about the water, so that they preferred to roam the dry land in search of food. The frogs and the fishes died in millions, while at home, the chicken raked round the compound with their claws to the point of ploughing the hard baked soil with hope of getting worms wriggling in the earth, but to their disappointment, they saw dust. The herbivorous animals were less palatable to the carnivorous because they were thin, and emaciated, but they sufficed their need. Every creature was leading towards its desolation.

To make up for their survival, some pseudo soothsayers, and the local meteorologists acting independently of Opuk, blamed for the drought on many people because of one thing or another. A man was blamed for the drought because he had hang his dog which he considered useless, because it always hunted for his laying hens at home and ate their eggs, besides, it never barked even when an elephant came home, so that his home was no better than those with cats only and whenever he took it out in the forest for hunting it always kept near him for safety. The killing of dogs was prohibited at the beginning of the rainy seasons. Because of the belief, the man was asked to sacrifice a sheep to the gods of rain to cleanse the blood of the dog, which was holding the rain up in the sky. He did. The sheep was slaughtered, but more sun shone.

With almost nothing to do during the period of the drought, the women around the Mission spent their free, boring times on a rocky hill near the Mission, chipping and shaping the rocks for their grinding stones, hoping that the rain would one day return, and the stones would be useful. The pseudo-soothsayer claimed that the gods residing on the hills were annoyed with the women because of the earsplitting noises the women were making on the hill as they shaped their grinning stones. The gods' resting place had been violated. To appease the gods, the pseudo-soothsayer prophesied that the gods residing on the hills would be happy to pour down the rain only if each woman sacrificed a white cock, a pot of *lacoi beer* and a gourd full of simsim oil. The women did as required but the gods gave more drought.

"Ala! What's wrong? " people interjected.

The road constructor had knocked down a tree where they intended to construct a road. The pseudo-soothsayers lost no time again in excusing themselves over their many failures in their prophecies. They claimed that the tree was another resting place for the gods of rain. It was also the site where the gods were offered sacrifices to appease them if ever they closed the supply of rain as they were doing, or gave too much unwanted rain for a season. They said that the gods were very annoyed because they were insulted by exposing them in the sun without shelters. Therefore, because of that, they took vengeance upon the people of Coomit by shutting up the rain, so that they also experience what it was like to be baked in the sun. The pseudo-soothsayers added, because of the gravity of the offence, the gods had demanded the heart of a human being with hernia of umbilicus.

David had it. Everyone in the village knew that he had the type of umbilicus wanted. Therefore, when words went out off the pseudo-soothsayers about the demand of the gods of rain, everyone had an eye on him, as the likely sacrifice to be offered. Anyadwe feared that her child could be kidnapped for the devilish sacrifice, which would not produce any results, because of that; she gave him maximum protection every day.

That year, Kinyera the chief, had enrolled two of his children Atokany, and Amal, in Primary one in Coomit Primary School. David walked with the children of Kinyera every morning to school but in the afternoon, they returned home alone. The stormy, thunder return of the rain after twelve months of drought that year, struck a little after mid day coinciding with the time when the pupils of Primary one and two should return to their homes. Because of the long drought, which had lived with the people at that time, no one bothered about the clouds, which had been incubating the first torrential rain ever in the year since dawn that day. Everyone thought it was the usual teasing from the gods of rain, with rain laden clouds, which they were not willing to let a drop seep on the ground before they ate the human heart they requested. Because of that, when the school closed for Primary one and two, their teachers set them free to go home notwithstanding the rain preparing. Most of the pupils left for their homes, but a few stayed behind. Amal had asked her brother Atokany to stay with her and a few other girls in Lugeny's shop, to observe the weather but Atokany declined the invitation of his sister, and continued to run home with seven of his friends, with the hope of beating the rain should it rain at all. However it soon began to rain. The storm gathered momentum as the boys ran further and further away from school.

Half way home the stormy thunderous rain, with the hailstones, checked their movements so that they were forced to shelter behind a leafless tree, which stood near the road.

While at school, the sudden out bust of the rain and hail stones in the class, through the shutter less windows, interrupted all the classes, and the pupils collected their books ran with them in panics for shelter in corners of their classrooms. After about four hours of continuous rain, hailstones, storm and thunders, the rain ceased abruptly as it came, and the place became as quiet as a vacuum. The dry stunted grass and flowers, on the lawn, were covered with a white carpet of hailstones. After the rain, the pupils ran out wet all over yelling with triumph for having escaped the storm alive.

There was much destruction caused by the storm. Several houses in the Mission lost their roofs altogether, while others had their roofs badly damaged. The church had half of the roof folded over the other half. The roof of Kul's house was blown off and carried away by the storm. Trees uprooted by the storm lay with their roots sprawling in the air, while some had their trunks smashed off their stems. The hailstones knocked down all scanty withering leaves on some trees. Many badly starved creatures caught in the storm were drawn to death.

Kul closed the school immediately that day with all the teachers and the pupils drenched by the rain. On their way home, David and his friends kept on encountering the havocs, which had been caused by the storm one after the other. They found dead pets, and chickens floating in the running rainwater. After the first turn on the road from school, there stood an old fig tree about one hundred yards away. The branches of the tree towards the road had covered three fourth of the road at a safety height for all vehicles.

As David and his friends came nearer the tree, they saw what had looked like some logs piled up at the roadside. David noticed a strange feeling in himself as they neared the objects. He felt his heart pumping faster, and he became nervous and anxious to know what they were. They reached the objects. They were stunned and horrified at what they saw, the eight bodies of the children who had ran in the storm laid piled on top of each other. Their arms grasped one another as they sought protections from each other during storm. David, without realizing, found himself full of vigour. He with Olel, and Kijang, rushed to the bodies of the children and began to unpack them one by one laying them separately on the ground. To them, all the children were dead. Instead of running home in panic as some pupils did, David and his friends ran back to school to inform the school authorities about the incidence. Padre Enriko and Brother Albertini, immediately brought them back to the scene in their Jeep, accompanied by the Headmaster Kul and two other teachers. The report, David and his friends made, that all the victims were dead was right with the exception of only one boy whom they had found lying sandwiched between two other dead boys. The eight boys were rushed to Gulu Hospital where the seven boys were confirmed dead by Padre Agustino the doctor in-charge of the hospital, and the surviving boy, was revived by Oxygenation.

Anyadwe was caught by the storm while preparing lunch. She had just returned from her first leg of the morning work, scraping the hard dried ground in an attempt to sow some millet seed to wait for the rain in the ground.

She, as everyone else, did not think the clouds, which had been roaming the sky since dawn that day, were going to throw a drop of water down. She looked at the clouds, and shrugged her shoulders with presentment and whispered: "If this is the beginning of the rain, then thank you God." And she entered her kitchen. When the storm struck, she got out and collected the chicken together in their hut before she ran back to her hut almost out of breath. She came and sat near the door alone watching how the storm was bull-dozing the trees and her granaries trying to stand them upside down. The storm became very strong as the hailstones increased their bombardment on the ground. After a while, not an object was visible. Anyadwe retreated inside her hut when the storm started jetting the rain and the hailstones into her hut. She slammed the door closed and found that the small shutter less window above the hearth in the kitchen was hurling in the hailstones and rain like a sprayer in operation. She got a rug of cloth made it into a ball, a little bigger than the window and forced it in the opening to block the hailstones and the rain water. But it wasn't long before the ball of cloth was shot out. The rain and the hailstones gusted in. She quickly rolled the cloth into a ball again and forced it back into the hole and held on it. She felt the force of the wind from outside nearly pushing her away. It was like supporting a collapsing wall. She held on like that until the rain stopped. When she left, her arms were tired. She opened the door with no hope of finding any of her granaries on its stands, but to her surprise, they were there, not a single grass from their roofs was lost, only rainwater, and thawing hailstones kept dripping down from the roofs down in the pool of water below. She ignored what was happening outside after seeing that all were safe, and turned her attention to what had happened in her hut.

She swept out the water, which had come in through other openings and the heap of soot, which fell down in the hut from the roof. It was not until she had finished clearing the hut that she began to think of her son David. She found out that she was not concentrating on what she was doing. She imagined him being brought home to her dead. She nearly wept at the mere speculation. From time to time, she looked out of her kitchen to see if he was coming, but she saw the hailstones thawing, which she was beginning to hate, accusing them for having buried David on his way home. She tried to resist the temptation of going to find out about him from the children of Kinyera, but in the end, she admitted a defeat when it started getting dark without David at home. When she got to Kinyera's home, she found Aremu, the wife of Kinyera clearing water from her kitchen. Her crippled son Otto, and her dumb and deaf daughter and a sleeping sickness patient Alanyo, were in the living room of their father. Their last-born Apire was playing in the doorway with a few blocks of hailstones.

"Hey Apire what are you doing here? Isn't it cold for you?" Anyadwe said, held him with the arm and walked with him to his mother in the kitchen.

*Hodi;* Anyadwe asked for admission as she approached the door.

"Ho; Anyadwe, it's you, you're welcome. Where've you picked him up?" Aremu asked.

"I got him playing with the hail stones at the door way there," she said pointing towards the door.

"Come in, my place is wet all over," Aremu said inviting her in.

"Whose is dry?" Anyadwe asked.

"It was a terrible rain wasn't it? If this is how it is going to go on then it has better not come at all," Aremu said.

"I thought my hut was going to collapse on me," Anyadwe remarked.

"Every place in my hut was vibrating. My goodness, has David come back home?' Aremu asked Anyadwe.

"No, he hasn't; actually, that is why I am here. I wanted to find out if Atokany and his sister have come back and if they had seen David anywhere before they came away," Anyadwe said with a note of anxiety in her voice.

"Even these two haven't come back. Let me hope that they haven't been caught up in the storm," Aremu said concerned.

"Children are funny. They could just be playing in the rainwater with the hailstones thawing. They find lots of fun in strange things like the rain water and the hail stones they have not seen in the last few months," Anyadwe said comfortingly against her owns feelings. She knew Aremu had all the reasons to be worried because her children should have come back anyway. In her case, there was still room for waiting. David could show up any time because the upper classes closed late.

"Let's hope that they come soon. It's getting late," Aremu said and walked out of the kitchen with a saucepan full of water she had collected from the kitchen. She went and poured the water away into the rubbish pit behind the kitchen. As she returned, she saw her daughter Amal coming wet all over. Aremu was almost cheering up that everything was all right with the children because, one of them had at last shown up. She was certain that Atokany was at his sister's heels somewhere at the corner along the path. "Hey Amal, you're wet have you been running in the rain!" Aremu exclaimed.

"No, we had sheltered in Lugeny's shop when the storms blew off the roof leaving us in the open. Everything in the shop including us was sodden by the rain." Amal replied.

"Poor Lageny, I'm sorry for him". Aremu said to her daughter.

"All the things in the shop are spoiled Mama."

"I know they must be. Where is Atokany?"

"He had come running home before the storm with some boys who we-we found dead under the fig tree near the last turn to the Mission. Aremu's heart missed several beats when she heard the information from her daughter. In spite of the cold weather, she began to sweat and shake. She stared at her daughter, with an open mouth not knowing what to say as if Amal had transformed into a dragonfly. Anyadwe heard them talk and walked out with Apire to join them. I think Atokany is in danger. She's telling me that he came before her, but the group in which he came was all found dead under that fig tree near the last turn to the Mission." Aremu said in a hoarse voice. Anyadwe did not know what to say. She stared at Amal thoughtlessly. Although she had wanted to ask Amal about David she found a big lump in her throat which shocked her speechless. As if she had bugged into her brain. Aremu in a dreaming voice asked her daughter, whether she had seen David anywhere before she came away home.

"Yes, we were together when we found the dead bodies of the boys. He and two other boys went and unpacked their bodies while the rest of us ran away home."

"Were they lying on top of each other?" Anyadwe asked talking for the first time since she joined them.

"Yes." Amal replied.

"Poor boys, why did you do that?" Aremu said lamenting. She went inside the hut, threw the saucepan in, and walked outside with tears streaming down her cheeks. Alanyo with her sleeping sickness, laid asleep on the mat in their living room snoring not bothered about the latest development in the family. Otto crawled out of the house to hear what was happening. When he saw his mother weep, he regretted his crippleness. He wished he had power in his limbs; he would have gone out himself to find out about his missing brother. Regretfully he wept bitterly.

"Let's go and find out what happened," Anyadwe suggested.

The two women left to go and see the bodies of the dead boys with Aremu trotting in front of Anyadwe.

"Why don't we find out if David's back so that he tells us more about the children?" Aremu suggested.

"It's alright we could do that," Anyadwe replied. Nevertheless, before they branched off, with the poor light of the setting sun exaggerated by the cloudy weather, they saw a boy running towards them. His mother, identify the boy that was David coming. She resisted the excitement of running to meet him on the way, and carry him on her head because of Aremu, who stood at her side with tears in her eyes waiting for David to tell her more about her darling

Atokany. They stood at the junction and waited for him their hearts pounding in their chests, lifting their breasts up and down. David came running; he saw the two women and recognised his mother and Aremu. When he got to them, he nervously went through the story for them.

The bodies of the seven boys, including that of Atokany, were returned from Gulu Hospital late the following day, and were distributed to their parents for burial with the only surviving boy fully recovered. The people of Coomit were awe-struck by the deaths of the children. The strange visiting stars in the west had all but one disappeared.

"Hmm, did I not tell you all these when you brought your sacrifices to me?" Opuk told the mourners during the funeral ceremony of the dead children.

"I told you that there was going to be a long drought and that there would be a great famine from which some people would die. I told you that the rain would come and some people would be killed. We lost our sons, seven young boys; they died because their parents refused to appease the gods. Is Kinyera not among those whose sons died? Did he not refuse to give in his sacrifice to the gods? The gods must have excused Anyadwe this time because of her brother's son who died at her home only a year ago from snakebite. The storms, the hailstones, are all signs that the gods are angry with us. Look at the damages inflicted in the Mission. The roof of the church, the sacred resting place of Christians God was blown off. Did any of you lose your *Abila* in the storm?" Opuk asked them. "No" they replied.

"Why?" Opuk asked again. When he did not get any answer from them, he cleared his voice and said, "It is because our gods are stronger, more powerful than the Christian God, secondly they couldn't have destroyed their own sacred resting places. The only few left. The roof of Kul's house, one of the Christians sympathisers, was also blown off; did any of you lose his hut in the storm?' Opuk asked again.

"No" they replied.

"Well my dear sons and daughters. Let us not be fools and blind, we must repent now that one star is still left. Someone or some persons must die before it disappears. We should repent and make appeasement with the gods. We have lost seven of our sons. Seven of them.They are gone never to come back to us again because of the obstinacy of their parents who would not accept our gods any more. Sons and daughters of Coomit, you'll continue to lose your young children if you do not turn back to your gods," Opuk said with a drowning voice and began to weep.

That year everything went wrong. When the rain returned, it kept on raining almost every day for the rest of the remaining year so that the crops planted grew tall and wild into weeds. Beans of all kind failed to flower, groundnuts hardly produced any pod. The maximum one got was a pod per plant. Millet seed only rotted and none germinated. Even the cassava and potatoes failed to tuber. So, at the end point was a severe famine. Most people ate once in two days just for survival. Children died because of malnutrition like flies sprayed with insecticide. Pregnant women regretted their pregnancies when they look at their stomachs leading them wherever they went. Pets were left to take care of themselves. Any loss in human life was regretted on humanitarian ground but it was an encouragement to the survivors because it meant additional food. Thefts for food increased in the villages. These nocturnal thieves' looted granaries stocked with foodstuff. Anyadwe and David had enough food for the two of them in their granaries to last them one year under that adverse condition. Because of the food raiders, who went emptying people's granaries at night, they cleared all the raw foods from their granaries and transferred them into their pots in the huts where they slept.

Even the Primary Leaving Examination was not well done that year. The famine, which withered everyone in the country, bore the blame. The teachers came to classes just to assign the pupils exercises to do during the class periods while they went out to look for food for their families. As the result of poor teaching and coaching for the examination that year, none of the pupil in the primary six scored the total mark required to win the first scholarship award. Latigi beat David with one mark to procure the minimum marks required to win the second class scholarship. The number of failure was high. Three girls including Latigi passed to be accepted in St.Theresa girls Junior Secondary School in Gulu while David and five other boys were accepted in St.Dominic Boys School.

One Sunday after the school had been closed for Christmas holydays, David went to church early for confession. When he got to the Mission, he found Padre Enriko just ending the first mass. Padre Egidio was walking back and forth across the cemented dais in front of the church's entrance. He walked limply from one end of the dais to the next dragging his feet on the cemented dais painfully. He had been with that pain on the legs on and off since early that year. He has had treatment for it but was never cured. David approached him from behind and greeted him. Padre Egidio recognised his voice, and turned painfully holding his knees to talk with him.

"Good morning David and how are you?" Padre Egidio asked him.

"I'm fine father thank you." David replied.

"You're very early today. Where is Mama?" Padre Egidio asked.

"I left her still at home. She's coming."

"Will you please tell your mother when she comes that I would like to see both of you after the mass?"

"Yes Father I will tell her." David replied and entered the Church as Padre Egidio walked to the Presbytery.

After the mass, Anyadwe and David walked to the presbytery and sat on the waiting bench on the verandah. Padre Egidio had offered the second mass in spite of the pain on the legs because Padre Enriko had gone out to say masses in two other chapels each of which was ten miles from the Mission. After Padre Egidio had removed the garments he used for saying mass in the vestry, he walked in great pain to the presbytery where Anyadwe and David were waiting for him. They exchanged greetings and Anyadwe said,

"You have bad legs?"

"I have no legs at the moment." He replied jokingly with a painful weary smile.

"My joints are aching very badly. I have not been sleeping well for the last two nights.

The sisters have given me all the treatments they have but they do not seem to be making any change at all this time. I think I must go to Gulu tomorrow for check up."

"It is a pity Father; I'm, sorry about it," Anyadwe said.

"I'll be okay." Padre Egidio said trying to comfort himself.

"I have some good news for you David." He said changing their topic of conversation.

"Yesterday I got a letter from the Secretary to the Bishop saying that, due to the national problem of weather disaster and famine the country is under going this year, the Bishop has decided that, the pupils whose marks fell short by a range of one to five marks in order to win any of the scholarship awards, in every Mission schools in the district, should all be legible for the awards.

Therefore, in our school here, we have you and Latigi both in the second scholarship awards. The first scholarship award remains unclaimed, because Latigi was short of seventeen marks to win it. The first two years of your education in the junior secondary will therefore be free. We will only pay the third year before you complete your junior secondary education. Congratulations," he said and shook David's hand before he shifted his hand on his head and ruffled his hair affectionately. "On top of this, the Bishop has also decided to reduce the school fees for all the classes next year, but the amount to be deducted has not yet been worked out. I think that has been very wise decisions taken otherwise many children were going to remain at home next year," he said and paused before adding.

"We are going to begin collecting your items next month after Christmas. Okay? Anyadwe that is the brief news I wanted you to know. I must go and rest, the pain in my joints are becoming too much for me to sit up with. I really do not know what this is," he concluded as he struggled up on his feet, which were refusing to carry him.

"Oh dear," he moaned as he stood up right.

"Thank you very much Father for the news. However, we are very sorry for your legs. I hope you will get well soon," Anyadwe said sympathetically to Padre Egidio who had already started dragging himself towards his room.

"He's feeling terribly bad," David said as they walked away.

"Yes he is. I've never seen him like that," Anyadwe agreed.

"Do you think it's because of old age?" David asked.

"Could be, but even if he is an old man, his joints don't have to ache like that.

He is actually in acute pain not the type of rheumatism old men complain about."

"It's important they take him to Gulu immediately." David said.

The leg of Padre Egidio worsened in the night. He was very restless so that he lay awake writhing in bed all night. He developed cough, severe pain in the chest around the heart and severe dysponea. Very early in the morning on Monday, he was rushed to Gulu hospital by Padre Enriko. Unfortunately, when they got to the hospital, Dr.Agustino the only doctor, and a Father in the hospital then, had gone for a tour of the Dispensaries and Health Centres which were built by the Mission in many places through the Northern part of Uganda, a routine one-week tour, which he made once every month. Whenever, he went on such a tour, he left Sister Domitilla, Brother Marko, who did most of the paramedical services in the hospital, and some of the locally trained staff, to handle the situation until he came back. Nevertheless, he always gave them the rough programme of his tour showing them where he was expecting to sleep, in case, they needed him urgently, and this was because they never had any telecommunication system in that part of the world.

The rain, which had been pouring throughout the year, had not ceased even at that time which should have been dry and hot. The surfaces of the murram road, the only class of roads available at that time, were badly eroded by the rain water so that the road workers were kept busy throughout that year trying to combat the rain water making road communication impossible. They dug drainages at the roadside, filled potholes in the middle of the roads and put some murram on the road to level the badly damaged areas.

This attempt to improve the road surfaces was impeded by the continuous down pour of the rain, which more often than not drove them away during their working hours, and washed away the murram put. Motor cars got stuck in the muddy road like flies walking on glue. The owner always spent hours on the road struggling to dig out their vehicles, which were always swallowed deep in the mud.

Padre Enriko rushed Padre Egidio to Gulu Hospital under that condition on Monday morning. It was raining and wet. They tore through the mud with their Jeep skidding occasionally turning uncontrollably across the road and coming to a stand still. They struggled on. The bumping, swaying and jerking movements made Padre Egidio even sicker so that by the time they got to the hospital he was critically ill. However, he was quickly oxygenated to aid his breathing.

Immediately Padre Egidio was admitted, Brother Marko and Padre Enriko followed Dr. Augstino to inform him about the case. They went in the Jeep, which had brought Padre Egidio to the hospital. Brother Marko, a slim tall young Italian, slid behind the steering wheel, shifted the gear into free and ignited the engine. Padre Enriko squeezed himself next to him in the co-driver seat, rolled the window glass down and rested his elbow on top of the glass, and stared fixedly in front without a word. They both crossed themselves and began to pray for safe journey as Brother Marko released the Jeep down the muddy road, the speedometer needle began to swing as he accelerated the Jeep between eighty and ninety miles per hour.

Dr. Augustino, after a difficult rough drive on the way, managed to get to Alunya Mission his first stop over safely with the stock of drugs he had to distribute to the various Health Centres and dispensaries. He was welcome by Padre Zakayo, the Parish Priest of Alunya Mission. Alunya Mission was situated on top of hill overlooking the main road. The School buildings, the Church, and Missionaries' residents stood up conspicuously on top of the hill giving the atmosphere of a young town growing in a jungle. The avenue, which connected the Mission to the main road, although, had murram surface, was better maintained than the main road. The sides were lined with rows of eucalyptus trees, which made one hate walking along it whenever it was chilly. Dr.Augustino spent the weekend with Padre Zakayo and Sister Cecilia organizing their Health Centre, and he attended to a few patients who needed a doctors' consultation, and treated them that Saturday afternoon. On Monday morning, he saw a few patients up to quarter to eleven o'clock before he left for Palaro.

Meanwhile Padre Enriko and Brother Marko after a long rough journey got to the avenue leading to Alunya Mission. As they turn in the avenue, Padre Enriko remarked, "Someone has just driven out or in."

"It looks like the thread on the tyres of our Land Rover." Brother Marko said.

"You mean to say Dr.Augustino has just pulled out?"

"It could be him or someone else. He said he was going to spend the weekend here," Brother Marko said. They soon got to Alunya Mission, drove straight to the presbytery, and parked. Brother Marko observed that the tyres marks left on the ground originated from the garage of the Priests.

It could not be anybody else other than Padre Augustino who has just cleared out.

He walked to the door step expecting Padre Zakayo to spring out from his room to give them his usual fraternal welcome but no one was in except a cat which came purring, rubbing its body on his feet, and entered between his legs welcoming him. He squatted down to talk to the cat but all it said was "mew."

"There is nobody home. Let's try at the sisters," Brother Marko said while caressing the back of the cat from the head right down to the tip of the tail. When they got to the sisters' home, they found Sister Cecilia alone at home. She was fully dressed in her religious attire. Sister Cecilia was commended by everyone for her charming beauty. You need not look twice to see it. Everyone wondered why she had decided to put celibate veil on her head, crucifix on her chest, and loaded her waist with rosaries, instead of loading her fingers with some golden engagement and wedding rings and lipstick on those rosy lips. It was difficult to resist that beauty and Sister Cecilia herself knew the impact her beauty was having on men even those as holy as monks. Sr.Cecilia watched Padre Enriko and Brother Marko go round in front of their house and parked their Jeep facing the way they came. She had not seen the Jeep before, but she was sure the occupants were Missionaries. She walked towards them to give them a general welcome nevertheless she was surprised to see Brother Marko jumping out of the driver's seat, took off his hat, and came towards her to shake hands with her.

"Hey, Brother Marko, it is nice to see you in a new Jeep! How are you?"

"I'm fine Sister thank you and how are you? You are all alone. Where have the rest gone?" Brother Marko allowed his question to follow.

"I'm fine thank you Brother. Sister Helen and Brother Aldo went to Pinyomor last Saturday and they were supposed to have come back yesterday but they have not shown up. We are expecting them any time today. Padre Zakayo had gone to the village. He feels very lonely when Brother Aldo isn't around, so most of the time he prefers to go and chat with the people in the village."

Padre Enriko, who had also got out of the Jeep, came towards them where they were talking.

"Sister Cecilia, meet Padre Enriko of Coomit."

"How do you do Sister?" Padre Enriko said, extending his right hand for handshake while removing his hat with the left hand.

"You haven't met before have you?" Brother Marko asked Padre Enriko.

No I think I've only heard of their arrival, weren't you in Sister Agnes' group?" Padre Enriko asked Sr.Cecilia.

"Yes Father and two Brothers, Simon and Romano."

"I was very busy then, I could not come to meet you in Gulu. You know Padre Egidio I suppose; he came to meet you in Gulu?"

"Oh, yes he is a nice humorous man. How is he?"

"He's not fine. He is infect very ill; I brought him and left him in Gulu hospital.

We are trying to catch up with Padre Agustino somewhere. Padre Egidio needs his attention very much." Padre Enriko said.

"In fact, Dr.Agustino left here for Palaro let me see, she said looking at her wrist watch.

He left at a quarter to eleven and now its half past twelve. He is about an hour and forty five minutes gone."

"How far is Palaro from here?" Padre Enriko asked.

"It's a bit far, about one hundred miles away." Sr. Cecilia said.

"That is far."

"Yes. Sr. Cecilia agreed and added. If I may ask Father, what is wrong with Padre Egidio?"

"Well, he has been complaining of painful joints particularly his knees since the beginning of this year but became worse last week. Sister Veronica treated him but he never responded to the treatment. It became serious last night. He was very restless, and worst of all he had severe dysphonia with pain in the chest around the heart. When I brought him to Gulu this morning, Sr.Domitilla ausculated his heart beats, she said it was beating irregularly and there was a murmur of the heart. She stressed that the doctor attends to him as soon as possible." Padre Enriko explained.

"I think, if all went well with him he's now about half way to Palaro," Sister Cecilia added sentimentally.

"Well we must be going." Padre Enriko said and began to walk towards the Jeep. Padre Enriko, and Bro.Marko still behind the steering wheel, set off in pursuit of Dr.Agustino. They waved to Sister Cecilia who waved back to them as they disappeared down the Mission avenue to the main road to Palaro. The marks left by Dr. Augustino's Land Rover had already started looking older. No other vehicle had passed that way after him since he left in the morning. They observed that the slippery muddy road very often roughened him as his Land Rover swayed and skidded on the road.

After about forty-five minute drive on the muddy corrugated road they came to an area on the road, which had just been filled with loose earth.

The rain, which had poured that morning, made the place very muddy and slippery. "The place looks very bad let me see how I am going to transverse it." Bro.Marko said as he slowed down the Jeep to a stop.

"You stay in let me see." He said to Padre Enriko, and got out of the Jeep and went to inspect how he should maneuver the Jeep through the muddy road.

"How is it? Possible?" Padre Enriko asked him when he returned to the Jeep.

"Should be if we detour out off the center of the road. The mud is many feet deep. I will go through it slowly on special gear we should be able to manage it." Br.Marko said and started to scrawl slowly in special gear at the side of the road skidding and throwing the mud from the rear wheels of the Jeep several feet behind them. It took them about five minutes to go through the muddy area.

"Beautiful," Padre Enriko commented Bro. Marko when he finished going through the mud, successfully.

"Thank God we didn't get stuck," he added.

Padre Enriko and Br.Marko noticed that Dr. Agustino with the help of some village people spent some time towing his Land Rover out of the mud. The bare footprints of the village people were left scattered all over the mud. The sticks and the rocks which they had used to tow the Land Rover from the mud were thrown at the roadside coated with mud just beginning to dry in the warm humid afternoon wind.

"Dr.Augustino got stuck here," Bro.Marko said affirmatively.

"He must have," Padre Enriko agreed.

When Dr.Augustino was towed out of the mud by the help of the villagers, he thanked them before he drove off. He looked at his watch; it was twenty-five minutes to two in the afternoon; the time he predicted if all went well he should be leaving Palaro for Palabek. I am very much behind schedule. I should have been several miles away from here he thought as he accelerated the Land Rover. Although the road thereafter was bumpy, it was not muddy. Therefore, it was a matter of maneuvering the vehicle between the rocks and the potholes. He tried to make up for the time he had lost on the way so that at times, he drove suddenly in pot holes in the road which tossed him several inches off his seat, rocking and swaying the Land Rover from side to side like a canoe on stormy lake. It was here that he started having a strange feeling that something was wrong somewhere. He felt very tired and wanted to go back to Gulu as soon as possible.

"Should I continue to Palabek when I get to Palaro or return to Gulu? Nevertheless, coming back this way again in this weather in the near future might not be easy and it is expensive. I think I should complete the journey," Dr. Agustino thought as he sped along the fair road.

Twenty minutes drive from where they successfully transverse the mud, Padre Enriko and Bro.Marko got to the place where Dr.Augustino started feeling nostalgic. The road there according to general condition of the road was excellent. So, Br.Marko accelerated the Jeep, the speedometer needle flickering between 140 and 150 miles per hour while Padre Enriko, sat beside him, rested his back solidly on the back rest of the seat, his elbow resting over the glass window rolled in, stared in front of them as if to survey ahead for any bump or ditch which might surprise them and tossed them several feet in the air.

They drove up a slope and they were descending it at a high speed. Down that slope, there were two homes on each side of the road only few yards from the main road. As they swept down the slope, in one of the homes, there were children playing in the compound chasing each other. Two of them immediately ran in the road only a few yards away from the Jeep. Bro.Marko braked suddenly and they shot forward crushing their foreheads on the metal bars of the front windscreen. Bro.Marko lost control of the Jeep as it continued to skid and swayed across the road. The Jeep hit the road bank and went over, and came back with its rear wheels digging in the wet road before it turned over with the wheels rotating freely in the air.

Padre Enriko sustained a cut on his forehead and he was bleeding profusely. Blood flowed down his eyes and down the bridge of his nose. His neck seemed to have sunk into his chest by an inch or more. It hurt so much that all other parts of his body ached in sympathy with the neck. Bro.Marko sprained his left wrist, and it got swollen. His left tibia ached. He limped in great pain, and sat near Padre

Enriko who was fighting to stop the bleeding from his forehead. He was swinging his head from side to side as if to bring out the shrunken neck. There was no one to nurse them, so they nursed each other, and sat on the rag they had pulled out of the Jeep. The time was three in the afternoon. The rain was due to strike any moment. They did not know what to do.

"How far is Palaro from here?" Padre Enriko asked.

"About twenty miles," Bro.Marko answered.

"What are we going to do now Brother?"

"I just have no idea at the moment. The motor car seems to be in perfect condition may be for the bumper and the roof only. If we could only get it up on its wheels, we should be all right. The question is how?" Br. Marko said.

"That is the worry, let's find out from these children where we could get help," Padre Enriko said and got up at once and walked to them holding his forehead with his left bloody hand while Bro.Marko struggled up slowly and limped after him.

## Chapter Eleven

The rain, which had been preparing to pour down, was very ripe and it started beating the ground throwing down big large drops here and there before it started pouring profusely. Padre Enriko and Bro.Marko followed the children into one of the homes for shelter. The children were afraid of them and they quailed away from them except an elderly boy about twelve, who welcomed them in and offered for them two mushroom stools to sit on. The rest of the children walked out and sat at the doorway, and looked at the two Missionaries fearfully.

"Where are your parents?" Padre Enriko asked the boy who let them into the hut.

"They've gone fishing and they won't be back until tomorrow morning."

The boy told them.

"Are you here on your own, not even a big person looking after you?"

"Yes we are alone. We are able to take care of ourselves."

"You cook for the children, do you?" Bro.Marko asked affirmatively.

"Yes I do."

"There is no other home around here beside these two?" Padre Enriko asked touching the bandage, which he had swathed on his head, which was soaking fast with blood.

"There are not very many homes around. The next homes are about two miles beyond the river down the road to Palaro. I think there is an old woman with some young girls left to look after the homes. The rest of the homes are scattered about in the forest. Do you want men to help lift up your motor car for you?" they boy asked.

"Yes", Padre Enriko agreed.

"I can do it for you." The boy answered.

"You are joking boy, you can't even rock that motor car from its present position and how can you talk of lifting it?"

"Do you want the motor car on its wheels?" the boy asked.

"Yes".

"Well, instead of taking all these kids with me, I will go and do it alone for you," he said. Padre Enriko did not know whether to get annoyed with the boy or laugh it off. He knew they needed help desperately and instead of talking sense, the boy seemed to enjoy the situation in which they were.

"You want me to do the job for you?" the boy insisted.

Brother Marko noticed that the blabbing of the young boy was exasperating Padre Enriko. He sneered at the boy and said, "It's okay boy, you go and put the Jeep on its wheels for us. We will be very grateful to you. Perhaps I should give you a hand if you don't want to take these young children to help you."

"I would rather take them than take you. By the way, do you realise that you are worrying yourselves over trifle?" Do you feel the weights of ten flies on your back when they land on you? The boy asked.

"Are you comparing the weight of that Jeep to the weight of ten files?" Padre Enriko asked.

"To me, yes, and at the same time, I want to tell you that the pressure, or the force, all of you can exert to help me put your Jeep up on its wheels, to be a little less than the pressure that ten flies exert on your back when you give them a ride."

"Do you boy know the weight of that Jeep," Padre Enriko snarled.

"That is why I cautioned you not to worry over a trifle. Do not mind the weight of that Jeep. It might be heavier than an elephant but I know I can easily put itup on its wheels for you.I guess you have come here on an important mission. Why don't you be serious about it?" The boy warned. The two Missionaries glanced at each other and Padre Enriko said, "Okay go and put the Jeep up for us."

"I am going to lift your Jeep gratis because you have saved the lives of my brothers.

You sit here do not go out; do not peep to see what I am going to do. You understand. But remember to, pray for me and Opuk." The last remark of the boy trepidated Padre Enriko so much, so that he did not know exactly what to make of the boy. "Pray for me and Opuk." What did he mean? Padre Enriko thought glancing at the boy who had sat at the side of the door in front of them.

"What's worrying you Father?" The boy asked bringing Padre Enriko in an upright position.

"How did you know Opuk? Which Opuk are you talking about by the way?" Padre Enriko asked.

"How many do you know?" The boy asked back.

"I know one in Coomit."

"Yes that is he, the one I am talking about." The two Missionaries stared at the boy perplexed.

It had stopped raining but the clouds were still hovering over head giving the sky a smutty appearance. The boy went out and soon returned with his body smeared with mud. He looked more squalid than he was before.

"Your motor car is ready to be driven away. You can come out and see. I have straightened the bumper, which was bent. You will do a bit of repair on the roof and I guess your motor car will be as good as new." He said and shook hands with them in the kitchen where they were sitting and walked out fast leaving them inside. The rest of the children, who had sat at the door, had remained as mute as eggs. However, when the boy who had lifted the Jeep disappeared behind the kitchen; they all stirred, and became more frightened by the presence of the two Missionaries in their kitchen. The young ones began to cower away behind the older boys holding them by the skin of their buttocks or hands.

"Where has he gone?" Padre Enriko asked the children. Nevertheless, they were too frightened to answer him, only a girl who was carrying another child on her back gathered a bit of courage and stood away from them.

"Don't be frightened children we aren't going to hurt you. We are human beings, like you. We want to talk to you." Padre Enriko pleaded to them convinced that boy who had just stood up their Jeep was not real. Their eyes were then opened to the fact of the uniqueness of the event.

"Who could this boy be?" They thought.

"I'm sure this Jeep needed ten strong men to put it on its wheels and this boy did it alone! I can't accept him as an earthly boy he must be one of the Holy ones sent by the Almighty God to help us." Padre Enriko said feeling his heart beating faster and burning with fear. The girl talking to them began to retreat towards the next home across the road as they advanced to catch up with her.

"I want to know that boy." Padre Enriko said.

"Which boy is that?" The girl asked and glanced behind her before she continued to retreat backwards keeping watch on them.

"The boy who lifted the Jeep."

"I don't know him."

"But he was in your company and he told us that he is looking after you here."

"Well, there is no boy bigger than myself among us here as you can see.

"Okay my dear young girl." Padre Enriko said touching his wound on the forehead.

"Where are your parents?" Padre Enriko asked to confirm what the boy told them.

"They have gone to fish for food in the river. You are aware that crops of all kind have been spoiled by this excessive rain, and big people go to the river every evening to fish for food even if the high water does not allow them to have a good catch. "

"At what time are you expecting your parents back from the river?"

"Tomorrow morning, the best time for fishing begins from mid night until down. That is when they come out of water and collect their catch together."

"I want you to tell me the truth Padre Enriko pleaded to the girl, are you sure, you didn't see any boy among you, who welcomed us in and offered us mushroom stools to sit on? He sat on the floor near the door while the rest of you sat behind him. The young girl shook her head and said, "I'm telling you the truth, that I didn't see any boy. There was not and there is not any boy among us bigger than myself." The girl stressed.

The rain was again preparing to pour for the sixth time in the day. Clouds laden with rain drifted as low as tree tops.

The girl looked up and said, "I must go, and she began to run away towards the other home across the road with the child she was carrying on her back bumping up and down.

"What do you make of this Brother?" Padre Enriko said wiping the small beads of sweat on his long hooked nose.

"I do not understand anything. I am very stunned father." Brother Marko replied.

"Okay Brother, let's go. I'll drive; you have a bad hand and leg; you can't control the Jeep well now. I'm well enough to do better."

Dr. Agustino, reached Palaro Health Centre at three thirty p.m. Palabek Health Centre was only forty miles away. He had made up his mind to continue to Palabek, deliver the drugs and equipments and come back to spend the night at Palaro. Sister Francisca was the sister in-charge of St.Paul's Health Centre at Palaro. Dr.Augustino got her very busy with her patients in the clinic.

"Hallo Father, you are most welcome." She said and walked out from the table where she had sat nursing her patients.

"Thank you very much sister."

"How was the trip?" The sister asked.

"The road is very bad. My Land Rover got stuck on the way in a deep mud but some kind village people towed me.

"That was very kind of them."

"Yes, they were nice men."

"Have you seen Padre Topone already?"

"No. I am straight from the road to your clinic. I'm intending to go to Palabek come and spend the night here so that I get to Gulu early tomorrow."

"Why don't we go and talk to him about that. It is not yet late to cook enough supper if you are coming to spend the night here. The road to Palabek is not very bad. It is mostly rocky," Sr.Francisca said. As they move to meet Padre Topone, Sister Francisca cried out, "Hey Father, have you been driving on a flat tyre?"

"Oh my God, what happened to the tyre? It was alright up to your clinic."

"A puncture may be," Brother Ceaser suggested.

"What could have caused it? Moreover, the tube and the tyre are all new. We have just replaced them a week ago." Father Agustino remarked disappointedly. Sister Francisca cried out again, "It is a nail! Look, its here." She said pointing at it. A six-inch nail had gone into the tyre passed the tube up to the metal rim.

"Oh my God, what an unkind nail! Why did you do this?" Dr. Agustino said as Brother Ceaser extracted out the nail from the tyre.

"I'll mend it for you." Brother Ceaser said. He got up and walked towards their garage to collect the instruments while Dr. Agustino began to roll up his sleeves in readiness to help him.

The sun had set. At least it looked set because it had been obscured throughout the day by the cloudy rain weather. Dr.Augustino had given up his idea of going to Palabeck. Instead, he had decided to leave all the medicine, and equipments he had brought for them with the Sisters at Palaro, to forward them to Palabek Health Centre.

Brother Ceaser was fastening the last nut on the wheel after he had mended the puncture tube, when they saw Padre Enriko drive in with the top of the Jeep covered with mud, and stopped right behind the Land Rover of Dr. Agustino.

"Oh dear you had an accident?" Brother Ceaser said and he got up from where he was squatting, cleaned the sand from his knees, and wiped the sweat from his forehead with the sleeve of the overall he had on.

"We over-turned about ten miles away from here," Padre Enriko said.

"Poor you, that was very nasty". Dr. Agustino said and moved near to examine their conditions.

"You need baths and proper dressing." He cautioned.

After they had washed and changed their dresses, they told their stories. Padre Enriko narrated the story in detail starting from when Padre Egidio became sick and how his illness worsened. He also told them how they traveled from Gulu until that time he was talking to them.

"He's quite ill. We don't know what has happened to him now." Padre Enriko said, swinging his neck from side to side which had just been anointed with liniment, and pressed lightly on the new smart bandage sister Francisca had just swathed round his head, giving him the look of an Arab. Brother Marko who was unable to rest his bad leg on the ground pulled one of the empty chairs and stretched his legs over it while he carried the dislocated wrist on his thigh. When they had finished telling their stories Dr. Agustino told them how he also traveled from Gulu via Alunya up to Palaro where they got him. Then individually, they began to put the zig saw puzzles in the events, which had happened to them on the way and tried to see their significance.

Dr.Augustino who was reading the latest Medical Bulletin from Italy, found out that he was unable to concentrate on what he was reading, because he was thinking about the story Pare Enriko had just told them.

From time to time, he folded the magazine and looked blankly in space in front of him. "I got stuck in the mud, what importance has it got with the chains of these events. Why was I feeling strange after I was towed out of the mud? Why was I inclined to return to Gulu as soon as possible? Padre Enriko and Brother Marko overturned when trying to save the lives of those kids, and they sustained injuries, which disabled them to attend to their Jeep. Moreover, the most fascinating part of their story, that boy. Definitely, he must be a heavenly body who has masqueraded that boy. He cannot be anybody else. In addition, my tyre, ripped through by this nail stopping me from going to Palabek. This is interesting," he thought.

Meanwhile Padre Enriko never bothered thinking about any of the other events, which happened to them or to Dr. Agustino. He only concentrated on that boy who conversed at length with them, teased them in many ways, and put their Jeep on its wheel probably by rolling it over with the stick he had in his hand as a child rolls a motorcar toy from side to side. "No wonder he didn't allow us out of the hut to go and see him do the job. How foolish I was to have got annoyed with him." Padre Enriko thought and crossed himself and began to recite an act of contrition. The Fathers and the sisters in Palaro although ate separately, normally ate their suppers at half past seven o'clock, but that day, because of the unexpected visitors, supper for the Priests was not ready until quarter past eight o'clock. When supper was being prepared, Dr.Augustino found out that he was wasting his time pretending to be reading the Milan Medical Bulletin. He tossed it on a verandah table near him on top of other newspapers, and got up. He dug his hand in his pocket and fished out his rosary, made a sign of the cross and walked out of the verandah into the compound.

The brightness of the pressure lamp they had impended on a stout wire from the roof at the verandah had illuminated about one hundred yards away. Padre Agustino walked the whole length of the illuminated area back and forth following the entrance to the Father's home reciting his rosary and at the same time thinking about Padre Egidio. "What am I going to do to help him? Pain in the joints sounds more like rheumatism; but of what type, old age, infection, or physiological! The dysponea, the murmur and the pain of the heart, do signify enterocarditis, which could be very fatal," he thought prognosticating the ailment of Padre Egidio. "I do not think sister Domitilla will handle his situation alone. I must go back as soon as possible, preferably tonight. If I start now, I guess by early morning tomorrow I should be in Gulu to attend to him. It might make a difference, rather than spend the night here and start tomorrow in the morning," Dr. Agustino continued to think and found that he had almost forgotten reciting his rosary in the fifty decades.

When Dr. Augustino came back from saying the rosary, during their supper time, he announced to his colleague that he was going to Gulu that night. Although they all heard him well, none of them answered him immediately. They all went on with their eating, glancing at each other over their food. At last their host, Padre Topone, sat up, inclined his knife and fork he was eating with at the edge of the plate and continued munching the mouth full of macaroni he had packed in his mouth, stared at Dr. Augustino who was picking his food with the fork like a stubborn child who wouldn't eat a damn because he believes eating is hazardous to his health. Dr. Augustino lifted up his head and their eyes met as the ball of food in Padre Topone's mouth started its journey through the peristalsis waves down his potbelly.

"You can't make it in the night. The road is quite bad now. It might do you a lot of good to get stuck in the mud tomorrow during the day than to go now, and bury yourself in the mud in the dark, rainy, muddy night." Padre Topone cautioned with concern. The rest of them who were eating in silence sat up to listen to him.

"I've decided to go Father, because I don't know how Padre Egidio is doing. According to what they have said, I suspect his condition needs a prompt and accurate medical attention. Otherwise, we stand a good chance of losing him. If I set out from here now, I might be able to get to Gulu by eight o'clock in the morning tomorrow. This might be of help to his life. We have to try to help him. What is the point of me sleeping here and start tomorrow at dawn just for my convenience? I have decided to go Father. You do not have to worry. I will be all right. Nothing will happen to me. I'll try to be careful not to bury my motor car in the mud."

"Well, if Dr. Augustino has decided to return, we'll accompany him," Padre Enriko said.

"No, you don't have to come with me. None of you is in good shape to drive from here to Gulu. I am going because I want to see if I could help Padre Egidio. You can come when you feel better." Dr. Agustino said.

"Is your Jeep alright?" Brother Ceaser asked Brother Marko who had sat next to him.

"I should think so." Padre Enriko drove it after the accident, he should know better.

"As a matter of fact, besides the dent on the roof there is nothing wrong with the Jeep. The bumper which was badly cramped after the accident was straightened by that boy we told you about."

"I think you will all go as Padre Enriko said, it will be easier to help on the way in case of an emergency. I do not see the sense in going and being stranded on the road until tomorrow. If that is the case then it's even advisable to remain where we are and going tomorrow as I had suggested earlier on," Padre Topone advised.

"Okay if they're ready to go back we could start immediately after supper. I'm not going to sleep here tonight." Dr. Agustino said determined.

"If that is the case I will come with you." Brother Ceaser announced his decision. When they all finished eating Padre Topone, led the prayers after the meal.

"I think we should go and let the sisters know about your decision before you leave," Padre Topone said after their prayers and they all walked out to the sisters' quarter.

But your conditions aren't good enough to travel in this cold night." Sister Francisca protested to Padre Enriko and Brother Marko when Padre Topone revealed to them that they had decided to go back to Gulu.

"We will be alright, we appreciate his decision. Padre Egidio needs him badly. We cannot let him go back alone. If the road was good, well, we would have let him go while we wait over night here." Padre Enriko said.

"You're not going to be of much use on the way either." Sister Francisca said. There was a pause between them and Padre Topone said.

"Will you take the spades with you? You might need them. Pick what you think will be useful for you on the way." They collected everything they needed into the vehicle and Fr. Agustino tested the tyres of his Land Rover by kicking gently on the four wheels.

When he was content that they were all right, he opened the door of the Land Rover and slid behind the steering wheel and, Brother Marko accompanying him, sat on the passenger seat. Dr. Augustino got the key from his pocket inserted it in the keyhole to ignite the Land Rover, as Padre Topone moved to talk to them.

"I'm sorry my dear brothers in Christ that you've to leave in such a hurry. I understand you. It is because of the life of one of us, which is in danger. May the Lord guide you and you reach home safely to help him."

"I'll go and see what I can do for him." Dr. Agustino said and started the engine.

The others, Padre Enriko, and Brother Ceaser driving the Jeep, followed them and they were soon swallowed up by dark night, only the red rear lights of their vehicles glowed for a while before they were completely out of sight in the dark night.

It was striking four o'clock. About nine hours since Padre Enriko brought Padre Egidio to Gulu Hospital critically ill. His condition continued to worsen with every second that ticked by. Sister Domitilla left alone to look after Padre Egidio in the acute care unit tried all the possible treatment she thought would help Padre Egidio but his condition continued to deteriorate. She knew that if Dr. Augustino did not return by Tuesday, he would only get the corpse of Padre

Egidio waiting for burial. She informed the Bishop, the other priests, Brothers, and Sisters in the Mission about his deteriorating condition. They all came to see him. They knew there was very little chance for him to survive so they anointed him with the sacrament of the dying, to prepare him for his death. They went in the church and spent hours praying to Almighty God to work a miracle to make him survive. At six o'clock Padre Egidio lost his consciousness, the rest of them thought he was dead but Sister Domitilla assured them that he was only unconscious. At nine o'clock, Padre Celestino of Gulu Parish came to the hospital again to check on Padre Egidio whether he had come round. In his rubber boots, he walked like a ghost gliding amid air. He came and stood near Sr.Domitilla. She was auscultating Padre Egidio's heart beat. She looked gloomy and sick.

"How is he?" Padre Celestino whispered in sister Domitilla's ears.

"No use Father."

"What do you mean no use?" Padre Celestino said moving forwards wishing he knew how to use the stethoscope he would have examined Padre Egidio himself.

"I mean he's getting worse." Sister Domitilla said, and pulled off the stethoscope from her ears, rolled it on her wrist and stood looking down at the dying Padre Egidio. Tears stole their way down her cheeks as a sign of surrender.

"He won't make it Father, I'm sorry. He's about dead," she said to Padre Celestino who was as red as baked brick.

"Is there nothing you …"

"I can't do anything Father, if there was anything I could do to help him, do you think I could be standing here to watch him sink?" she said regretfully.

"I'm sorry Sister."

"I know what you mean Father."

The journey to Gulu was quite a tough one. Dr. Augustino driving in front kept thinking about Padre Egidio, trying to diagnose him from the clinical history he was given by Padre Enriko. He wanted to treat him immediately on arrival for suspected septicemia.

"At least if I eliminated septicemia, I could have a chance of working on him better." He thought as he drove. The more he thought about him, the more he accelerated the Land Rover. Nevertheless, the rain, which was pouring, and the mud on the road could not enable him to achieve the speed he had wanted to drive at. They drove through the houndred miles in rain and mud, so that when they got to Gulu at 6 O'clock in the morning, there was not an inch of their vehicle without mud, except for the path of the wipers on the front windscreens. Their effort did not achieve its aim. The moroseness they saw on the face of everyone they met that morning told them that they were too late.

"He's dead," Sister Domitilla told them amid tears as they lumbered in the acute care unit in the hospital where his body still lay.

"He died at ten in the morning. He became unconscious at six in the evening but he never came round and died." She said and broke into bitter sobbing.

Dr. Augustino hysterically moved to the corpse of Padre Egidio, took his wrist in his hand, and began to feel for his pulses disbelieving what sister Domitilla had said, or was it a doctor's reflex action, which made him behave like that? He stood holding Padre Egidio's wrist for a while, while looking down at the dead face and dropped it with disgust and slowly moved away towards the door, stopped, turned to the group who came with him and said. "No good, he's dead."

The black long coffin, with big white crosses on top and all the sides for Padre Egidio was ready by one o'clock in the afternoon when he was put in it to rest. It was then taken into the church where it was laid surrounded with wreaths of sweet smelling flowers.

Burning candlesticks, two towards his head, and legs stood on the stools. The coffin, which could be opened and locked like a suitcase, was left open for the other Missionaries to pay their last respect to him before he was taken to Coomit where he had directed he should be buried. Padre Constantino was one of those who visited Padre Egidio in the hospital before he lost his consciousness. It was through him that the directive from Padre Egidio that he should be buried in Coomit Mission and a note he wrote for the new Parish Priest of Coomit was received.

The death of Padre Egidio deprived all the Christians under Coomit Parish of a priest they had loved. He had been a kind, humble and a simple man. It was his simplicity, which had earned him admiration and love from everyone who knew him. He never segregated anyone. Everyone received the same treatment from him as human beings of one family. He condemned racism. He compared the racist British colonialists to machines, which do accurate work but do not understand what they are doing or appreciate their existence. To Anyadwe and David, the death of Padre Egidio meant a lot more than it meant to any other Christian in Coomit Parish. For them, they lost a spiritual Father, and a benefactor, who had helped them in all aspects of life. They all knew that the end of David's education was in sight, and he was not going any further than his junior two in St.Dominic Boys Junior Secondary School in Gulu, which were the two years of the scholarship award he won in the examination that year. The source of financial support seemed cut off.

The thought haunted Anyadwe wherever she went. She never slept properly at night so that each day when she woke up in the morning, she looked very weary and moody. She thought of the last talk they had with Padre Egidio, on the last Sunday they saw him alive with the excruciating pain all over his body. She thought of the aid Padre Egidio promised them, which then appeared dreams to them, and as remote as the sun in the sky.She always sat with her head in her hands, remising the death of Padre Egidio she hated the world; she spent most of her time praying for Padre Egidio. She was more affected than the Missionaries themselves.

Eleven days had passed since Padre Egidio had died and was brought to his grave in Coomit. The weather was a bit fine.The excess rain had stopped. David and his mother were sitting in their compound after their evening meal when Padre Enriko called in to see them, riding the motorcycle, which used to belong to Padre Egidio. Padre Enriko had the note, which Padre Egidio wrote and left for him before he, became unconscious. The note was concerning the assistance, which Padre Egidio, on behalf of the Mission, was rendering to Anyadwe and her son David Acellam, particularly towards David's education. Given that the weather was fair that evening, Padre Enriko decided to come and break the news to them at their home.

"I should have told you this last week on Tuesday when we brought the body of Padre Egidio for burial but I was busy with the guests. There was a note which had been left by Padre Egidio before he died to the next parish priest of Coomit, which according to the instruction I've received from the Bishop in Gulu, is me."

He said and fished out a letter written on a sheet of paper torn out of a book, and began to read for them. *"Brethren, Rev.Padre Egidio send you all in the Parish greetings. I am writing this note to you from my hospital bed. My condition looks critical. I don't know what is going to happen to me, but I am almost certain I will not walk out of it. If I do, then it will be God's wish. The subject of this note to you is to introduce to you the widow of Ogwok, Ajulina Anyadwe, who has survived her late husband Ogwok, by a son David Acellam. I am appealing to you, to continue the assistance the Mission has been rendering to them, particularly towards the education of her son David. The Mission has been paying his fees through out his Primary education. I have found him a reliant boy and the family of two an upright one. You will find that out yourself. The man, Ogwok, was killed by a lion many years back. Without him, we would have probably not founded Coomit Mission. I personally believe we owe him quite a lot. Besides, he was a reliant, diligent man who, when he was still alive, worked with us in the Mission. He did most of the work in the name of our Lord Jesus Christ. He never wanted to be paid for them. When he died, I thought it best for the Mission to look after his widow and the son. For the next two years in his Junior Secondary education, the Mission will only assist him in buying the school requirements because he has won the second scholarship award. This also tells you what sort of a boy he is. For this year, I have already bought some of the school requirements for him and they are in a carton on top of the cupboard in my room. Please let him have them. If you could also organize his transport to and from School, that will be appreciated. May the good Lord bless and help you and all under you in your work. Sincerely yours, Rev. Padre Egidio.*

When he finished reading the note to them, Padre Enriko folded the letter slowly and slipped it into the envelope he used for carrying it before he put it in his pocket.

"We shall keep this letter safe in Administrative file so that whoever comes as a Parish Priest here in Coomit tomorrow, or whenever, will honour it. You should not have any fear of dissertation. I have approved all what he stated in this letter. I know you well. If I leave in the same way as he has left us or otherwise, before you are able to manage your own affairs, I will acknowledge this very note to the next Parish Priest in the same manner. The Mission is committed to your husband's examples, of a good disciple. Look at the many Christians we have here today, this is because of his initiative, he welcomed the servants of God and aided them to preach the words of God to all the pagans. Jesus himself said to his twelve Apostles when he was sending them out to preach the words of God. He said, I'd send you out as my father has sent me. Anyone who welcomes you, welcomes me, and anyone who casts you out, casts me," et cetra.

"So you can actually see the immense debt which we owe your husband, no human wealth can pay it back." Padre Enriko concluded. Anyadwe was very touched by the information. She began to think of her hay days with her husband who was then about fifteen years old in the ground. She thought of how Padre Egidio used to come to their home, sit with them, before her husband took him out in the village to meet the pagans. She thought of how her husband organized them to put their first chapel, St.Joseph Chapel in Coomit. She thought of their wedding in the Chapel. She traced all what they did when her husband was still alive in the company of Padre Egidio including the birth of the new Sub-Mission in Latinnyer.

Without realizing what she was doing, she was startled by the warm drops of tears on her bare chest.

Three days later, Padre Enriko, came riding on his motorcycle. Their supper cooking on fire in the hearth had made the kitchen warm and because of that, Anyadwe and David, sat at the doorway in the light of the evening setting sun. Padre Enriko came and stopped his motorcycle near the granary, which was nearer the kitchen. On the pillion, of the motorcycle he had tied the carton Padre Egidio had mentioned in his letter. They exchanged greetings and Padre Enriko began to untie the rubber used for holding the carton on the pillion. David moved forward and lifted the carton off the pillion for him and put it down on the ground, went back inside the kitchen and got a mushroom stool for him to sit on. They sat outside talking as the smoked meat on the fire continued to cook issuing very appetizing scent.

Padre Enriko like Padre Egidio had found a secret which most whites or may I say the Italian Missionaries didn't discover in the delicacy of the Acholi dish of smoked meat cooked with simsim or groundnuts paste *Olel soup* preferably with *kwon bel*. Padre Egidio used to buy some meat, smoked it, and brings it to Anyadwe to prepare it for him. Now that his favourite Acholi dish was being prepared Padre Enriko made no hurry in introducing his topic, and disclosing the contents of the carton he had brought. His only worry was that he did not tell Bro.Albertini that he would be out for supper. How he wished there was any telecommunication system anywhere in that part of the world.

"I hope you are aware that your school starts next month on Tuesday February the second?" Padre Enriko asked David after their supper.

"Yes Father."

"I've brought here what Padre Egidio had bought for you.

He had in fact bought most of the items except, I think, he didn't buy a basin and a box which I'll purchase for you soon." He said and pulled the carton near him and opened it. The contents of the carton fascinated Anyadwe and David. The paper box had been neatly packed with item, which was far from their reach like the stars.

A blanket, a pair of bed sheets stripped, red, green and yellow, a pair of canvas shoes bearing the manufacture label inside *made in Italy* two pairs of woolen stocking, stationeries, cutleries, washing and bathing soap and school uniform, were packed in the carton.

Two days later, Padre Enriko came back with the items he had promised to buy for David, a basin and a beautifully embroided tin box with a complex lock, dangling on the metal hasp shutter of the box.

# Chapter Twelve

Tuesday February second the beginning of the school year came too soon for David. On the eve of his departure to school in Gulu, David had sleepless long night because he was worried of going away to Gulu leaving his mother alone at home. After long wait daybreak came at last, David got up and bundled his mattress he was taking to school rolling it in a palm leaves mat, bought for him by his mother. The mat was to be used on top of the bed, to prevent any spikes on the bed from tearing the mattress.

The sun slowly crept out from behind the Eastern horizon expelling the cold wind of the morning, which kept most people chafing their hands on their bodies, or lit fire in the compounds to warm themselves before the aggressive heat of the dry season sun took control of the day. It was about eight o'clock in the morning, when his mother put in front of him his breakfast of chicken meat with *Kwonbel* to eat before he left for Gulu.

After his meals, David went into his hut to dress. Anyadwe followed him a short while after he had left. She found him already dressed, sitting on the bed weeping.

"My dear son, take it easy. I know it is the first time for you to go out of home.

You are going to be all right when you meet your friends at school. Be a good boy, and behave yourself when Padre Enriko comes to pick you up. I do not want you to start those tears in front of him. You are a big boy who should not be weeping like that because of leaving your dear mother behind. I will miss you too, but I am bearing it because I know you are going out for the better if you go and work hard. After three months only, you are going to rejoin me here at home.

You'll get me as strong as ever, with a lot of stories to tell to each other". His mother advised him. Anyadwe had just finished talking to David when Padre Enriko and Sr. Veronica in the front seat of the Jeep drove in with a few other passengers in the rear, some of whom were patients being taken to Gulu Hospital for treatment. He made a 'U' turn in the compound parked the Jeep facing the path along which they had come through, and got out to help David who was already walking towards the Jeep lugging his bundle of mattress in one hand, and the tin box in the other.

"Good morning David, you're ready to go?" Padre Enriko asked as he picked up his mattress and tossed it on the rack, on top of the Jeep.

"Yes Father", David replied.

"That's good and where is Mama? Still sleeping?"

"No, Father she is inside there, about to come out." David said and gave his box to Padre Enriko who again tossed it on the rack of the Jeep.

Anyadwe came out following David carrying the basin. After they had exchanged greeting, Anyadwe gave the basin to Padre Enriko who had stood on the rear bumper in readiness to fasten the rope. When Sr. Veronica heard Anyadwe talked, she got out of the Jeep and came to talk to her. "Good morning Ajulina."

"Good morning Sister."

"We're taking him away from you today." She said with a huge smile and patted David on his back. The statement made David fidget. He did not want to be reminded about his departure from his mother although it was apparent.

"We will miss each other alright but we shall get used." Anyadwe said deliberately when she detected uneasiness in David.

"Of course you will, particularly him who is going to meet many friends and he might not even think of you for weeks," Padre Enriko, said.

"Come on let's go we're getting late," Sr. Veronica said and dragged David by the hand to the front seat, and sat him between her and Padre Enriko. Anyadwe went and peeped through the window of the Jeep at the side of Sr. Veronica to wish her son good-bye. David looked at his mother and looked up at the roof of the Jeep, and blinked rapidly in an attempt to reverse the direction of flow of his tears, but nature was too great for him. He exploded and the tears oozed out from his eyes draining into his ears.

"Come on, David!" Sr. Veronica said wiping off his tears with her handkerchief. "Don't be a naughty boy. You are not going away for good. You're going to come back to your Mama in a matter of weeks only." She explained to him.

"I wish you could talk to him more Sisters, he has been worried throughout last week, and he hardly slept well at night." Anyadwe said.

"Why should he be worried? Is it because he is leaving you here alone?"

"I think so." Anyadwe replied.

"Your mother is going to be alright David, don't worry about her. We will keep in closer contact with her this time and we will inform you about everything happening at home either by letter or personal contact.Okay Ajulina, we must be going, see you later when we come back."

Sr. Veronica said impatiently and shook hand with her. David extended his hand for a brief handshake with his mother, but she clang on his hand, even when the Jeep had started rolling, she held on his hand wishing him all the best of luck in the world. Padre Enriko looked at them, smiled, and drove away. They waved back to Anyadwe who stood alone in the compound with the chicken, the granaries, the huts, and the trees looking after her son, David, being taken away in search of higher knowledge.

The official opening of the school was marked by the welcome speech of the Principal, Padre Quirino. In his succinct speech, he welcomed all the pupils to school. He told them to be disciplined, obedient, and to respect all the teachers, the pupils in authorities, and among themselves. He warned them against violence, drunkardness and immodest behaviour in general, but more specifically with the girls in the neighboring school, which he spelt out clearly to them that, no male pupil, was allowed without permission, to leave a foot mark in the girls compound under any circumstances, unless authorised by the Headmasters or the Teachers of either of the two schools. He sternly warned them that any of them, who will be found, or reported having done so, would leave the school instantly. Finally, he urged them to be friendly among themselves, and to attend all prayers every day.

David met his old friends he knew in Coomit Primary School and soon got used to school life without his mother around him. He was hard working pupil in the class so that he excelled all students in his class in all subjects taught. These criteria earned him more new friends not only among the students but also among the teachers. If ever he remembers his mother then it was during his prayers.

Padre Enriko visited him in school often whenever he came to town. He always conveys to him his mother's love and greetings. The first two terms in school made David aware that he was to work even harder in future if he was to improve the standard of living in which they were with his aging mother.

The school year ended with the usual farewell advice from Padre Quirino in the Assembly Hall. He advised the students that, while they are at home, for their holidays, they should obey and help their parents, and all the people in the village whenever necessary and to be good example to the Christians by going to church on every Sunday. He warned them against pomposity and diddling, the illiterates in the villages, and above all, he warned them against indecent public, or private behaviour. With these words, Padre Quirino closed the school.

David was one of those who were promoted to junior two together with his friends Ocune and Olel. Padre Enriko of Coomit brought them back home for their holidays. David found his mother busy collecting her crops. She was happy to have him at home for Christmas holidays and David was very happy to join her. Whenever David was away at school, Anyadwe was not building the fire in the compound. She always stayed in the kitchen using the fire in the hearth which she had used for her cooking to warm herself and she went to bed earlier than when he was at home for his holidays. That evening, when David returned home for his Christmas holidays, he built their usual small bonfire in the compound. After their supper, they sat outside near the fire talking of their past when David looked up in the sky and saw the only star which had remained after the death of Padre Egidio still twinkling in the clear night.

"Mama"

"Yes"

"What does Opuk say about that star which is still remaining in sky?"

"He says the gods are angry with me and Kinyera, plus few other people who would not yield to his explanation about the gods. He said Aremu would probably die this year. Her own son will kill her. We all wonder which son? Otto is a cripple and Apire is too young. Nevertheless, as for me the course of my death will not be known. He also said, he would not live to see us die. However, he stressed that we must repent to the gods by rebuilding our *Abila*, and offer sacrifices to the gods as others are doing, if we want to save our lives.

"Did he say that?" David exclaimed with deep concern.

"Yes, but don't worry, nothing will happen to us. I am trying my best to get him Baptized."

"How will you do that when he hates to hear anything about God, he doesn't even like to see a priest around him?"

"I have already had an open discussion with him once. He is not very adamant as he used to be. I do not know why I have a belief he will be baptised. Since Padre Egidio died he has been very happy, and he has been going everywhere in the village saying that the gods had told him that a white priest would die, and it happened as he had prophesied, and he threatened that he has been told that more of the Priests will die if they do not leave Coomit. Padre Enriko said he would continue to pray for him so that he also becomes a Christian one day."

"He's getting too old. He might die before he's baptized."

"The best time is at his dying hours. If God wants he will be baptized." Anyadwe said.

As they talked, they heard some people blowing horns as if they were warning the entire village of a danger.

"What is the matter Mama? Is there something wrong? " David asked

"I think those are the men who are informing their friends about the hunting expedition in Acut tomorrow."

"Oh I see. I thought there was something wrong somewhere."

"I don't think so. They have been doing that for the last few days."

The hunting expedition in Acut was always organized once a year, during the dry season. Okelokoko owned the hunting ground, which were so many hundreds of square miles. It was he, who authorised the hunting in the place after performing the ceremonial rites to the gods of peace, which he did annually.

Okelokoko, the brother-in-law of Opuk, was a short stout man who had suffered from Polio when he was a child. His left leg was several inches shorter than the right leg, so that he walked with springy motion. Every year at about that time, words were passed to as many people as possible throughout the District giving a period of about two weeks before the actual hunting day. The information were passed out mostly during public gathering like market days during local traditional dances and others, so that some people came from as far as fifty miles away to participate in the hunting in Acut. Whenever it was only a few days left, selected people were sent out to remind the hunters about the hunting day. They moved along the road carrying with them wet branches of trees, and blowing horns.

Their messages were always picked up by the men, and transmitted further a field in all villages. As a result, sound of horns and trumpets were heard everywhere. These same people who sent out reminiscence to the hunters, continued with their commissionable duties during the hunting time. It had been resolved by the elders of the front line villages embodying the hunting ground that, in appreciation of Okelokoko's good services to hunters during the hunting day, coupled with the fact that on that day he wasn't allowed to see the sun, as part of the ceremony for good luck to all hunters, those chosen people who wear crowns of leaves on their heads during the hunting time to identify themselves, were supposed to collect one front leg of any animal bigger than a rabbit and smaller than an elephant from everyone who had killed such animal. These collections were shared between them and Okelokoko. It was feared that anyone who tried to collect the meat fraudulently, met with bad omen. This fear was instilled in most people because of two incidences in which two young men tried to be smart during two different hunting periods. They had designed for themselves the crowns of leaves identical to those of the elites. In both cases, they had collected a number of legs of various animals. In the first incident, the young man got an arrow through his skull from a hunter who was aiming at an animal, which had stood between them. He died instantly from the shot.

## The Devout Woman

A lion killed the other boy, in a different hunting expedition practicing the same mischief.

Every year the men and the women from Coomit who went to hunt all assembled at Oyat's home the brother-in-law of Okelokoko before they moved in a huge group to the hunting ground.

That year almost all the hunters streamed past through Anyadwe's home, who wished them safe journey, success, and happy return. Chief Kinyera was one of those who went hunting that day. Only the old women and young children were left at home. All the girls and young women were all taken along to help carry the meat.

The earth gradually moved away from the bright hot sun, which eventually became a cool glowing red ball in the Western horizon taking with it the hot windy day hence surrendering the responsibility of lighting the earth to the moon, and the stars, which steamed the clear sky of the bright night. The night, as many other bright nights in the dry season, was a noisy one with insects flying about in the moonlight. David and his mother remained outside waiting for the men to come back blowing horns and trumpet happy as they did every year, but to their surprise, not a noise came, in spite of the fact that they were late in the night.

"What's the matter today, it's about bed time, and none of these hunters has come back." Anyadwe remarked. David who was almost falling asleep on the log on which he was sitting, stirred up to listen to what his mother was saying.

"May be they are still skinning the animal they have killed," he suggested.

"I do not think so; they normally delay like to-night only when there is trouble. Let's hope that's not the cause of their delay tonight," Anyadwe said.

David needed sleep more than waiting to see people stream pass with their bundles of meat on their heads.

"Mama I'm going to sleep," he suggested.

"I think we can both go. I'm also sleepy now, whatever has delayed them, we shall hear tomorrow." Anyadwe said and got up taking fire woods in her hands. As she turned round, she saw Kinyera walking quietly through the gate. He was carrying on his head a huge bundle of meat tied together with his gun, in a wet skin of an antelope.

"Ha, Kinyera, is that why you are unable to blow the horn because you're walking with the world on top of your head?" Anyadwe commented

"Help me to put it down, but pull the gun out first," Kinyera replied indifferently and crouched for her to reach the butt of the gun, which had jutted out of the bundle.

"I hope it is safe to handle," Anyadwe pondered.

"It is as safe as your baking stick." Kinyera replied.

After she had pulled the gun out of the bundle of meat, Kinyera dropped it down and sat down on the ground, his legs stretched out the left over the right, and sighed, like a boxer who was saved by the bell in a bout. He stared moodily in front of him like a man with package of sad news to deliver but did not know where to start.

"You're welcome back Kinyera; I hope no grass cut your feet as I wished you this morning."

"Oh no, I'm quite in one piece except that I am very tired and confused." Kinyera said.

"Confused? What do you mean? Is that why you do not look fine? "What happened?" Anyadwe asked and became more interested to know what had happened during the hunting time as sleep disappeared from both of them.

"Was there a fight? Someone got killed?" She continued to ask Kinyera.

"We've had an accident alright; he started to say, paused for a while and turned his head towards Anyadwe.

"What accident? Who was hurt?" She insisted. Kinyera sighed and said.

"Opuk misfired today," he added and shook his head regretfully.

"Don't tell me that Opuk also went for the hunt." Anyadwe remarked.

"I wonder why he did that. I think God had decided for him that way."

"Is he dead? Please, tell me the details". She asked desperately.

"We were not surprised when we saw Opuk, his son Ojuk, and his daughter Lanyero, Kinyera said and went on.

"We thought that Opuk was only coming to see us off, and may be briefly talk to us about his gods and spirits, give us some good luck wishes as he usually did and return to his home, but we were shocked to learn that he was to come with us. All of us were against the idea because we knew he was obviously going to hamper our movement. Nevertheless, he insisted on coming with us claiming that he has had a dream at night, which he interpreted to means that, if he went to hunt, both of them, that is, his son Ojuk and him, were going to kill an animal each. You know who Opuk was. He was a difficult man to be convinced against superstition and all his beliefs. So we went, of course because of him, we reached our wing late. When we got there, the operation started well. Akuta, the son of Balmoi, was the first to kill a cob, which was followed by a series of killings ranging from squirrels to a buffalo, which Ojuk killed. We fought very hard to kill the buffalo.

After we had finished skinning the buffalo at about three p.m. and had given the meat to the ladies to carry we continued to advance forward. We had crossed the stream Otwala and had left it about a quarter of a mile when we saw an antelope running away from us. Our men soon scattered around and encircled the animal. With the help of dogs, they managed to drive it back to the place where most of us were couching in the grass to ambush the animal. Among us were Opuk, and his son Ojuk.In front of Ojuk, stood a dry tree, which had lost all its bark. The antelope came running towards Ojuk passing near the tree. He suddenly sprang up and plunged his spear with the hope of fixing the animal; but his sudden appearance caused the animal to change its course very quickly towards his father who had squatted next to him. The spear Ojuk had plunged, missed the animal and zoomed towards the tree.The blade just missed the tree, but the handle hit the trunk of the tree and deflected the spear toward Opuk who was only a few feet on the other side of the tree. After his son had missed the animal, Opuk got up in an attempt to accomplish his dream he had in the night, when he met the spear of his son which had been deflected by the tree right on his left breast and went through his back. He fell down with a cry: "I'm dying." I was not far from him. I saw him receiving the spear on his chest. I ran to him. I pulled it out and pieces of meat came out with the blade. Blood spurted out from the wound. I held his head up and rested it on my thigh. His son came and fell on his knees crying.

"I didn't mean to do it." He cried. His father admitted it was an accident. Then do you know what happened, and what surprised us most? Opuk started to shout.

"I see a pit full of fire. There are people in the fire. They are crying. Don't send me in the fire, help, please help, I am burning." He cried.

"Then I told him that if he didn't want to go into the fire, he should accept the Lord Jesus Christ, and be baptised in his name. He willingly accepted then I baptised him using the water I was carrying in my gourd.

"You baptised him?" Anyadwe asked with a thick hoarse voice.

"Yes I did."

"How beautiful; you have done the very thing I was longing to do. I thought he would be saved. Thanks God for that."

I am sure Padre Enriko will be thrilled to hear the news," she said with tears of joy flowing out of her eyes.

"Well that's what I did. And more strange things happened I was saying Paul, I gave him the name Paul, because he first rebelled against God, I baptised you in the name of the Father, Son, Holy Spirit, and when I was dropping the last drop of water on his head he smiled and dropped his head on my arm and died. Immediately a strong whirlwind took off from where we were. It danced around us for about two minutes throwing the grass and dead leaves very high in the sky before it started spinning away from us with a loud noise. The ashes it was throwing up, stood like a pillar of dust, standing sky high. We didn't know what was happening and the explanation to the whirl wind." Kinyera paused and went on. "So, because of that, we could not continue with our advancement, we stopped there and came away home.

When we arrived at Opuk's home, of course, his wife was puzzled when she saw all of us coming home in a gloomy silence. She took a quick look around and noted that her husband was missing; she immediately asked where he was. Before any of us could say a word, she saw the corpse of Opuk, which was being carried by Otto and Onek. We had wrapped him up in grass reinforced with some long poles to facilitate carrying. She burst into a bitter cry demanding with rage the explanation for the cause of her husband's death. Tongpur, Oyat, and I took her by the arms into her kitchen to explain to her what had happened. With difficulties, we managed to mollify her, and Tongpur, being their nearest family friend, and relative, went through the whole story for her. You know what shocked us most; she denied that, that was an accident. She alleged that was a planned patricide. She said that Ojuk had all the time longed to kill his father because of that girl who eloped with him six months ago. His father, apparently, the way she put it, did not like the girl, but Ojuk had fallen for her flat on his face so that anyone who tried to discourage him, was his enemy number one. This was a family secret, which even

Tongpur did not know. I don't know whether you know anything about that."

"No, I didn't," Anyadwe said.

"Well there we are. The reasons she gave for Opuk disliking his daughter-in-law were that she was older than Ojuk; besides he believed she was full of bad omens. In addition, you know if Opuk had formed an opinion about you, only he could change it, no one else could. Therefore, it was, he had formed an opinion about this woman who, as I have already said, he believed was a taboo because she had got married three times, and each time she lost the husband. Furthermore, she is very lazy; she does not like to work. Opuk was worried about the type of life his son was going to lead. We tried to convince Lajok that, in this particular incident, we strongly believed it was accidental regardless of the grudges they had against each other. You know what she did, she ran out from the kitchen where we were talking went and fell in front of Ojuk her son, and ordered him to kill her as he had done to her husband, but the poor boy just sat there crying, confessing to his mother with all sincerely that he didn't deliberately kill his father. Nevertheless, his mother could not listen. That was when I remember Ojuk saying lamenting about three times on the way when we were coming back, that his mother would not accept that it was an accident. She was already prejudiced about all he did to his father to be planned anti-Opuk act.

We were holding Lajok, trying to talk to her to behave, not bothering about Ojuk. Our backs were all on him. His sister Lanyero had stood not very far away from the corpse of her father crying when Ojuk idiosyncratically drew out his skinning knife from its sheath hanging from the belt tied around his waist, and drove it through his heart up to the hilt. His sister Lanyero saw it too late, and shouted, "Ojuk has knifed himself."

"We all turned around just in time to witness his fall. Tongpur jumped across and pulled out the knife, which gave way to a fountain of blood. He blamed his suicide on his mother who incessantly refused to accept anyone's explanation about his father's death. After a short

## The Devout Woman

time only, he kicked, stretched, gasped, and laid his head down to rest. So there are two corpses there, we are going to bury. I don't know, one might have fallen again after I left, we'll go and see," Kinyera concluded his story shaking his head in deep regret.

Anyadwe sat there transfixed by the story so that if it were not because of the occasional blinks of her eyes and the throbbing of her heart, which could be seen from a distance, one could have mistaken her for her portrait. After Kinyera had finished his story, he shared some of his meat with Anyadwe before he got up and struggled with his bundle of meat on his head once more and left for his home with promise that he would see them again in the morning.

At day break, Anyadwe and David walked out in the bright cool morning with the sun creeping up slowly behind the Eastern horizon throwing its rays on trees, houses, granaries and projecting their long grotesque shadows right across the compound when Kinyera arrived at Anyadwe's home. They exchanged greeting and he sat down on a mushroom stool David had brought for him. When all were set, they left for the burial of Opuk and his son. The small home was thronged to capacity with wailing women, and men blowing tolling solemn funeral tunes through the horns.

The two deceased were buried. After the death of Opuk and his son Ojuk, the only remaining star in the west became hazy in appearance but did not completely disappear.

"What is the meaning of all these?" People of Coomit inquired. Opuk had said Aremu and Anyadwe would die this year if they do not repent to the gods by rebuilding their *Abila* and offer sacrifices to the gods, and he had said that he would die before them. Now he and his son are dead. The only star left is disappearing. Does it mean it has not completely disappeared because of Aremu and Anyadwe? If so why don't they see the danger they are in and listen to Opuk's warning?"

Aremu would have stopped her son Apire earlier if she did not over trust her husband's carefulness in handling his gun. Each time

Kinyera came back home from his hunting exercise as he had called it, he made sure that not a single unfired bullet remained in the magazine in the gun. Furthermore, he always left the safety catch on. His wife was aware of his perpetual carefulness in handling his gun, so that she was not frightened at all by the threat of her son Apire, who very often whenever his father was not at home, took the gun and went with it wherever she was and, he always called for her attention. Once he had it, he would then tell her, "Mama, I'm going to shoot you."

Then he would pull on the trigger, which would only click, and his mother would laugh and ask him to take the gun back in the house. Apire would submissively return the gun and come back to his mother saying: "Tomorrow I'll go with Baba in the forest and when we see an animal I'll take the gun from him and I'll fire at the animal with only one shot "TWA!' and the animal will fall down dead." Aremu would then flatter him saying, "I'll love to eat the meat of the animal you killed, my son." This practice went on and on without her husband knowing anything about it. Only Aremu and the children knew about the potential, lethal, joke she and Apire were enjoying at that time.

One day, late in the evening, after his hunting exercise Kinyera hurriedly left home for an urgent duty without putting the safety catch on or removing the bullets from the magazine of the gun beside he had left it cocked. He had hardly gone far from home, on his bicycle when his son Apire entered the living room of their house, and the first thing he saw was the gun inclined in one of the corners leading to the bed room of his parents.

He immediately picked it up and walked out with it. His mother was peeling sweet potatoes near the kitchen, and Otto sat out on a mat near the door where Apire was standing with the gun, the butt resting on the ground with the barrel a few inches taller than he was. Then he called his mother. When she saw the gun, her heart leapt and she began to wonder if her husband had removed the bullets and put on the safety catch. She remembered when her husband returned; he went and had a quick bath, dressed and left almost immediately.

"May be he has put on the safety catch even if he didn't remove the bullets," Aremu thought. It was the first time that the sight of her son, pointing at her with the dark nozzle of the barrel of the gun, frightened her. She was frightened, and the son saw that she was. He became more interested in the fun than he had ever been before. She was opening her mouth to tell him to return the gun, when he also decided to pull on the trigger showering his mother with the bullets. The *bang* of the gun startled him to madness. He threw the gun down and ran for protection to his mother whom he had just shot. His mother fell with a shot on her forehead, which blew, off the top of her head.

After his wife's death, Kinyera lived with his children who had been handicapped by various debilitating diseases. Unfortunately, his children who were normal were not doing well at school. Already, his first-born Inyamonyuk had disappeared in the King African Rifle, nowhere to be heard of. Since he left home, about sixteen years ago, he never wrote home. When his mother died, it was not possible to contact him anywhere. Amal, who had escaped the storm in which her brother Atokany was suffocated to death, had just given up school and was then roaming the village like a bitch on heat.

His last-born Apire, who gunned down his mother, was struggling at school without any hope of passing the Primary Leaving Examination, as he was always at the bottom of the class. The sight of futureless children crowding near him, day and night, worried him more than the death of his wife.

# Chapter Thirteen

It was certainly a strange year for Anyadwe as Opuk had said. Anyadwe started it off with ill health of all severity ranging from common cold to generalized oedema. She had been in and out of the Sister's clinic for most of the time that year. She feared that she was not going to get enough food for them as she was laid off by the sickness most of the time that year. She hardly stayed out of bed for as long as a month. There was diarrhoea today, rheumatism tomorrow, and fever the next day. She had all types of injection until her buttocks became callous. She drunk and swallowed all mixtures and tablets to a sickening point. She began to dislike the smell of medicine, which was making her sicker. If Opuk were still alive, she would have obviously talked to him for some Acholi herbs. It looked to her that the white men's medicine was failing to cure her. For the reason that David study would be affected if he learned of his mother continuous ailments the Prists and the Sisters in the Mission kept him ignorant of it.

Meanwhile at school, at the end of August, David had dreams, which gave him a presentiment that something was wrong at home. One bright dreamy night, David found himself with his mother at home. She was looking healthy, fatter and younger. While at home with her, she asked him to accompany her to the river to fetch some water. He accepted and they went. She was walking in front of him carrying a water pot, balanced on her head on *Otac*. He walked behind his mother carrying a similar smaller pot on his head. As they neared the river, which was swollen with the rainwater overflowing its bank, they got to a sloppy slippery place.

His mother slipped and fell. Her water pot and the *Otac* on which she was balancing the pot rolled down the river and in no minute the current of water swept the pot and the *Otac* away. They stood at the bank of the river laughing mirthfully as they watched the pot and the *Otac* being carried away by the angry water. Overlapping the first dream, when they came back from the river, they went and set bush fire around their sisals fence. As the fire burned, a strong whirlwind came and swept through the fire carrying with it a burning nest of a bird. The nest kept burning in the air as the whirlwind carried it towards their kitchen. The roof of the kitchen arrested the burning nest and started the hut burning. Thick and dark smoke like that from the chimney of a steam locomotive engine issued from the burning hut. Again, instead of attempting to fight the fire, they merely looked at the burning hut and laughed.

When he woke up in the night, David was troubled greatly by the dreams. It was the first time he tried to query himself about the meaning of dreams. He had never believed in a dream nor did he want to do so, but by the mere fact that those two dreams implicated his mother in a unique way, they worried him and he kept thinking trying to make something out of them. He tossed from side to side, on his stomach, on his back, on the bed in an attempt to sleep but no sleep came thereafter.

"Shall I get some sad news from home tomorrow? That is, if one of the Priests from home comes tomorrow to tell me that my mother is dead. What am I going to do? " David thought, especially when he recalled what his mother had told him that Opuk had said, Aremu and herself were going to have a sad year. 'Aremu died of gun shot as Opuk had said. Will my mother also die?" David thought. He tried to dismiss the thought from his mind but they kept finding their ways back into his head as flies do on rotten meat. He wept at the mere imagination of seeing his mother dead and being put into her grave to rest leaving him alone, and the last of his father's family on earth.

"It's terrible, really terrible," he whispered to himself as more and more tears streamed down his cheeks.

When he woke up the following day in the morning, he expected some sad news from home in connection with the dreams he has had at night, but to his relief he saw no one.

It was not until the seventh day on a Monday, since he last had the dreams that he saw through the window of their classroom during the Geography lesson, the spectacular Jeep of Padre Enriko sorrowfully rolling into the school compound through the gate, turned at the round about in front of the headmaster's office and parked at the side of the lawn. Padre Enriko got out of the Jeep, and walked to the headmaster's office. David realized that his blood flow had quickened. His pulses went up about five times its normal rate, his heart thumping; slamming against his chest made *pump, pump* sound loud enough to be heard a yard away. His breath became rapid and irregular. He felt warm, and small beads of sweat formed on his fore head and the tip of his nose. His palms became moistened with sweat, so that from time to time he wiped them on his thighs alternatively as he copied the Geography notes Padre Richard had jotted on the blackboard. After he had finished jotting the notes on the blackboard, Padre Richard sat on the teacher's table facing the pupils and watched them copy the notes in their notebooks. That was when he noticed that David was not looking fine. He was glancing out of the window very often. Padre Richard stepped down on the floor, came and stood at his side.

"What is the matter? You look hot," Padre Richard asked him.

"Nothing is wrong, I'm alright Father", David replied. All the same Padre Richard put the back of his palm on his fore head to find out if he was feverish, ignoring his answer that he was fine. Padre Richard walked back in front of the class without any comment. He had just sat down on the teacher's chair, when the Headmaster came and knocked on the door of the classroom, and invited him to his office. He got up and followed him into his office where he found Padre Enriko seated on one of the office chairs next to the Headmaster's table, with his fore arms resting on the table, his finger clasped together, he looked directly into the eyes of Padre Quirino who had just regained his seat.

## The Devout Woman

"I don't know how we are going to let him know about it," he heard Padre Enriko saying. "Hello Father, good morning," Padre Richard said and stretched out his hand for hands shake with Padre Enriko.

"Hello good morning", he said and shook hands with him before he focused his attention back to Padre Quirino anticipating the reply to his question he had just asked.

"What's the problem?" Padre Richard asked Padre Enriko as he lowered himself on an empty chair in front of the Headmaster.

"Padre Enriko has brought David's mother to the hospital. She is critically ill, and she is blown up all over; generalised oedema."

Padre Richard raised his eye brows and said: "Oh, sorry to hear that. Have they found out the cause?"

"No. Not yet; he has just brought her. I do not know if the hospital laboratory will be able to ascertain the cause of the oedema. Dr. Agustino might have to treat her on suspicion, hoping that he will be lucky, and strike on the right nail. Bro. Marko pointed out in our last hospital committee meeting that he is lacking many chemicals, and equipment in the laboratory, besides the routine microscopy examinations, and urinalysis, he can almost do no other test. Oedema of that type points out mainly to the deficiency of protein in the body, and it could be brought about by defect in the function of the heart, liver, and kidneys, or malnutrition etc. So you see it is not going to be very easy to fire in the dark and hit the target here," explained Padre Quirino who seemed knowledgeable in human medicine, to the two priests who looked very blank about the difficulties expected in treating Anyadwe.

"What you got us discussing is, how we are going to let David know that his mother is dying in the hospital without destroying him completely. You are aware of his family background I think. The fraternal love exaggerated by their solitude, make them inseparable from each other like the heart is from the body." Padre Quirino said.

"I think he knows about that already," Padre Richard comented.

"What! How did he get the news?" Padre Enriko asked surprised, and lifted himself from the table sat with only half of his back resting on the chair and swept his straying hair backwards with his left hand.

"How do you know he knows about it already?" Padre Quirino added leaning on the table towards Pader Richard.

"He was behaving funny in the class. I think he saw Padre Enriko drive in and started sweating. I did not know why he was behaving like that. I thought he was getting sick. I asked him what was wrong, but he said he was alright even if he was perspiring." Padre Enriko sighed and looked at Padre Quirino, rubbed his nose and stared back at Padre Richard.

"Who might have told him the news?" Padre Enriko asked.

"I don't know but he's reacting like someone who is anxious to hear some sad news."

"Well, if he knows about the news already, and he's ready to accept it as a young man, then let's call him, and explain to him about his mother's condition and give him all the necessary encouragements," Padre Quirino said.

It was break time, ten o'clock in the morning. The pupils were all out playing with each other in the compound while some stood in groups discussing their class problems. David, who always loves to participate in such discussions with his friends, isolated himself like a wounded buffalo, went and stood alone near where Padre Enriko had parked his Jeep. Olel and Ocune saw him looking depressed and dejected. They walked to him to find out what was the matter, but David dismissed them.

"May be he has received some bad news from home." Olel said affirmatively.

"But he would have told us about it! He was all right this morning and he has not talked to Padre Enriko who should have told him something if any. It could be one of the bad days; people get occasionally when you feel like not talking even to yourself." Ocune commented as they walked away towards the Headmaster's Office.

Padre Quirino opened the door of the Office and walked out. He stood on the verandah of the office and saw Olel and Ocune, approaching him. He asked them to call David into his office. David went to the office like an espionage being led to a court hall to hear his execution verdict. The three Priests were seated waiting for him like a team of juries. David went in looking frightened. When he entered, Padre Quirino waved him to sit down on an empty chair next to Padre Enriko.

"How are you David?" Padre Enriko asked him.

"I'm fine Father thank you." David replied forcing a smile, which disappeared faster than it came, and looked away avoiding their eyes.

"How are studies?"

"Fine," he replied curtly. David got more suspicious that something was seriously wrong with his mother, because usually whenever Padre Enriko went to see him, he never talked with him in the office although many a time he talked with him in the presence of other priests outside in the compound. The three Priests looked at each other, and Padre Quirino nodded to Padre Enriko indicating he was the right man to let David know about the story. Padre Enriko cleared his throat, and adjusted himself on the chair like an internist preparing to give an impromptu speech to a class of Professors on the subjects he wasn't sure. He didn't know where to start. He was not sure if he would be convincing enough to make him understand and accept the reality of life, that some people have their hells while still alive.

"Have you met anyone from Coomit within the last weeks?"

"No. Why Father?" David asked as his heart beat heavily in his chest when he recalled the dreams he had about his mother.

"I'm wondering if you've already received some information about your mother's illness."

"My mother's illness! No, I haven't."

"Well I brought her to the hospital this morning," Padre Enriko said.

"What is the matter with her Father?" Is she very ill? Is she dying? David asked and broke into tears.

"She has since been complaining of malaise, insomnia and generalized oedema of the body which came late in the evening. Sr.Veronica has been attending to her complaints and she was showing some improvement. However, as time went by, she began complaining about her chest, and pain on the waist in addition to those she had before.

It was only last Sunday that the condition deteriorated very sharply and when she reported to the Sister, she could not allow her to go back home. She asked her to stay in the clinic in the Mission until this morning when I brought her to the hospital. In fact, it was very fortunate that Sr. Vernonica detained her in the Mission, because she lost her consciousness in the night. I am afraid David I have to be frank with you, your mother is ill, Padre Enriko said while smoothening the knee of David nearer to him with his open right palm. David never moved. His blood seemed to have stopped flowing. He fixed his eyes on the opposite wall on the picture of the Sacred Head of Jesus without blinking. His breath came stealthily like that of a woman who discovered a thief under her bed at night.

"You don't have to be too worried David" Padre Quirino said taking over from Padre Enriko; your mother will be all right. She is now in the hand of a very efficient doctor. You'll go with Padre Enriko to the hospital to see her, and he'll bring you for lunch."

David without looking at any of them sighed, thanked Padre Quirino, got up and walked out of the office weeping.

Doctor Agustino had consulted all the volumes he had on his bookshelf for the possible guide to the treatment of Anyadwe's oedema with unconsciousness and fever. "I will first check her blood for malaria parasites. Now all I can think of are some liver diseases with hypoglycemia or renal failure with azotemia. She is not diabetic because the urine has no glucose not even a trace. I think I will be on the safe side if I revive her with dextrose drip and give her some quinine for malaria when she comes through." He thought as he put back the first volume which could not give him enough information on the possible cause of oedema with unconsciousness, and picked on the next volume entitled 'Renal Diseases' and sat down to read it. He finally sighed, got up and talked to himself, "I hate blind treatment in complicated cases like this one, without the laboratory guides. It takes long before you strike on the right treatment, if you are lucky, but if the patient is unfortunate you may never get the right problem and you waste the drugs and everything. Perhaps some detail clinical history from her if she should come round will put me on the track of the disease". He thought as he walked back to the ward where Anyadwe was put on dextrose drip. The drip was halfway gone. He felt for the pulse. It was high and the blood pressure was high too, 170/140. He slightly increased the rate of the drips from fifteen to twenty per minute. It was when the dextrose was getting finished that Anyadwe began to stir, opened her eyes, and stared blankly at the strange environments she found herself in. Like someone recovering from vodooism she began to shout.

"Sr. Veronica where are you?" She called Sr.Veronica of Coomit.

"Where am I?" She asked again. As she talked, Dr. Agustino, who had gone to call Sr. Domitilla to come and attend to her walked in the ward with her at his heels.

"Take it easy Anyadwe you're in the hospital. You're sick." Dr. Agustino said.

"What happened to me and how did I reach here?"

"You were unconscious when Padre Enriko brought you here this morning.

Now lie down and rest. Dr. Agustino told her. Meekly she lay down on her back but soon got up lifted her chest up on her elbow and asked;

"Does my son David know I'm here already? Poor son, dear son. I do not know how he is going to receive the news that I am here dying. She said and fell on her back, on the bed, weeping.

"He will be alright." Sr.Domitilla said reassuringly, as she removed the needle from her vein to disconnect the drip.

"No sister you don't know that boy. He's going to be knocked out by the news that I'm stretched up here dying," she said as she continued to weep.

As they argued about David, Padre Enriko parked his Jeep in the parking lot next to the ward where Anyadwe had been hospitalised. He led David to the door of the ward where his mother was. Across the wooden door of the ward, a mahogany strip of timber had been screwed with the words "Acute Care Unit' artistically engraved on it.

The letters were painted white and they stood out distinctly against the brown colour of the Mahogany wood. Padre Enriko had raised his hooded fingers to knock on the door when it swung open revealing Sr.Domitilla at the door way.

"Don't knock me, " Sr.Domitilla said with a huge smile on the face.

"Why did you take it away before I hammered on it? Did you fear I'd make a hole in it?" Padre Enriko joked.

"I didn't want to nurse your finger. Prevention is better than cure." The sister returned his joke.

## The Devout Woman

"How is she anyway?"

"She is much better than when you brought her in this morning. Dr. Agustino is now talking to her. He thinks they should be left alone. He wants to find out all from her about her disease. Because he thinks, he might diagnose her condition and base his treatment on what she will tell him clinically. David will be allowed to see how she is improving, but I think now you should leave them on their own for a while.

He is not going to take very long. Do you mind waiting for him in the office?" The Sister said and descended from the doorway and closed the door behind her.

Padre Enriko held David by the hand, and followed Sr. Domitilla to the office of Dr. Agustino. They had sat for about thirty minutes only when Dr. Augustino came out of the ward. He looked thoughtful and worried. With the stethoscope hooked around his neck, he walked to his office while reading the clinical notes he had taken from Anyadwe. He opened the door while reading his notes not knowing that his office was occupied.

"Sorry. I'm really sorry you'll excuse my intrusion," he apologized.

"We're sorry for violating your office Father", Padre Enriko said.

"It's quite in order no problem," Dr. Agustino said and glanced at the notes he was reading. He wished he did not get them in the office he would have given himself more time to fit the zig saw puzzle about Anyadwe's sickness together.

"Dr. Agustino, have you met David Acellam, the son of Ajulina before?" Padre Enriko introduced them.

"I met him. I remember well. It was on the Pentecost day I spent with you in 1939 in Coomit. Don't you remember he gave me that snow, white, lovely cock, which I said I would not slaughter but keep?"

"You're right. It had slipped out of my mind." Padre Enriko said.

David never paid any attention to any of their talk. He was only thinking about his mother.

"How is she?" Padre Enriko asked when he saw that David looked anxious to know the effort his mother was putting up to recover.

"She has done quite well since you brought her this morning although she is secreting a lot of protein in the urine. I have just been testing her urine in the laboratory. She is losing well over one thousand milligrams of protein per milliliter of her urine. I don't know the cause yet."

"Could we go and see her now?"

"Sure; why not! You can go and see her. I am sure Sr. Domitilla will be glad to take you to see her. Won't you Sister?" He said and looked at her, dismissing them from his office preferring to be left alone to study Anyadwe's clinical history. Sr. Domitilla understood the message he was politely conveying to her. She willingly accepted to take David and Padre Enriko to the wards to see Anyadwe.

When they got to the ward, David could not believe he was seeing his mother. She was blown up in every cell on her body. She was twice her original size. Was that the condition revealed to him in his dream he had about a week ago, that he went home, and found his mother looking healthy, fatter, and younger? In addition, is the prophecy of Opuk coming true? He began to weep, ran, and fell on his knees at the bedside of his mother, and buried his face between her breasts. On her part Anyadwe cupped his head between her arms and started to weep too.

Padre Enriko, and Sr. Domitilla, stood and watched them piteously without saying any word. On their way out of the ward, Sr. Domitilla reassured David that they were going to do their best to save the life of his mother, but she warned that if it were God's wish, then no human hand could divert it. She advised him to go back to school and continue with his study.

## Chapter Fourteen

One week had past, because of the bed rest and the diuretic drugs Anyadwe was put on, oedema subsided well. Once more, the veins on her feet and hand could be seen. Again, her face became thin from the puffiness she had because of the oedema, but the root cause of the Oedema remained mysteriously occulted, and this was the greatest worry to Dr. Agustino. Aware of this problem, Dr. Agustino took blood from her and sent the serum to Italy by an urgent airmail for analysis; to find out how her liver and kidneys were functioning. He had examined her physically and from the simple laboratory investigations from the hospital, he was more suspicious of the kidneys to be defective.

"All I am going to do now is to control the hypertension and check the urine protein regularly. If there will be decrease in proteinuria with the decrease in blood pressure, then the biochemical result from home on blood urea will confirm what I'm suspecting now." Dr. Agustino thought. The result of the blood tests he sent to Italy came back after one month. All the liver function tests other than the total serum protein which was severely reduced, and the serum electrophoresis which showed marked decrease in the albumin band with increase in the globulin fraction were all normal. Her blood urea was slightly increased. Serum electrolytes were all normal. With these findings, combined with the normal physical examination he made of the heart, with his stethoscope confirmed with the electrocardiogram he took, his suspicion laid solidly on the kidneys even if the intravenous pyelography he performed on her to check on the nephrons of her kidneys did not reveal any abnormality.

"What could be the cause of this proteinuria resulting in the oedema?" she is hypertensive. In addition, what is the cause of the hypertension? She is a person who has been subjected to many worries. Could it be the mental stress, which has triggered off the hypertension? The intravenous pyelography did not show any abnormality. There is no stricture, not gall stone in the bladder, nor any ulceration," Dr. Augustino continued to think as he compiled the medical reports on Anyadwe.

David was visiting his mother every evening after school during the school days accompanied by his friends Olel and Ocune. Nevertheless, he spent most of his Saturdays and Sundays at her bedside in the hospital. When her Oedema had subsided, Anyadwe wanted to go back home. She complained to David about her crop being spoilt unattended.

"You can't go back home before the doctor said you are alright." David one day told his mother who wanted Dr. Agustino to release her from the hospital so that she went home to look after her crops.

"I know my dear son, but what are we going to eat next year if I don't go and look after the crops? I am now well enough to work. May be it is this continuous lying down that is causing the pain in my waist. If I were doing some exercise with my hoe, I am sure I would have been a lot better off than I am now."

"No, you'll stay here until the doctor tells you to go. I don't mind going on an empty stomach, so long as you're alive and well," David stressed. His mother giggled and asked, putting her hand on his head. "Why do you always doubt my living?"

"Of course I do not doubt your living. I only mean to say that you are the only life I want and desire for day and night. I don't want you to walk out of the hospital before you are cured."

On the Sunday when his mother's health mysteriously deteriorated, David had come to see her in the hospital as he always did. His two friends Olel and Ocune always companied him to see his mother in the hospital. That day the two friends went back to school because Anyadwe was looking tired and sleepy and could not talk to them. David saw them off at the hospital gate before he went back to his mother in the ward. David was not feeling well that morning. He felt as if he had malaria.

When he came back to the ward, he told his mother about his feeling and drew the stool he was sitting on nearer her bed. His mother did not answer him, but turned her head wearily on the pillow and looked at him, her eyes looking somnolently like someone falling asleep from an over dose of sedative drugs. David lifted up his head in time and their eyes met.

"What is the matter Mama? You look tired today. Do you want to sleep?" David asked her. "Yes, to prepare for the long journey I'm going to make today." She replied with a drawling voice.

"What are you talking about? Don't you understand that you are not well enough to walk anywhere and you are not going to try it? In any case, if you want to go home, you are not going to walk home. Padre Enriko will come and pick you up. You get well first, and you'll go." David stressed to his mother and sat up on his stool, folding his arms on his chest. His mother smiled sleepily and said in drawling voice.

"My dear son, you don't understand. I must go today where no one else can accompany me. I am even seeing the people with whom I am going to stay." David was perturbed by his mother's statement he thought she was becoming psychosomatic. After a moment of silence, she closed her eyes and started to sleep. David remained sitting near her bed for sometime watching her sleep, snoring lightly and breathing very rapidly.

Because he wasn't feeling well himself, David thought it was better for him to let her rest. He walked out and sat on a flat form on the lawn in the hot sun thinking.

"What does she mean by saying she is going away today, and to her people? I'll tell the doctor or the sister about her plan. But she looks too weak to be thinking of escaping from the hospital. All the same I will tell them so that they keep good watch on her."

After a short while, David saw Sr. Domitilla and a nurse pulling a trolley packed with all kinds of medicaments from the male wards going with it towards the female ward 'A'. David got up and went to them.

"Excuse me Sister." David said.

"Yes please David you are excused." The Sister replied.

"I would like to tell you something about my mother."

"What about her?" The Sister asked, left the handle of the trolley and moved towards David while the nurse held on the trolley and watched them attentively.

"My mother is talking of going away to her people by all means today; I fear she might escape from the hospital," David said.

"Is it so?"

"Yes Sister."

"Don't worry David, your mother is only joking with you, she can't go anywhere, she is one of the most co-operative patients we've ever nursed in this hospital. She will be all right. I will talk to her all the same when we get to her ward. Is that why you're out to see if she will escape?" The Sister asked.

"No, Sister; she's sleeping. She said she must prepare for the long journey and beside I am not feeling well. David replied.

"What is wrong with you David? The Sister asked.

"I have general weakness of the body."

"I will see you after this, okay. Do not worry yourself over nothing; your mother will be all right." The Sister said and began to push the

## The Devout Woman

trolley as the nurse pulled it to female ward 'A'. The nurse, who was only listening to them, was a bit concerned about the information David was telling the Sister.

"Who is this patient that boy is talking about?" The nurse asked.

"Ajulina, that's her son. The only family left alive with her." The Sister answered.

"Oh I see. Nevertheless, you know Sister, sometimes certain patients when they are about to die, talk stupidly like that but I do not think she is in any danger to die. She has been doing quite well for the last one month."

"Oh yes, she's much improved. In fact Dr. Agustino is waiting for Padre Enriko from Coomit to come, possibly tomorrow, before she is discharged from the hospital." The Sister said as they entered the ward.

Dr. Agustino had finished seeing some of the critically ill patients who needed his observation on that Sunday morning in the male wards, and moved within the inner passage to the female ward 'B' and into the side room where Anyadwe laid snoring.

A specimen of urine she had taken earlier in a bottle labeled with her name and the laboratory form stood on the side locker near her bed. Dr. Agustino came and stood at the foot of her bed, the sphegmanometer in his left hand, his stethoscope hooked round his neck, he watched the way she was panting in her sleep. He also noticed the spasm on her body. He wanted to check her blood pressure but since she was sleeping the sleep, which he described as abnormal, he only checked the pulses, which he found to be very high indeed.

"What is happening?" He thought and took the specimen of urine and the laboratory form standing on the side locker and rushed with them to the laboratory to check for the protein in her urine. He had put her on anti-hypertension drugs for the last one month. The result was very encouraging. He had knocked down the blood pressure from 170/140 to 110/80 and he maintained it there and kept close observation on her. The proteinuria was tremendously reduced from 1000-milligram percent to zero. His findings encouraged him. He thought he had found the root cause of her problem.

After he had talked to the sister, David went back and sat on the bench worried about what his mother might do, notwithstanding Sister Domitilla's assurance. The Sister and the nurse, came out of the female ward 'A' with their trolley, and were going to female ward 'B' where Anyadwe had been transferred. The nurse had just pushed the door to the ward open with her left hand, while pulling the trolley of medicine with the right when they heard a voice through the half-opened door, which startled everyone in the vicinity.

"Acellam, Acellam, come here. Where are you?" The voice called. David unmistakably recognized the voice of his mother calling him.

"Yes mama," David replied, got up and ran quickly to the ward.

"Acellam," the voice went on, "come and let me shake your hand for the last time my only child. I'm leaving you and going far away to my home. I can see them. They are waiting for me. " David had torn through the half opened door, shoved the nurse, the Sister, and the trolley aside. The malaise he had was gone. He ran and fell at the bedside of his mother on his knees. All the other patients in the common ward sat up on their beds wondering what the commotion was all about. Those who were well enough got up from their beds and went to crowd the doorway to the private room where Anyadwe was.

Even if you had never seen anyone yelling for mercy in the hands of Death, if you saw one, you won't mistake it for a comic, because its tragedy is very typical and yet unique in death. It enters the victim in the unique way, and the strangulating transfiguration it confers on the victim is characteristic to no other joker but Death. When David saw his mother dying, he didn't mistake it for a temporary fare well. He knew that his mother was dying. Hysterically, he got up from where he was kneeling and thrust himself in the open arms of his mother and began to cry bitterly as his mother continued to convulse.

## The Devout Woman

Because of lack of telephone in the hospital, Sr. Domitilla ran out to fetch Dr. Agustino to come to their aid. She met Bro.Marko along the corridor to the theatre with the heap of X-ray films on the trolley he was pushing along to the X-ray Unit.

"Where is Dr. Agustino?" she asked.

"I guess he should be in the laboratory if he isn't in any of the wards."

"He isn't in any of the wards", the Sister replied moving restlessly wringing her fingers.

"What is happening in the ward?" Bro.Marko asked.

"Ajulina is dying."

"Oh, Noooo! That can't be," Bro. Marko lamented parked his trolley against the wall and rushed to the ward; while Sr. Domitilla rushed to the laboratory where she found Dr. Agustino drawing the conclusion of urinalysis for the dying Anyadwe.

"If only she could use the anti hypertension drug regularly as I'll instruct her, I'm sure she'll be all right", he thought with the proteinnometer held at eyes level, his back against the window, he interspersed the test tube containing Anyadwe's urine among the reference standard tubes on the stand. It was when he was smiling to himself about his achievement that Sr. Domitilla hurriedly opened the door, which swung violently on its hinges and crushed on the wall the doorknob bang against the wall. Dr. Agustino was startled and he turned angrily to see who was pulling the door down. He saw Sr. Domitilla at the doorway looking frightened as if someone had told her that the end of the world was in sight, and she discovered that she was not ready to meet the Lord, the judge, so she rushed to him, the nearest priest, for purification.

"What is biting you outside Sister?" Dr. Agustino said controlling his temper.

"Don't just sit there admiring those tubes, Ajulina is dying."

The Sister said and disappeared behind the door like the Christmas ghost.

Dr. Augustino banged the proteinometer on the bench spilling some of the tubes out of the stand.

"Impossible," he said slamming both hands on his thighs. "I can't believe it," he said and started to follow Sister Domitilla to the female ward 'B' where Anyadwe was dying. Dr. Agustino came, and took the hand of Ajulina to detect the racing pulses he had detected a few minutes ago, but it was like recording the pulses of an iron rod. He ausculated her heart to monitor how it was behaving but not a *thud* was heard. Her chest was as quiet as a tomb. He looked at Sr.Domitila, and Bro.Marko who was then holding David by the hands and shook his head and whispered, "she- is- dead!"

The body of Anyadwe was shrouded in a white sheet and laid in a black coffin with a big white cross on top. The coffin was left in the small chapel of the sisters waiting for Padre Enriko to come and take it back to Coomit for burial.

Padre Enriko, making his routine Monday trip to Gulu that morning, was connived beyond doubt that, one of those he would bring home that afternoon cured, and well would be Anyadwe. Because, according to Dr. Agustino, during his last trip to Gulu, Anyadwe was definite to be discharged from the hospital during his visit he was making that Monday morning. Padre Enriko drove and parked his Jeep in the parking lots near the female ward 'B', walked into the ward and into the side room where Anyadwe had been. She wasn't there. Her bed was smartly made. Her medical record, which was hung at the foot of her bed, had all been removed. Her belonging were not in the shutter less side locker.

"Well, it looks she has been discharged and she is waiting for me in some place," Padre Enriko thought and walked out of the ward greeting the patients in the wards as he walked out.

## The Devout Woman

Sr. Domitilla and the nurse had finished dispensing medicine to patients in female wards 'B' and they had just gone into female 'C' ward when they heard the door to the female ward 'B' squeaked opened and closed again. They knew that someone must have gone in and out of the ward.

Sister Domitilla walked to the window and looked out of the ward to see who the person was. She saw Padre Enriko walking away towards the office of Dr. Agustino. She quickly walked out of the ward after him leaving the nurse alone to continue dispensing the medicine to the patients. Padre Enriko heard the door opened behind him. He turned and saw Sr. Domitilla following him.

"Hey, I didn't think there was anyone around," he said with a juvenile smile as he walked back to meet her.

"Good morning father." The Sister greeted him.

"What's the matter Sister, you don't look fine are you sick?"

"No, I'm not sick but we—we," she started saying, trying to find the best way of putting the news across to Padre Enriko who until that moment was convinced that Anyadwe was alive and well sitting somewhere with her bundle of luggage waiting for him to take her home.

"How about the we?" Padre Enriko asked studying her face.

"Ajulina," she said and touched him on the arm and began to walk away towards their chapel. Padre Enriko did not understand what Sr. Domitilla was driving at.

"What could have connected Anyadwe to the chapel? Did she do anything sacrilegious in the church?" He thought. The idea that her corpse was in the chapel waiting for him was too remote to worry him or did it cross his mind at all.

He meekly followed Sister Domitilla into the chapel and to the small alter, where the black coffin with a big white cross laid on top of two stools like a bridge of timber across a river, yonder which, there is no more sorrow, pain and suffering of any kind.

"There she is", Sister Domitilla, said in a whisper.

"No!" It cannot be! It's untrue, Padre Enriko yelled slamming his open palms on top of the bench they were resting their hands on and immediately crossed himself paired his palms together looked up in the air and inwardly uttered prayers for Anyadwe's soul to rest in eternal peace.

When they walked outside, Padre Enriko stopped suddenly causing Sister Domitilla to do likewise. He scratched his head, stared at the Sister and asked, "What happened?"

"She died. She was very well on Saturday throughout the day and night. She even walked out of bed in the evening and went to church for confession. After her confession, she came and stayed with us for about one hour before she went back in the ward. There was not any sign of serious sickness in her. Nevertheless, on Sunday morning she did not come to church. We thought she over slept. Then at about ten o'clock, as nurse Philomena and I dispensed medicines to the patients in the wards, David was sitting outside on that bench," she said and pointed at a bench, which was in the hospital compound near ward 'B'. "When he saw nurse Philomena and I going to the female ward 'A; he walked to us and told me that his mother was talking of going on a journey, to her people. He was worried that his mother might escape from the hospital before she was discharged. Nevertheless, I assured him that she was a nice patient who would not do such a thing.

I did not think of anything strange. Nevertheless, later, nurse Philomena warned me that some patients when in the agony of death, utter such talks but she also did not expect it to be the case with Anyadwe, because she had really improved Father. David went back and resumed his seat on the bench because Anyadwe was sleeping at that time. After we had finished dispensing medicine to all the women in ward 'A', and we were going to ward 'B' as we were entering the ward, we heard Anyadwe shouting and calling David, we all rushed to her room. We saw her fitting and convulsing, and I immediately ran out to find Dr. Agustino to come and help us. I found him in the laboratory working on her specimen, which according to him, the result was encouraging. When we came back to the ward, she was already dead," Sr. Domitilla narrated the story to Padre Enriko.

"Oh God, where is David now?" Padre Enriko asked very concerned with his whereabouts.

"Oh Father the boy is broken down completely. He is in a very bad state. He is threatening to kill himself. We tried to dissuade him yesterday not to commit suicide, but it seems his mind is made up. He sees no use to live without his mother. We have sedated him now. He is sleeping in our place. I am worried about him, Father. I don't know what will happen to him." the Sister said wringing her fingers.

"That has always been my first worry Sister. I have been all along imagining all the bad things, David would do if the condition of his mother did not improve. They were committed to each other; a fraternal love, which is not common in most families.

There is a cause for him to feel like that. She was the only relative. Any child with such a single love for his dear mother should feel the same. I have a duty now, to make him understand the position as it is. We aren't going to make him sleep for ever, the earlier I make him accept the truth in life the better," Padre Enriko, said.

"I will be very grateful to you Father if you will make him cool down, and give up the desire to commit suicide. I sincerely tell you that you will find it difficult to convince him." Sr. Domitilla stressed.

On that Monday, when the corpse of Anyadwe was being returned to Coomit for burial, Kinyera remembered that Padre Enriko had told him that Anyadwe was returning home that evening. Therefore, he decided to go and clean her compound to welcome her back home. After he had cleaned the huts and the compound, he went to the forest to collect some firewood for her. He brought the firewood and packed them at the side of her kitchen. Lastly, he went and fetched some water for her in her water pot. However, when he was doing all the services he felt mysteriously anxious. The anxiety, which reminded him of the day, his wife was shot by his son Apire. When he was satisfied that he had done a fair job to welcome Anyadwe back home, he started to walk back to his home thinking about her. He crossed the main road, turned towards his home, and at a distance on the straight road, he saw the spectacular Jeep of Padre Enriko approaching him. As the Jeep drew nearer and nearer, he heard the sound of people wailing in the Jeep as they saw the coffin of Anyadwe. He felt his heart pumping faster, he felt as if he was fainting.

Padre Enriko saw him, and stopped to talk to him. Kinyera moved nearer and saw in the front seat, between Padre Enriko and the Mission Catechist David Acellam, still sleeping from the sedation he got from Sr. Domitilla in Gulu. Marks of tears dried at the corners of his eyes. They were all looking morose and dismayed.

"Hello Father, what misfortune has befallen us?" Kinyera asked and leaned against the Jeep.

"Oh, Kinyera; this is one of the sad thing which has to happen at one time or another. Ajulina is dead. I'm sorry about what I told you last week, although she was really well, no one knows what happened to her exactly," Padre Enriko said brushing his hair backwards with both hands and clasped his fingers at the back of his neck.

"You don't mean it Father". Kinyera said regretfully, while staring at David.

"I don't blame you Kinyera for doubting what I'm telling you. I know you and everyone else, including me, will find it difficult to believe that she has left us. This is what happens when you lose an intimate friend," Padre Enriko said.

Kinyera fought his tears back and asked Padre Enriko: "What are you going to do with this boy Father?"

"Up to now I don't know. Nevertheless, I am going to try to make him happy. My first task will be to make him understand that the misfortune, which has happened to him, is natural and that we have to be prepared to welcome good and bad from God at all times. This needs courage and prayers." As he talked, Kinyera broke down and began to dab tears from his eyes with the sleeves of his shirt. In a sobbing voice, Kinyera asked him where he was going to bury Anyadwe.

"We are going to bury her in the Mission Cemetery, and it should be tomorrow after the seven o'clock mass between ten and eleven. Will you come to give us a hand tomorrow?"

"Certainly, I'll come."

"Okay Kinyera, control yourself. You can do a lot better by praying for her soul than cry for her company. See you tomorrow Kinyera," he said grinning at him shook his hand and ignited the Jeep and drove off.

Before the residence of Coomit knew about Anyadwe's death, her only surviving brother Kolo, was already informed by Ibinonga, his neighour about, the death of Anyadwe. Ibinonga was in Gulu hospital in the same ward in which Anyadwe died. Ibinonga had been attending to his daughter who was ill, suffering from pneumonia. When Anyadwe shouted and began to convulse, fitted and died, Ibinonga was one of those who went into her room to see what was amiss.

He saw her face and thought he knew her. Because she resembled her brother Kolo, Ibinonga did not have difficulty in suspecting and associating her with Kolo. Ibinonga had seen Anyadwe once when she took the cows to Kolo's home sixteen years ago.

"I'll let him know about her as soon as I get home today," he thought as he packed the luggage of his daughter discharged from the hospital on that Sunday.

When Ibinonga got home and told Kolo about her. Kolo thanked Ibinonga for the message and set out for Coomit the following day Monday. He was determined to finish the two days journey in one day. He was lucky, ten more miles before he reached the ghosts plain, a lorry came from behind him going towards Coomit. He waved for a lift from the driver who stopped, and offered him a ride on his lorry.

They got to Coomit about one hour after Padre Enriko had met Kinyera and informed him about the death of Anyadwe. When Kolo reached his sister's home he expected to find people mourning his sister but the place was quiet. Instead he found that the grasses around the compound were dug not more than five hours ago. It was swept and kept clean, typical of his sister's tidiness. The firewood Kinyera heaped at the side of the kitchen gave him the second thought that his sister was not dead after all.

"That must have been a different lady who resembled Anyadwe that Ibinonga saw in Gulu hospital. My sister is alive strong and well. She must have gone out somewhere", Kolo thought as he put down his luggage and sat on his mushroom stool. As he sat waiting, he felt like going to ease himself in the toilet. He got up, walked past the newly dug compound, and discovered that the footprints of the person who had cleaned the compound were scattered all over the newly dug place around the home.

Although the person wore a pair of sandals made of motorcar tyre, the footprints were definitely not his sister's. They were too big to be a woman's footprints.

"Who could have done this work for her?" Kolo thought as he walked out of the pit latrine. He immediately decided to walk to Kinyera's home to find out what was happening.

www.ingramcontent.com/pod-product-compliance
Lightning Source LLC
Chambersburg PA
CBHW072329080526
44578CB00011B/39